Proofreading & Editing Precision

6th Edition

Proofreading & Editing Precision

6th Edition

Larry G. Pagel
Professor
College of Business
Northern Michigan University
Marquette, Michigan

Barbara Norstrom
Professor
Office Technology
Kaskaskia Community College
Centralia, Illinois

SOUTH-WESTERN
CENGAGE Learning™

Australia • Brazil • Japan • Korea • Mexico • Singapore • Spain • United Kingdom • United States

SOUTH-WESTERN
CENGAGE Learning

Proofreading & Editing Precision,
Sixth Edition

Larry G. Pagel, Barbara Norstrom

VP Editorial Director: Jack W. Calhoun

Editor-in-Chief: Karen Schmohe

Acquisitions Editor: Jane Phelan

Consulting Editor: Mary Todd

Developmental Editor/Editorial Assistant:
Conor Allen

Associate Marketing Manager: Laura Stopa

Director, Content and Media Production:
Barbara Fuller-Jacobsen

Content Project Manager: Emily Nesheim

Media Editor: Mike Jackson

Senior Frontlist Buyer: Charlene Taylor

Production Service: S4Carlisle Publishing
Services

Senior Art Director: Tippy McIntosh

Cover and Internal Design: Grannan Graphic
Design, Ltd.

Cover Image: ©Masterfile

Senior Text Permissions Manager:
Mardell Glinski Schultz

Senior Images Permissions Manager:
Deanna Ettinger

Images Permissions Researcher: Darren Wright

For product information and technology assistance, contact us at
Cengage Learning Customer & Sales Support, 1-800-354-9706
For permission to use material from this text or product, submit all
requests online at **www.cengage.com/permissions**
Further permissions questions can be emailed to
permissionrequest@cengage.com

Exam*View*® is a registered trademark of eInstruction Corp. Windows is
a registered trademark of the Microsoft Corporation used herein under
license. Macintosh and Power Macintosh are registered trademarks of
Apple Computer, Inc. used herein under license.

Student Edition ISBN-13: 978-0-538-45046-1
Student Edition ISBN-10: 0-538-45046-0
Student Edition with CD ISBN-13: 978-0-538-45045-4
Student Edition with CD ISBN-10: 0-538-45045-2

South-Western Cengage Learning
5191 Natorp Boulevard
Mason, OH 45040
USA

Cengage Learning products are represented in Canada by Nelson
Education, Ltd.

For your course and learning solutions, visit www.cengage.com/school
Visit our company website at www.cengage.com

Printed in the United States of America
16 17 18 19 20 24 23 22 21

Brief Contents

Contents

For professionals whose responsibilities involve working with written or printed communications, the ability to proofread and edit is extremely important. Proofreading and editing skills are critical for students, administrative professionals, paralegals—indeed, for all professionals who strive for excellence in their communications.

Excellence in proofreading and editing can be developed. Excellence means accuracy, which is the gold standard in every business. Employers value workers who have the ability to ensure that all business communications are clear and well written, which then reflects well on the sorganization.

Proofreading & Editing Precision, 6th edition, is a comprehensive activity-oriented text-workbook designed to sharpen your proofreading and editing skills using hard copy (handwritten or printed) and computerized activities. It provides a thorough review of the rules governing language arts and document preparation and applies them in realistic business documents. This text-workbook will be helpful to you in any course that requires the production of written communications. The proofreading and editing skills you learn will also apply to your other courses, including keyboarding, word/information processing, office procedures, business communications, and business English.

The skills and confidence this text builds will pave the way to a bright future career!

» Helpful Features

You'll find these features in each chapter of *Proofreading & Editing Precision*, 6th edition:

- Spotlight on Accuracy that highlights the importance of precision in written communications

- Documents updated to the new Microsoft Word defaults

- Activities that make use of a variety of documents, including letters, memos, e-mails, reports, resumes, minutes, and news releases

- Commonly confused and misspelled words cycled throughout the documents

- Teamwork exercises to build peer editing skills and to foster collaborative learning

- Foreign language exercises designed to sharpen attention to detail

- Emphasis on proofreading at the computer

- A new, fully-featured Web site with activities and tools to enhance chapter content

- A list of proofreaders' marks on a handy tear-out card for easy reference

- Two comprehensive projects that provide practical hands-on experience in proofreading, editing, and formatting real-world documents

» Chapter Profile

The chapters in *Proofreading & Editing Precision*, 6th Edition, contain brief reviews of proofreading concepts in order of increasing difficulty. Concepts include identifying errors in keyboarding, spelling, capitalization, abbreviation, number expression, sentence construction, and punctuation; proofreading and editing at the computer; formatting business documents; and editing for errors in content, clarity, and conciseness. To provide a variety of opportunities for applying the principles reviewed in the chapter, chapters include the following:

- **Proofread and Mark.** These exercises apply one rule or a short series of rules just presented.

- **Spelling and Word Usage Check.** This exercise provides a list of frequently misspelled words and three sets of commonly confused and misused words for students to review and then apply within documents.

- **Word Division Check.** Applications apply word division; the rules are located in the appendix.

- **International Vocabulary.** This exercise is made up of a list of foreign language words for students to proofread. You do not need to understand the foreign language to complete these activities. You'll compare a list of correctly spelled foreign language words in the first column to a list of foreign language words that contain spelling errors in the second column. This is an excellent activity for building foreign language awareness as well as a means to focus on the task of proofreading.

- **Proofreading Applications.** The Proofreading Applications include a series of business documents that apply the same concepts emphasized within the chapter.

- **Proofreading at the Computer.** This exercise consists of business documents (on the student CD) that provide extensive practice in proofreading, formatting, and editing documents that occur in everyday business situations.

- **Cumulative Application.** The final application encompasses all of the concepts presented to this point in the textbook.

≫ Student CD

Packaged with the text, the student CD contains word processing files for proofreading, editing, and formatting.

≫ New! Proofreading & Editing Web site

 www.cengage.com/keyboarding/pagel

New for the 6th edition, *Proofreading & Editing Precision* offers you a feature-packed Web site with tools and activities that will enhance your mastery of new proofreading and editing concepts.

Student Resources

- Flashcards
- Interactive grammar games
- Proofreading challenges
- Chapter quizzes
- Web links with activities

Instructor Resources

- PowerPoint presentations for each chapter
- Chapters tests
- Supplemental proofreading challenges

Good luck in your proofreading and editing studies . . . we wish you the best in work and life.

Errors! Errors! Errors!

Spotlight on ACCURACY

In an e-mail message, a writer forgets to include the time for a meeting. This error of omission may cause confusion, or it may inconvenience the recipients of your message. What is the impact when errors are published in thousands of copies of books? Yes, even professionals in the textbook industry make errors. Some are simple typographical errors. Others are more serious content errors. In one textbook revision, a state review committee discovered that Christopher Columbus sailed for the New World in 1942. In another book, the Statue of Liberty was said to be made of bronze, rather than copper. And one world history text omitted an entire Chinese dynasty.

Of course, anyone can make an error—and everyone does at one time or another. The point of proofreading, though, is to eliminate errors—or at least to minimize them. Whereas mechanical or format errors may cloud a message, content errors may completely obscure it.

Adapted for use from Dona Orr, Carol W. Henson, and H. Frances Daniels, *Proofreading: A Programmed Approach*, 4th edition, Cincinnati, South-Western/Thomson Learning, 2003, p. 213.

Objectives

- Understand the importance of proofreading.

- Identify the most common types of errors when proofreading.

- Explain and apply the various methods of proofreading documents.

- Use references to verify information when proofreading.

You receive a letter in the mail. You look at the envelope. What do you find? Errors! Your name is misspelled. Your house number is incorrect. Even your street name is misspelled. As if that were not enough, your ZIP Code is wrong too. The letter itself might contain more errors. You take a quick glance and think to yourself, "More errors." You notice that *February* is spelled F-e-b-u-a-r-y and that the letter address is incorrect, just as it was on the envelope.

You wonder: "Why didn't someone proofread this letter? Who wrote this letter? Who signed the letter without first checking it for accuracy? What does this mean about company employees? Do I want to do business with this company?"

» Importance of Proofreading

Documents that are error free create a favorable impression. Letters that look attractive, contain no misspelled words, and use correct grammar and punctuation indicate to the reader that the sender is a competent person who is concerned about quality. The reader of such quality documents judges the individual to be a professional with whom he or she can conduct business.

On the other hand, errors reflect carelessness and incompetence. Most people are annoyed when their names are misspelled, even though they may not say so. Grammar errors, too, are distracting; and the reader may assume that the sender is uneducated.

People expect letters, memos, reports, and tables to have a certain look. Readers expect documents to be prepared in a standard format, making them easy to read. Irregular formats are distracting because they cause the reader to think about how the letter looks rather than what it says.

Errors are inevitable. Everyone makes them. Errors can be found in all types of handwritten, keyed, and printed materials. Errors occur in business letters, faxes, e-mails, memorandums, reports, and other kinds of documents. Errors also occur in newspapers and in magazine headings, articles, and captions. Uncorrected errors are embarrassing; they may cause misunderstandings and confusion, and they may become expensive. Why? Errors cause delays in the delivery of goods or services. Apologies must be made when an incorrect price is quoted or an invoice total is wrong. Sometimes a phone call must be made or follow-up message must be sent to explain how the error was made and how it will be corrected. All of these steps mean additional time, effort, and expense. How the sender might wish he or she had taken the time to check for accuracy in the first place!

Today computers, high-speed printers, and other electronic equipment enable documents to be produced faster than ever before. Form letters can be prepared for large audiences in an amazingly short period of time. If documents are not prepared correctly, however, this same equipment can produce errors just as quickly.

Accuracy is the most important standard in the business world. Businesses constantly seek qualified employees who pay attention to detail. Therefore, the ability to produce accurate documents is a necessity.

As a person who will soon be working in the business world, you must develop an attitude of excellence. You must not be satisfied until what you have produced is error-free. This means carefully checking names, numbers, dates, content, spelling, grammar, and punctuation. After all, you are responsible for the work that leaves your desk. Your image and that of the company depend on your ability to proofread well.

» What Is Proofreading?

Proofreading is the process of reading handwritten, keyed, or printed material and marking errors to indicate corrections. Thus, proofreading is essential to ensure the accuracy of your work.

As errors are identified, they are marked with special symbols called **proofreaders' marks.** Each symbol not only highlights an error but also indicates the correction to be made. Proofreaders' marks are standard symbols. They should be used by executives, managers, document specialists, and all other office workers who proofread and make corrections on an original document. The person who makes the corrections will then be able to interpret them accurately. The chapters in this text present the most common proofreaders' marks. A list of these also appears at the back of this text.

People hired primarily to proofread are known as **proofreaders.** Proofreaders may also be responsible for setting format standards and training other office workers to follow the same standards.

Proofreading requires both knowledge and concentration. It demands patience and attention to detail. Information cannot be proofread by skimming. You may think that when you have finished composing or keying a document, it is correct. You might say, "Well, I'll read it through quickly just in case I missed something." Or you might say, "I used the spelling checker to search for errors, so I don't have to worry." Your task is not done, however, until you have carefully reread the document. Instead, you should say, "I know there is at least one error here; I just have to find it." In other words, you must develop the attitude that proofreading is vitally important in the preparation of documents.

Proofreading is an essential task that you need to take seriously. The more important the document, the more time you need to devote to proofreading to ensure accuracy. The best proofreaders are effective because they do the following:

- Pay attention to detail.

- Take time to proofread carefully.

- Recognize frequent types of errors.
- Use a variety of proofreading methods.
- Are good spellers.
- Know and apply the basics of correct grammar and punctuation.
- Use appropriate reference materials to guarantee accuracy.

» What Kinds of Errors Are Most Common?

Errors may be classified as either mechanical or content. Because these are two different kinds of errors, it is important to read the material once for mechanical errors and a second time for content errors. If the material is long and complex and has many numbers or other details, proofread the material a third time to ensure that all of the errors are found.

Mechanical Errors

Mechanical errors are those that can be recognized when looking at the material without having to reference the meaning. These errors include transposition (the reversing of letters or words), capitalization, spacing, punctuation, and spelling errors. Can you find the mechanical errors in these three sentences?

1. Place thier agenda the in folder.
2. The color choices are red, blue and green
3. please send this to your assitant.

In sentence 1 *their* is misspelled and the words *the* and *in* are reversed. Sentence 2 should have a comma after *blue* and a period at the end of the sentence. In sentence 3, the first word should be capitalized and the last word should be spelled *assistant*.

When proofreading for mechanical errors, slow your reading rate to "low gear." Read the copy letter by letter, word by word, phrase by phrase, or line by line, pronouncing each word as you read. Pronouncing each word forces you to slow your reading. This is the most effective way to proofread.

Another proofreading technique is to read from right to left. This focuses your attention on each word, letting you check for mechanical errors.

Content Errors

Content errors are errors of information or fact. They are more difficult to locate than mechanical errors because once information is in print, you tend to think of it as being correct. Content errors cause confusion and misunderstanding.

To locate content errors, read the material more slowly than your normal rate. Read complete sentences. Instead of reading word for word, concentrate on the meaning of what you are reading. Ask yourself questions such as these:

- Does the content make sense?

- Are the facts accurate and complete?

- Do I understand what the writer is trying to tell me?

- Do the subject and verb agree?

- Is there number agreement (singular versus plural)?

When proofreading for content errors, particularly when dates, numbers, names, or other details or important facts are included in the copy, check the accuracy of the information against the original source. Be prepared to check references, such as those listed in the next section. Proofreading for content errors should be done at least twice—once for grammar errors and once for other content errors.

Can you find the content errors in the following sentences?

1. The summer meeting in Des Moines will be on February 1.

2. On April 31 the tour will stop at Denver.

3. The flyers can be sent to the members which are orange.

In sentence 1, a summer meeting in Des Moines would be during summer months. In sentence 2, the date is wrong because April has only 30 days, not 31. Sentence 3 needs a shifting of words because it sounds as if the members, not the flyers, are orange.

» Where Can a Proofreader Get Help?

A skillful proofreader does not rely simply on memory. Competent proofreaders verify facts and rules in a variety of sources. The first source should be the copy from which the information was taken—the *original* source. The original source might include address files, price lists, sales receipts, vouchers, checkbook records, purchase orders, or invoices.

Use references such as these when you proofread:

- Atlases
- Calendars
- Dictionaries
- Reference manuals

- Online references
- Spelling/word lists
- Statistical sources
- Thesauruses

© GETTY IMAGES/PHOTODISC
References are an invaluable aid to proofreaders.

» Methods of Proofreading

You can improve your proofreading by applying the methods described in this section. Use the first two methods when you read the material by yourself. Use the third method when you proofread with another person. Other helpful hints for proofreading are included in each chapter where you see the PEP (*Proofreading* and *Editing Precision*) Tip icon.

Comparative Proofreading Method

The comparative proofreading method involves comparing one document with another. Follow these steps when using this method:

STEP 1   Place the document to be proofread next to the original copy.

STEP 2   Place the documents being compared as close to each other as possible. This decreases unnecessary eye and/or neck movement and allows for more accurate proofreading.

This method is especially useful when you proofread statistical or technical material that contains many numbers or specialized vocabulary, such as that found in medical, legal, and scientific material. This method can also be combined with the team method, which is explained later in the chapter.

On-Screen Method

When preparing documents on a computer, you need to proofread the documents before and after you print them. Follow these steps:

STEP 1   Proofread on-screen once for mechanical errors and once for content errors. (Proofread sections of the document or one full screen at a time.)

STEP 2   When proofreading for mechanical errors, move your cursor and carefully pronounce each word as you read.

STEP 3   Check for words that may have been omitted or added when copy was revised.

STEP 4   Although most word processing software hyphenates words according to its built-in dictionary, check all of the line endings for inaccuracies. Words are sometimes hyphenated in odd places. Check to make sure that large gaps do not occur at the ends of lines because words have not been divided. Also check words that were hyphenated originally at the ends of lines but are now in the middle of lines because of lengthy revisions that caused different word-wrapped paragraphs.

STEP 5   Use the spelling checker to check the spelling in the entire document. (This procedure is discussed further in Chapter 2.)

STEP 6   Print the document after you have proofread it.

Team Method

As the name implies, the team method involves two people. One person reads the draft or original copy aloud while another person follows along, reading and marking the other copy. When the copy is quite long or complex, the two people take turns reading aloud and checking the copy. The team method is especially effective when checking the accuracy of technical or statistical copy or copy that has long lists, many names, or numbers. When using this method on lists of names, the readers *must* verify accuracy of spelling. The team method ensures that copy has been proofread carefully because two people have checked it.

The team method of proofreading is effective for technical documents.

©ANDREW TAYLOR, 2009/USED UNDER LICENSE FROM SHUTTERSTOCK.COM

* When proofreading for mechanical errors, read the material from right to left instead of the usual left-to-right method.

Proofreading & Editing Tips

PEP Tip

≫ What's Ahead?

Beginning with Chapter 2, you will learn how to find specific kinds of errors and how to mark the errors using correct proofreaders' marks. Errors will occur in spelling, capitalization, number usage, punctuation, format, and content. You will also learn how to make editing corrections.

Within each chapter you will be introduced to several basic rules. You will then have an opportunity to test your understanding of the rules and to apply them in several ways.

- In Proofread and Mark activities, which immediately follow the introduction of specific rules, you will be asked to proofread in the context of short sentences.

- The Confused and Misused Words section lists groups of similar words whose meanings and usage are often used incorrectly. The complete listing of these words is located in the appendix.

- The Proofreading Applications begin with activities that concentrate on the types of errors introduced in the current chapter.

- The Spelling and Word Usage Check is next. This section includes several words that are commonly misspelled. You will be asked to identify those words that are spelled incorrectly and use appropriate proofreaders' marks to make corrections. A listing of misspelled words is located in the appendix.

- The Spelling and Word Usage Check is followed by one of two things: (1) International Vocabulary: This activity includes a list of Spanish and French words. Although you may not recognize the words or understand their meaning, this exercise will help you increase your ability to find words that are misspelled; (2) Word Division List: This is a proofreading exercise that contains a list of words separated by syllables. Some are divided correctly and some are not. You must use proofreaders' marks to correctly identify errors. Guidelines for word division are located in the appendix.

- More proofreading applications follow in which you proofread two or more realistic business documents that contain errors discussed in the chapter. Some of these documents will be computerized applications (Proofreading at the Computer) available on a student CD. (Your instructor can tell you if you will be completing these exercises.) The purpose of these exercises is to provide additional proofreading and editing practice. You may also be directed to a Web site on which you can complete additional proofreading challenge activities.

- Most chapters conclude with a Cumulative Application that includes one document focusing on all proofreading topics covered up to that point.

As you complete the assignments in this text, keep in mind the importance of proofreading. With the proper attitude, you will succeed in developing good proofreading skills. You will also become a valuable, efficient, and productive employee.

Keyboarding Errors

Spotlight on ACCURACY

If you are a bad speller, you may think you will always be a bad speller. The good news is that approximately 90 percent of all writing consists of 1,000 basic words, a manageable number to learn.

Objectives

- Recognize transposition errors, added copy errors, omitted copy errors, incorrect letters, numerical errors, and word division errors.

- Use appropriate proofreaders' marks to correct these errors.

- Spell correctly 12 frequently misspelled words.

- Use correctly three sets of commonly confused and misused words.

>> Spelling Errors

The most frequent types of errors found in business documents are spelling errors. These errors result from striking the wrong character on the keyboard or actually misspelling the word. Regardless of the cause, the proofreader's task is to locate the errors and indicate exactly what corrections are needed. In Chapter 2, you will learn to identify spelling errors that result from transpositions, additions of extra letters or spaces, omitted letters, and misstrokes.

To locate spelling errors, read very slowly, letter by letter. If the material has been keyed from another source, such as a handwritten document or a rough draft, check the final printed copy against the original copy.

If you are using a word processing program equipped with a **spelling checker,** use it to check for spelling errors. The spelling checker compares each word in the document to the words in the program's electronic dictionary. Words that do not match the dictionary of the spelling checker are clearly marked on the screen. Although the spelling checker will identify errors such as *bisiness* or *oppertunity*, it does not read for context. Therefore, it will not recognize errors such as *form* for *from* or *short* for *shirt*. The spelling checker does not recognize **homophones,** words that are pronounced alike but are spelled differently, such as "when he through the ball" (should be *threw*) or "the third addition of the textbook" (should be *edition*). To locate misused or inappropriate words, you must read the copy carefully. For more details on the spelling checker and grammar checker, see Chapter 3, "Proofreading and Editing on the Computer," pages 28-29.

DIGITAL VISION/GETTY IMAGE
Read copy carefully.

>> Transposition Errors

Letters, numbers, punctuation marks, words, or even sentences keyed out of order are called **transpositions.** Transpositions frequently occur in vowels (rec*ie*ve), short words (*adn*), and word endings (availab*el*). Letters that are adjacent on the keyboard, such as *r* and *t*, *v* and *b*, *n* and *m*, and *s* and *d*, are frequently transposed.

Sometimes transpositions result in words that look familiar. However, when the entire sentence is read for meaning, it becomes obvious that the word is used incorrectly. Careful proofreading is required to find transposition errors such as *form* for *from*, *board* for *broad*, *trail* for *trial*, *sacred* for *scared*, *sued* for *used*, *untied* for *united*, and *dairy* for *diary*.

To show any copy that is not in the correct sequence, use the transposition symbol. You should also write this symbol in the left or right margin of the document to alert the reader to an error in the line. Notice how the transposition symbol is used to mark errors in the following examples:

	MARKED COPY	CORRECTED COPY
Transpose (reverse order).	The handel is broken.	The handle is broken.
	"Start the meeting by noon".	"Start the meeting by noon."
	The report due is on Monday.	The report is due on Monday.

Exercise 2-1 • Proofread and Mark

*Proofread these phrases for transposition errors. Use the transposition symbol to show corrections. If the phrase is correct, write **C** to the left of the number.*

1. on Wedensday morning

2. quick answer is necesasry

3. the real prolbem

4. to be aware of the

5. frequent fylers

6. needless say to

Exercise 2-2 • Proofread and Mark

*Proofread the keyed copy for transposition errors by comparing it to the correct handwritten copy. Use the transposition symbol to show corrections. If the sentence is correct, write **C** to the left of the number.*

1. Thank you for your response.

2. The next meeting is in September.

3. Call us before noon.

4. Our motto is "Friendly Service for All."

5. The committee meeting will be held on Tuesday.

1. Thank you your for response.

2. The next meeting is ni September.

3. Call su before noon.

4. Our motto is "Freindly Service for All."

5. The committee meeting will be held on Tuesday.

≫ Added Copy Errors

Another common spelling error is adding extra letters, spaces, numbers, or punctuation marks. Additions can be caused by faulty keying or by incorrect copying from the source document. Unnecessary words, phrases, and even sentences often occur in documents that have been composed and edited using a word processing software program. Writers may insert new text but fail to delete the old text. Similarly, when making changes in documents that have been printed on paper, writers often fail to cross out unwanted text.

As you proofread, be alert for the following added copy errors:

- Words repeated at the beginning of a line (particularly small words such as *in, for, that, with,* and *as*)

- Extra letters added in long words and words with double letters (*schedualed, immmediately, reccommend, tommorrow*)

- Words that may appear correct (singular versus plural; homonyms) but are not because of an extra letter (offic*es* for office, pleas*e* for pleas, time*r* for time)

- Numbers repeated in a list

- Phrases or an entire line of text repeated

When proofreading, use the delete symbol to show that extra copy should be deleted and the close-up symbol to indicate that extra space should be omitted. Use both the delete and close-up symbols when letters or characters should be deleted within a word.

Errors can be embarrassing.

		MARKED COPY	CORRECTED COPY
Delete or omit copy.	℘	Purchase your͓ supplies in Boston.	Purchase your supplies in Boston.
Close up space.	⌒	Hire four new employe͟es.	Hire four new employees.

Exercise 2-3 • Proofread and Mark

*Proofread the following phrases for added copy errors. Use the delete and close-up symbols to show corrections. If the phrase is correct, write **C** to the left of the number.*

1. an approppriate response

2. take a morning nap

3. some requirred reading

4. provided some an swers

continued

5. discusssed the situation   **8.** work with with the manager

6. a completed application   **9.** lack of preparattion

7. during our bussiness   **10.** one problems to settle meeting

Exercise 2-4 • Proofread and Mark

*Proofread the keyed copy for added copy errors by comparing it with the correct handwritten copy. Use the delete and close-up symbols to show corrections. If the sentence is correct, write **C** to the left of the number.*

1. *Your tax return is due.*   **1.** Your tax return is due.

2. *Answer the customer's request.*   **2.** Answer the cusstomer's request.

3. *The decision made by the faculty was final.*   **3.** The decicision made by the faculty was final.

4. *Preside over the meeting.*   **4.** Preside over the the meeting.

5. *Clean the conference room.*   **5.** Clean the conferrence room.

» Incorrect Letters

Keying an incorrect letter results in a misstroke. Misstrokes are easy to overlook in long words or in such words as *quarantee* (incorrectly spelled with a *q*) for *guarantee* (correctly spelled with a *g*). It would be easy to miss *change* for *chance* because both of the words are spelled correctly. The meaning of the sentence determines which of the two words is correct. Proofread carefully for misstrokes in short words such as these:

o*f*, o*n*, o*r*	the*n*, the*m*, the*y*	th*a*n, th*e*n
no*t*, no*w*, ne*w*	th*e*se, th*o*se	

Use the straight diagonal line to mark a misstroke, and write the correct letter above the misstroke.

	MARKED COPY	CORRECTED COPY
Change letter. /	It was a good opp*o*rtunity.	It was a good opportunity.

Exercise 2-5 • Proofread and Mark

*Proofread the keyed copy for incorrect letters by comparing it with the correct handwritten copy. Use the straight diagonal line and proper letter to show corrections. If the sentence is correct, write **C** to the left of the number.*

1. *Her name was added to the list.*	**1.** Her name was added to the last.
2. *She is our new manager.*	**2.** She is our now manager.
3. *Your help is sincerely appreciated.*	**3.** Your help is sincerely apprediated.
4. *Pay the insurance premium.*	**4.** Pay the insurance primium.
5. *They have increased. their services.*	**5.** They have increased their services.

» Omitted Copy Errors

Another common error is the omission of copy. Omissions occur whenever a space, character, or word is left out of a document. Entire lines and even entire sentences may also be omitted. Paired punctuation marks, such as brackets, parentheses, and quotation marks, are also common errors of omission.

Omissions of letters are common in long words, in words with silent letters (knowledge*a*ble and temper*a*ment), and in words with double letters (oc*c*urrence and ac*c*ommodate). Sometimes when you are scanning a document, the copy may appear to make sense, even though something has been omitted. An omission can change the meaning of copy—sometimes drastically. Note the difference an omission makes in the following examples:

OMISSION ERROR	CORRECT
under doctor's car	under doctor's care
send you response	send your response
sprig into action	spring into action
check their backround	check their background

To mark omission of spaces, use the space symbol (#).

To mark errors in omitted copy, use the caret symbol (^).

If space is limited, add the caret in the exact spot in the text where the omission occurs and write the insertion in the side margin. If several words must be added and insufficient space is available in the side margin, write the copy in the top or bottom margin of the page and extend a line from the copy to the caret.

		MARKED COPY	CORRECTED COPY
Insert space.	#	mail to#this address	mail to this address
Insert copy.	∧	premium is du∧e soon	premium is due soon
		Be sure∧the coverage ∧is extensive.	Be sure the coverage is extensive.
		Your∧job application is being reviewed.	Your job application is being reviewed.

Exercise 2-6 • Proofread and Mark

*Some of the following phrases have omitted copy errors. Use the appropriate proofreaders' marks to identify the corrections. If the phrase is correct, write **C** to the left of the number.*

1. the eletion results

2. when you message arrives

3. the resulting conseqences

4. soon to be released

5. an interestng person

Exercise 2-7 • Proofread and Mark

*Proofread the keyed copy for omitted copy errors by comparing it with the correct handwritten copy. Use the appropriate insert mark to identify the corrections that should be made. If the sentence is correct, write **C** to the left of the number.*

1. *Your evaluation has been scheduled for next month.*

1. Your evaluation has been schedule for next month.

2. *You will be recognized for your achievements on Friday.*

2. You will be recognized for you achievements on Friday.

continued

3. *The advertisement will appear in Thursday's newspaper.*	3. The advertisment will appear in Thusday's newspaper.
4. *If you are able to attend, please let me know.*	4. If you are able to attend, please let me know.
5. *Factory orders will be increasing.*	5. Factory ordrs will be incrasing.

» Numerical Errors

Accuracy of numbers is extremely important because many decisions are based on numerical data. Errors in dates, amounts of money, percentages, telephone numbers, social security numbers, and statistical copy can be very costly as well as embarrassing. Transposition of numbers is a common numerical error. Similarly, errors within listed items occur frequently, particularly as items are added to or omitted from a list.

Do not assume that a number is correct. In fact, check all numbers twice. If a number has been copied from another source, make sure it has been copied correctly. Verify all extensions and totals. Proofread numbers digit by digit. For example, read the number *1994* as "one-nine-nine-four" instead of "nineteen ninety-four." If numbers are to be spelled out and also written as figures, as required in many legal documents, make sure both numbers are the same; for example, six months (6 months). Finally, check your calendar to make sure the day agrees with the date listed. Is the correct date Friday, May 5, or Thursday, May 5?

Exercise 2-8 • Proofread and Mark

*Proofread the keyed copy for numerical errors by comparing it with the correct handwritten copy. Use the appropriate proofreaders' marks to show corrections. If the sentence is correct, write **C** to the left of the number.*

1. *The exam will have 35 questions.*	**1.** The exam will have 53 questions.
2. *Send a check for $139.52 with your order.*	**2.** Send a check for $39.52 with your order.
3. *His office telephone number is 555-0174.*	**3.** His office telephone number is 555-0147.
4. *Only 9 percent volunteered immediately.*	**4.** Only 29 percent volunteered immediately.
5. *Her address is P.O. Box 1327.*	**5.** Her address is P.O. Box 1327.

Exercise 2-9 • Proofread and Mark

*Mark any errors in the keyed list by comparing it with the correct handwritten list. Use the appropriate proofreaders' marks to show corrections. If the list is correct, write **C** to the left of the number.*

1. Carrie C. Wilson, No. 53118	**1.** Carriee C. Wilson, No. 531188
2. Doug E. Johnsson, No. 873241	**2.** Doug E. Johnsson, No. 873241
3. Michael Watermann, No. 318661	**3.** Michail Waterman, No. 381661
4. Kris R. Braun, No. 9733332	**4.** Kriss R. Braun, No. 973332
5. Roger C. Galvez, No. 35826	**5.** Rogre C. Galvez, No. 358362

≫ Spelling and Word Usage

Misspellings are a distraction to the reader. They are embarrassing to the writer and reflect negatively on the company. Learning to recognize these errors is critical to being a good proofreader. Develop the habit of checking a dictionary or spelling guide whenever you are unsure of a word. If you are using word processing software, use the spelling checker provided with your software. Remember, the spelling checker will miss words that are spelled correctly but used improperly. To find these errors, you need to use the spelling checker in addition to carefully reading your document.

The appendix of this text contains a list of frequently misspelled words and another list of commonly confused words. To strengthen your ability to spell these words correctly, 12 spelling words and 3 confusing words will be included in the Spelling and Word Usage Check of each chapter. In addition, these words will be applied in the Proofreading Applications at the end of each chapter.

CONFUSED AND MISUSED WORDS

addition   *n.* process of summing; an added part

edition   *n.* copies of a published book

The **addition** of new workers helped us complete the project on time. Our class is using the third **edition** of that textbook.

affect   *v.* to influence

effect   *v.* to bring about; *n.* result

How will the downsizing **affect** morale?

Smoking has a negative **effect** on your health.

all right   *adj.* (two words) all correct or appropriate

alright   unacceptable spelling of *all right*

Mia's answers were **all right**.

The terms of the contract seemed **all right** to Sean.

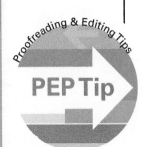

Proofreading & Editing Tips

PEP Tip

* Check short words such as *of*, *on*, *or*, *an*, and *at* for possible misstrokes.

* Proofread numbers carefully for transposition errors.

* Check for repetition of words and/or repetition of numbers in a list.

* Check separately for errors in numbers, dates, technical information, and names of people.

* When using word processing software, take advantage of the spelling checker. Remember, using your spelling checker is only one step in proofreading. You must also read each word carefully to make sure you intended to use that specific word.

PROOFREADING APPLICATIONS

Exercise 2-10 • Paragraphs

Proofread the following paragraphs to locate spelling and word usage errors. Use the appropriate proofreaders' marks to show the corrections.

Among the many profesional organizations is the Associated Writers of America (AWA). This is an organization for people who are keenly interested in writting as a profession and as a hobby. Two major events for the AWA are its annual national convention and its special fall conference, which features presentations of information for both current and potential writers.

The confrence is held in a different city each year with arrangements worked out by the AWA conference manager. He or she will work out details to quarantee that everyone attending the conference will have the opportunity to participate in a number of meetings.

At the last conference, the participants were addressed by a writer whose major occupation is serving as president of an electricle company. His talk on the struggled to perfect his writing style helped many in the audience apppreciate the challenge of good writing.

If you are interested in becoming a part of this group and in attending any of its regional or national conferences, simply watch your newspaper for informaiton on where to join.

Exercise 2-11 • Spelling and Word Usage Check

*Compare the words in Column **A** with the corresponding words in Column **B**. One of the words is spelled or used incorrectly. Use the appropriate proofreaders' marks to correct the misspelled or misused words. If both columns are correct, write **C** to the left of the number.*

Column A	Column B
Ex. and	and
1. writing	writting
2. potencial	potential
3. addressed	adressed
4. participate	participate
5. oppertunity	opportunity
6. electrical	electricle
7. participants	particpants
8. confrence	conference
9. appreciate	apperciate
10. guarantee	quarantee
11. institutoin	institution
12. responsibel	responsible

>> Word Division

Words are often divided at the end of a line to keep the right margin as even as possible. An even right margin makes the page appear balanced and attractive. Every worker who is responsible for producing business documents should know and apply the basic rules of word division.

1. Use a hyphen to show where a word should be divided.

2. Divide words between syllables.

3. Leave as much of the word as possible at the end of a line before dividing. This makes the word easy to identify.

4. Do not divide words at the end of more than two consecutive lines.

5. Do not divide the last word of a paragraph or the last word of a page.

Word division rules are located in the appendix. As you review the word division rules, note that some rules state "avoid dividing." This means that though it may be permissible to divide a word at a certain point, it is not recommended.

Exercise 2-12 • Word Division List

*Proofread the words in each line. If one or more words are divided incorrectly, correct the word(s) using the appropriate proofreaders' marks. Then write the word(s) on the blank line using hyphen(s) to show **all preferred points of division**. If all three words in a line are correct, write **C** on the blank line.*

Ex.	lit⌒tle	repre– sent	admis– sible	*little*
1.	stop– ping	corp– oration	worth– while	
2.	mort– gage	collect– ible	infat– uation	
3.	sep– arate	protec– tion	they'll	
4.	prefer– ence	curric– ulum	cooper– ated	
5.	posses– sing	prepa– ration	gas– oline	
6.	bro–therhood	immedi– ately	pros– ecute	
7.	compari– son	sister– in–law	mainten– ance	
8.	suf– ficient	assim– ilate	cons– cious	
9.	commit– tee	elec– trical	pharm– acy	
10.	practi– cal	trespas– sed	typ– ical	
11.	height	referr– ed	bull– etin	
12.	desira– ble	bene– factor	cler– ical	
13.	bil– lion	im– itation	custo– mary	
14.	extenu– ating	clarif– ication	reason– able	
15.	cross– filing	pass– ing	chron– icle	

Exercise 2-13 • Business Letter

Proofread the letter for spelling errors. Correct the errors using the appropriate proofreaders' marks.

WRITERS SUPPLIES, INC.

Suite 47—Hibbard Building
349 West Grandview Drive
Des Moines, Iowa 50313-1298
Phone: 515-555-0100 • Fax: 515-555-0101

September 23, 20--

Ms. Janet R. Jameson, Chair
National Convention Commitee
Associated Writers of America
3462 West Grant Avenue
Omaha, NE 68111-1742

Dear Ms. Jameson:

Yes, we except your invitation to particpate as an exhibitor at the June convention. We have been strong believers in the work of the AWA and its many proffessional activities.

Thank you for sending a copy if the layout for the exhibits area. We prefer to have the two booths numbered 32 and and 34 by the north entrance to the hall, with the edition of one double electrical outlet.

Please send us a price list of boothe supplies so that we can place our order as soon as possible. The list should be sent by fax or regular mail to the office address given above. Also, would you let us know to whom our payment should be snet? An adressed envelope is enclosed for your convenience.

Sincerely,

Calvin Brown, Manger
Sales and Marketing

tbe

Enclosure

Exercise 2-14 • Memo

Proofread and mark the spelling errors in the following memo.

Writers Supplies, Inc. Memorandum

TO: Department Heads

FROM: Dorothy Diekemper, HR

DATE: April15, 20--

SUBJECT: Casual Fridays

In May we will be allowing employees to to participate in casual Fridays.

Please advise the employes in your department that we still want to project a professional image to are customers and our cleints. We will approach this as a trial period through the summer months of May, June, June, and July. Advise your employees that if the trial period goes well, we will consider extending casual Fridays.

This is an effort to allow employees to feel comfortable at work. We hope this goes well. It may be necessary to set up a dress code in the future for casual Fridays. In the meantime, if you have any questions one what is acceptable and what is not, just stop by and we will discuss individual situations.

I will also be looking for feedback from the department heads. If this effects your department negatively in any way, I would like to be informed. Thank you for your cooperation in this matter.

tbe

PROOFREADING AT THE COMPUTER

Note to the student:

- Beginning with Exercise 2-15, standard procedures are provided for saving, printing, and proofreading the hard copy and reprinting the document. You will see these directions repeated for a few chapters. After that, you should continue to follow the standard procedures for all exercises presented in Proofreading at the Computer.

- Also, in later lessons formatting instructions may not be provided for the documents. If necessary, refer to your text-workbook for assistance.

Exercise 2-15 • Business Letter

1. Open 2-15 from the Chapter 2 folder on the student CD. (This is a computer copy of Exercise 2-13.)

2. Proofread the letter on the screen. Correct all errors on the screen copy that you indicated with proofreaders' marks in Exercise 2-13.

3. Format the letter using default left and right margins and a 2" top margin.

4. Save the letter as 2-15R. You can store the file in a variety of locations, such as in a folder on your hard drive, a flash drive, a CD, a disk, a shared drive on a network, or to other removable storage media. Check with your instructor if you have questions about where to store your file.

5. Print the letter.

6. Proofread the printed document. If you find any additional mistakes, correct the errors on both the hard copy and the screen.

7. Save and print the revised document.

Exercise 2-16 • E-mail Message

1. Proofread the e-mail below.
2. Mark all corrections with proofreaders' marks.
3. Open 2-16 from the Chapter 2 folder on the student CD.
4. Correct all errors you marked on the hard copy.
5. Save the e-mail as 2-16R, and print it.
6. Proofread the hard copy. If you find any additional mistakes, correct the errors on both the hard copy and the screen.
7. Save and print the revised copy.

From: jrubard@kitstrom.com

To: employees@kitstrom.com

Cc:

Subject: Health Insurance

As you know, we have recently changed carriers for out health insurance a Kitstrom. Attached iss a summary of the changes. We will have a webinar on May 1, 20-- at 1 p.m. to explain in more detail the the benefits you will have with the new carrier. We beleive you will be pleased with our new pollcty.

This will be an interactive webinar. You will have and opportunity to ask questions. Mabel Bauza from Human Resources will be conducting the webinar and a representative from Green Cross Insurance, our carrier, will be available to answer questions. The webinar should last approximately on hour.

The URL is www.kitstrom.com/benefits an the number to phone is 217-555-0130. Your acccess code 45619.

Jennifer Rubard, Human Resources

Bookmark It!

Want more practice? Go to www.cengage.com/keyboarding/pagel for more proofreading activities.

Proofreading and Editing on the Computer

Spotlight on ACCURACY

Technology is changing the way people work, both personally and professionally. Spelling checkers, grammar checkers, online dictionaries, and voice recognition technology all work to make tasks easier. But is the technology always right? How accurate was the spelling checker in the following?

- Isn't technology grate!!

- Know won knows better than me what a difference it makes. Me own spelling checker tells my that my righting is perfect. I've maid know errors!

- This whey I don't have too rely on some won else proof reading me work for me.

- So you sea, bee smart and play the game.

- Let you spelling checker due you work for you!

Objectives

- Understand and apply the principles of on-screen proofreading.

- Increase your productivity level in preparing written business documents.

- Improve the quality of your written business documents.

- Spell correctly 12 frequently misspelled words.

- Use correctly three sets of commonly confused and misused words.

Computers have made creating and revising documents easier and faster.

>> Introduction

The increased use of computers and information-processing programs has made the task of creating written materials easier and faster. However, the speed with which information is processed through computers and printers has placed a heavy responsibility for accuracy upon the operators of such equipment. The need for proficient proofreading and editing skills is critical when using a computer.

Most word processing programs have a feature that can merge addresses with a "shell" document to instantly create personalized sales letters for distribution to hundreds or even thousands of people. If errors exist in the shell document, all of the merged letters will have the same errors. Consequently, customers receiving those letters will have poor impressions of the company. The result may be fewer sales; or, in some cases, the company may have to send out corrected copies of the letter, which would substantially increase the cost of the mailing.

>> On-Screen Proofreading

The types of errors found in on-screen copy are the same as hard-copy errors, so the same proofreading skills are applied. However, there is a major difference between hard-copy proofreading and on-screen proofreading. In hard-copy proofreading, proofreaders' marks are written on the hard copy to identify the errors. In on-screen proofreading, when an error is located on the computer screen, the proofreader corrects the error immediately, saving time that would otherwise be spent rekeying. The diligent proofreader who detects and corrects all of the errors in the on-screen copy will produce a printed hard copy that is free of errors. Several tools and tips can simplify on-screen proofreading.

Spelling Checker

The **spelling checker**, found in most information processing software programs, should be used first—after saving the document. With this feature, the program compares the spelling of each on-screen word with the words in a dictionary stored within the computer's memory. If the on-screen word matches the stored dictionary word, the computer moves to the next word. If it does not, the on-screen word is highlighted. At this point, the operator must either purposely ignore the highlighted word and continue with the spelling checker or correct the misspelled word by selecting one of the suggested choices listed in the memory dictionary. The computer will not automatically correct the misspelled word; the operator must choose the correct word.

The spelling checker is an extremely valuable tool for the proofreader. However, the spelling checker will not locate inappropriately used but correctly spelled words, such as homophones. For example, in the following paragraph, the spelling checker would identify only one incorrectly spelled word. However, seven incorrect words appear in this copy. Can you find the errors?

> At the meering held last weak, the members decided
> that their should bee a committee too prepare a proposal
> four expansion of the west central office located inn
> Los Angeles, California.

In some word processing programs, the incorrect words will be indicated. In Microsoft Word 2007, for instance, the seven incorrect words in the previous paragraph may display with a blue squiggly line under each one, indicating a possible contextual spelling error. If you right-click on each flagged word, you will see a suggested solution. You can turn this option on or off in Word 2007.

Grammar Checker

The **grammar checker** is a feature of some software programs that allows proofreaders to identify and correct grammar errors in their written documents. The grammar checker may be employed after the spelling checker is used. Depending on the specific program, a grammar checker program analyzes the material on the screen for various aspects of writing, including correctness of grammar, sentence structure, punctuation, and spelling.

Grammar checker software lets you select the checking style that is best for your writing style. In addition, German, French, and Spanish versions are available from some companies.

Cursor Movement Check

A third step in on-screen proofreading is to use the cursor. When reading on-screen copy, the proofreader should use the cursor and the directional arrow keys to move through the copy. A simple technique is to proofread on-screen material by moving the cursor down one line at a time. When the cursor is at the bottom of the screen, continuing to move it down will bring a new line to the bottom of the screen. A line at the bottom of the screen is easier to proofread because there are no words below the line (see Figure 3-1).

Print Preview

Most word processors have a feature you can use to preview the document before it is printed. By using **Print Preview**, you can see if the formatting, spacing, and margins are correct. You can also see if the document fits on one page; if not, you must make adjustments to fit the document on one page or create a second-page header or footer. Using Print Preview before printing a document saves time and paper.

Figure 3-1
On-Screen Editing
in Word Processing
Program

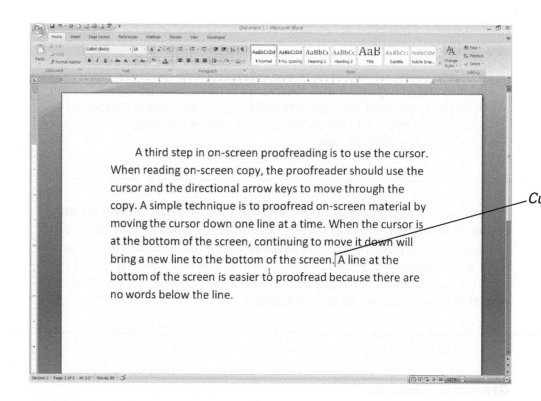

A third step in on-screen proofreading is to use the cursor. When reading on-screen copy, the proofreader should use the cursor and the directional arrow keys to move through the copy. A simple technique is to proofread on-screen material by moving the cursor down one line at a time. When the cursor is at the bottom of the screen, continuing to move it down will bring a new line to the bottom of the screen. A line at the bottom of the screen is easier to proofread because there are no words below the line.

Cursor

» Information Processing Tools

Whether proofreading on-screen or off screen, you will work with information processed in a variety of software programs. Familiarizing yourself with formats such as spreadsheets and databases will help you proofread more effectively.

Spreadsheet

An important tool used in business management is the **spreadsheet**. Basic information is entered into columns and rows. The spreadsheet program processes the information through a variety of calculations, and additional data is generated in other columns and rows, as shown in Figure 3-2.

Figure 3-2
Sample
Spreadsheet

	Acct. No.	Title	Budget	Used/Sep	Bal. 9/30	Used/Oct
1						
2	3721	Supplies	1500	250	1250	150
3	3722	Phone	100	10	90	15
4	3723	Travel	1000	0	1000	0
5	3724	Mags.	150	50	100	0
6	3725	Lecturer	500	0	500	0
7	3726	Film	125	25	100	20
8	3727	Misc	100	0	100	0

If the basic information contains errors, the resulting analyses will be incorrect. Therefore, the basic information entered into the spreadsheet must be proofread carefully.

Database

Another electronic tool used in processing information is a **database**. The database format is a structured way to store basic information such as names, addresses, and telephone numbers; product data; and information on services performed. The bits and pieces of the information are entered into fields. These fields form a separate record for each customer, person, or company. All of the records become the database, and the operator can use various commands to rearrange, sort, or select information from the database.

A crucial step in the preparation of a database is keying the initial information. Uncorrected errors will result in incorrect data. Each record should be carefully checked against the original information and all errors corrected.

Voice Recognition Software

Voice recognition software gives you the ability to transfer your spoken words directly into text. As you speak into a microphone connected to your computer, the software transforms your spoken words into text on the screen.

Because each person has a unique voice profile, the software must learn each person's voice pattern. Most programs first ask you to speak a sample list of words or sentences into the microphone. As you practice your speech skills, the software learns your voice and your unique way of speaking. The success rate for the software depends on your computer's speed, but it is not unusual to have an accuracy rate of 95 percent or higher.

» Communicating Online

It's a safe bet that most of the communicating you do today isn't formal or handwritten. E-mailing, texting, instant messaging, and social networking continue to increase in popularity. These offer unique ways to communicate immediately.

These methods of communication are more casual than composing a cover letter for a job application. While you probably don't spend the same amount of time proofreading a message you're posting on your friend's Facebook page as you would a business letter, that doesn't mean proper grammar and spelling aren't still important.

It's hard to guess who might see what you're posting online, and mistakes or carelessness may be noticed. We've all heard stories of employees who have been fired for material they posted online, never thinking twice about who might see it.

Remember that in most cases, online communication isn't as private as you might hope, and this is especially true when you're e-mailing at work. Numerous court cases have determined that company e-mail messages belong to the company, not the individual. If a subpoena is issued to your Internet service provider, everything you have done or said can be traced.

When communicating online, utilize the same good communication skills you would use in a more formal setting. Consider the following:

- Understand that your online communication represents you and that first impressions are important.

- Use correct spelling, grammar, and punctuation because they are still important.

- Write descriptive subject lines for your e-mails.

- Avoid sarcasm. In most cases, readers will be unsure of your true meaning.

- Do not use all capital letters (often perceived as *shouting*).

- Do not attach large files to e-mails without first receiving permission from your recipient.

- When forwarding messages, key your comments at the top.

- Do not overuse acronyms such as BTW (by the way), IMHO (in my humble opinion), and ROFL (rolling on floor laughing).

- Do not use e-mail for highly sensitive or confidential information.

- Don't respond to an e-mail that's upset you when you're still angry. The temporary satisfaction you may feel will fade.

CONFUSED AND MISUSED WORDS

accept   *v.* to agree to; to receive
except   *prep.* but; other than
Please **accept** my congratulations!
Everyone **except** Dusty arrived on time.

advice   *n.* recommendation
advise   *v.* to give advice; to inform
My **advice** is to arrive ten minutes before your interview.
I **advise** you to double-check your computations.

all ready   *adj.* (two words) completely ready
already   *adv.* before now or a specified time
Your order is **all ready** to be sent.
You have **already** received the shipment.

---

* Use the cursor; and proofread the bottom line of on-screen copy, advancing only one line at a time.

* Do not rely solely on spelling and grammar checkers to find and correct errors in your electronic communications. Remember to check for misused words that are spelled correctly.

* Proofread and edit your e-mail messages as you would any other written correspondence.

PROOFREADING APPLICATIONS

Exercise 3-1 • Spelling and Word Usage Check

*Compare the words in Column **A** with the corresponding words in Column **B**. Use the appropriate proofreaders' marks to correct the misspelled or misused words. If both columns are correct, write **C** to the left of the number.*

Column A	Column B
1. exceed	exceede
2. phenomenen	phenomenon
3. sufficeint	sufficient
4. negotiable	negotible
5. consceous	conscious
6. guidence	guidance
7. advantagious	advantageous
8. extraordinary	extraordenary
9. precedent	precident
10. occurrence	occurrence
11. extention	extension
12. unique	unikue

Exercise 3-2 • International Vocabulary

*Compare the French and Spanish words in Column **A** with the corresponding words in Column **B**. If the word in Column **B** is different from the word in Column **A**, use the appropriate proofreaders' marks to correct Column **B**. If the words in both columns are the same, write **C** to the left of the number.*

Column A	Column B
1. propuesta	propuista
2. encomienda	encomienda
3 versatile	versetile
4. asoleado	asolaedo
5. lendemain	lendermain

PROOFREADING AT THE COMPUTER

In this chapter, the exercises will give you an opportunity to proofread on-screen documents. In some cases, you will proofread the on-screen copy against a hard-copy draft. Proofread the on-screen copy very carefully. Your goal should be to print an error-free document the first time.

Exercise 3-3 • Business Letter

1. Open 3-3 from the Chapter 3 folder on the student CD.
2. Proofread the letter on the screen.
3. Correct all errors on the screen copy.
4. Save the letter as 3-3R. You can store the file in a variety of locations, such as in a folder on your hard drive, a flash drive, a CD, a disk, a shared drive on a network, or to other removable storage media. Check with your instructor if you have questions about where to store your file.
5. Print the letter.
6. Proofread the printed document. If you find any additional mistakes, correct the errors on both the hard copy and the screen.
7. Save and print the revised document.

Exercise 3-4 • Memorandum

1. Open 3-4 from the Chapter 3 folder on the student CD.
2. Proofread the memo on the screen, and make all corrections before printing the hard copy.
3. Follow the standard procedures for proofreading the hard copy. (Review the steps in Exercise 3-3 if necessary.)
4. Save your final version of the memo as 3-4R.

Exercise 3-5 • Short Report

1. Open 3-5 from the Chapter 3 folder on the student CD.
2. Proofread the report on the screen, and make all corrections before printing the hard copy.
3. Follow the standard procedures for proofreading the hard copy. (Review the steps in Exercise 3-3 if necessary.)
4. Save your final version of the report as 3-5R.

Exercise 3-6 • Statistical Report

1. Open 3-6 from the Chapter 3 folder on the student CD.
2. Work with a partner to proofread this document. Your partner should read from the correct handwritten document below while you make all corrections to the computer file before printing the hard copy.
3. Save your final version of the memo as 3-6R.

OFFICE FURNITURE AND EQUIPMENT COMPARISON

Central City Competitors

Model No.	Diff. Description	Our Price	Store A	Diff 1/2%	Store B	Diff 1/2%	Store C	Diff. 1/2%
DC-10	Desk Chair	$ 75	$ 90	120%	$ 95	126%	$ 70	207%
DT-21	Desk	320	410	128%	580	181%	300	206%
CT-28	Computer Table	250	220	212%	340	136%	250	None
CR-42	Calculator	15	20	133%	28	187%	20	133%
FC-58	File Cabinet	75	65	213%	90	120%	70	207%
ET-61	End Table	90	90	None	120	133%	75	217%
DL-36	Desk Lamp	45	50	111%	75	167%	45	None
TR-32	Desk Tray	10	12	120%	15	150%	9	210%
FM-15	Floor Mat	70	75	107%	90	128%	65	207%
FC-62	File Cabinet	90	85	206%	110	122%	85	206%

Exercise 3-7 • News Articles

When using desktop publishing programs, the writer and/or the editor often creates separate articles that are imported to specific locations on the newsletter page.

1. Open 3-7 from the Chapter 3 folder on the student CD.
2. Proofread the two articles on the screen, and make all corrections before printing the hard copy.

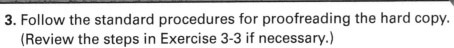

Exercise 3-7 • News Articles (*continued*)

3. Follow the standard procedures for proofreading the hard copy. (Review the steps in Exercise 3-3 if necessary.)
4. Save your final version of the memo as 3-7R.

Exercise 3-8 • Edited Memorandum

1. Open 3-8 from the Chapter 3 folder on the student CD.
2. Using the following list of changes, make corrections and changes in the document.
3. Proofread the material, and make any additional corrections on the screen before printing the hard copy.
4. Follow the standard procedures for proofreading the hard copy.
5. Save your final version of the document as 3-8R.

CHANGES IN MEMO	
Subject line	Insert "proposed" between "for" and "Denver."
New paragraph 1	Insert the following as the first paragraph: On May 1 the management council asked for information about the sales potential in the Denver metropolitan area. Contacts were made to conduct a survey.
Old paragraph 1 becomes new paragraph 2	In line 2 add "representatives of" between "by" and "City." In line 2 change "three" to "four." In line 3 add "eastside" between "the" and "shopping." Also change "survey instruments" to "questionnaires."
Old paragraph 3 becomes new paragraph 4	Start paragraph with "Because of national radio and television advertising," in line 2 insert "the names of" between "with" and "several." In line 2 delete "However."
Last paragraph	In line 1 insert "major" between "a" and "conclusion." In line 1 insert "viable" between "a" and "market." In line 2 delete "the process of opening" and replace it with "determining the feasibility of establishing."

Exercise 3-9 • Merged Documents

1. Open 3-9A from the student CD and print the recipient list.

2. Open 3-9B from the student CD and make any necessary corrections to the main document. Do not revise or remove the words ADDRESS BLOCK and GREETING LINE.

3. Click the Mailings tab and then Start Mail Merge. Select Letters. Still on the Mailings tab, click Select Recipients. Select Type New List, and then click the Customize Columns button at the bottom of the New Address List box.

4. From the list of Field Names, delete Company Name, Address Line 2, Country or Region, Home Phone, Work Phone, and E-mail Address. Click OK. Type your data list beginning with Mr. Salvador Rosario, keying Mr. in the Title Field and then tabbing to the next field. Key all five recipients, click OK, and save as 3-9List.

5. In the letter, select the words ADDRESS BLOCK. Click the Address Block button on the Mailings tab and click OK. Next, delete the words ADDRESS BLOCK in the letter. Select the merge code for Address Block and apply the No Spacing style to that line. Select the words GREETING LINE, click on Greeting Line, and change the comma to a colon. Delete the words GREETING LINE in the letter.

6. On the Mailings tab, click Finish & Merge, Edit Individual Documents, and OK. Save your merged letters as 3-9R.

Exercise 3-10 • Table

1. Open 3-10 from the Chapter 3 folder on the student CD.
2. Proofread the table against the amount of daily receipts from the calendar on the next page. Carry out extensions.
3. Make corrections on the screen, and print a hard copy. Follow the standard procedures for proofreading the hard copy.
4. Save the final document as 3-10R.

Exercise 3-10 • Table (*continued*)

March 2015

Sunday	Monday	Tuesday	Wednesday	Thursday	Friday	Saturday
1 648.50	2 546.80	3 585.50	4 684.90	5 585.00	6 748.60	7 800.46
8 685.00	9 475.10	10 648.63	11 670.91	12 678.82	13 759.25	14 900.14
15 789.46	16 300.45	17 458.63	18 654.28	19 649.14	20 686.90	21 1000.76
22 689.46	23 539.12	24 562.13	25 598.12	26 646.21	27 688.50	28 925.46
29 613.56	30 500.64	31 650.00				

Exercise 3-11 • Database

Open 3-11 from the Chapter 3 folder on the student CD. Proofread each record in the database against the information given on the registration cards that follow. Make corrections on the screen, and print a hard copy. Follow the standard procedures for proofreading the hard copy.

ANNUAL ARTS RECOGNITION DINNER RESERVATION

TO: AARD Chairperson, 357 Armstrong Avenue, Minneapolis, MN 55418-1833

Please make ___1___ (No.) reservation(s) for the AARD on May 8.

A check for ___$18___ ($18 per person) is enclosed.

Meal choices are as follows:

Reservation No. 1: Chicken _____ Fish ___✓___ Vegetarian _____

Reservation No. 2: Chicken _____ Fish _____ Vegetarian _____

Name: ___Julia West___

Address: ___4783 Dell Street___

City, State, ZIP: ___Hopkins, MN 55342-1862___

ANNUAL ARTS RECOGNITION DINNER RESERVATION

TO: AARD Chairperson, 357 Armstrong Avenue, Minneapolis, MN 55418-1833

Please make __2__ (No.) reservation(s) for the AARD on May 8.

A check for ___$36___ ($18 per person) is enclosed.

Meal choices are as follows:

Reservation No. 1: Chicken ___✓___ Fish _____ Vegetarian _____

Reservation No. 2: Chicken _____ Fish ___✓___ Vegetarian _____

Name:___Dwight Fern_____

Address:___27624 7th Street_____

_____

City, State, ZIP:___Edina, MN 55424-2388_____

ANNUAL ARTS RECOGNITION DINNER RESERVATION

TO: AARD Chairperson, 357 Armstrong Avenue, Minneapolis, MN 55418-1833

Please make __2__ (No.) reservation(s) for the AARD on May 8.

A check for ___$36___ ($18 per person) is enclosed.

Meal choices are as follows:

Reservation No. 1: Chicken _____ Fish ___✓___ Vegetarian _____

Reservation No. 2: Chicken _____ Fish _____ Vegetarian ___✓___

Name:___Walter Gappa_____

Address:___18321 Fairmont_____

_____

City, State, ZIP:___Crystal, MN 55428-1381_____

ANNUAL ARTS RECOGNITION DINNER RESERVATION

TO: AARD Chairperson, 357 Armstrong Avenue, Minneapolis, MN 55418-1833

Please make __2__ (No.) reservation(s) for the AARD on May 8.

A check for ___$36___ ($18 per person) is enclosed.

Meal choices are as follows:

Reservation No. 1: Chicken _____ Fish _____ Vegetarian _____

Reservation No. 2: Chicken ___✓___ Fish _____ Vegetarian _____

Name:___Felipe Baca_____

Address:___832 Chestnut Street_____

_____

City, State, ZIP:___St. Paul, MN 55125-2162_____

Exercise 3-11 • Database (*continued*)

ANNUAL ARTS RECOGNITION DINNER RESERVATION

TO: AARD Chairperson, 357 Armstrong Avenue, Minneapolis, MN 55418-1833

Please make __2__ (No.) reservation(s) for the AARD on May 8.

A check for __$36__ ($18 per person) is enclosed.

Meal choices are as follows:

Reservation No. 1: Chicken __✓__ Fish _____ Vegetarian _____

Reservation No. 2: Chicken __✓__ Fish _____ Vegetarian _____

Name: _____ Ester Birr _____

Address: _____ Box 83 _____

City, State, ZIP: _____ Byron, MN 55920-0083 _____

ANNUAL ARTS RECOGNITION DINNER RESERVATION

TO: AARD Chairperson, 357 Armstrong Avenue, Minneapolis, MN 55418-1833

Please make __1__ (No.) reservation(s) for the AARD on May 8.

A check for __$18__ ($18 per person) is enclosed.

Meal choices are as follows:

Reservation No. 1: Chicken _____ Fish _____ Vegetarian __✓__

Reservation No. 2: Chicken _____ Fish _____ Vegetarian _____

Name: _____ Senjen Vilaysing _____

Address: _____ 11362 Mill _____

City, State, ZIP: _____ Mound, MN 55364-2183 _____

ANNUAL ARTS RECOGNITION DINNER RESERVATION

TO: AARD Chairperson, 357 Armstrong Avenue, Minneapolis, MN 55418-1833

Please make __1__ (No.) reservation(s) for the AARD on May 8.

A check for __$18__ ($18 per person) is enclosed.

Meal choices are as follows:

Reservation No. 1: Chicken __✓__ Fish _____ Vegetarian _____

Reservation No. 2: Chicken _____ Fish _____ Vegetarian _____

Name: _____ Tara Mead _____

Address: _____ 628 Point Street _____

City, State, ZIP: _____ Barrow, MN 54812-1371 _____

Exercise 3-11 • Database (*continued*)

ANNUAL ARTS RECOGNITION DINNER RESERVATION

TO: AARD Chairperson, 357 Armstrong Avenue, Minneapolis, MN 55418-1833

Please make __2__ (No.) reservation(s) for the AARD on May 8.

A check for __$36__ ($18 per person) is enclosed.

Meal choices are as follows:

Reservation No. 1: Chicken _____ Fish __✓__ Vegetarian _____

Reservation No. 2: Chicken _____ Fish _____ Vegetarian __✓__

Name:___*Ruby Palo*___

Address:___*34 North 8th*___

City, State, ZIP:___*Durand, WI 54736-8034*___

ANNUAL ARTS RECOGNITION DINNER RESERVATION

TO: AARD Chairperson, 357 Armstrong Avenue, Minneapolis, MN 55418-1833

Please make __2__ (No.) reservation(s) for the AARD on May 8.

A check for __$36__ ($18 per person) is enclosed.

Meal choices are as follows:

Reservation No. 1: Chicken _____ Fish _____ Vegetarian __✓__

Reservation No. 2: Chicken _____ Fish _____ Vegetarian __✓__

Name:___*Gordon Maas*___

Address:___*Box 135*___

City, State, ZIP:___*Aitkin, MN 56431-0135*___

ANNUAL ARTS RECOGNITION DINNER RESERVATION

TO: AARD Chairperson, 357 Armstrong Avenue, Minneapolis, MN 55418-1833

Please make __2__ (No.) reservation(s) for the AARD on May 8.

A check for __$36__ ($18 per person) is enclosed.

Meal choices are as follows:

Reservation No. 1: Chicken __✓__ Fish _____ Vegetarian _____

Reservation No. 2: Chicken __✓__ Fish _____ Vegetarian _____

Name:___*Meg Reskin*___

Address:___*Box 322*___

City, State, ZIP:___*Baldwin, WI 54002-0322*___

Exercise 3-11 • **Database** (*continued*)

ANNUAL ARTS RECOGNITION DINNER RESERVATION

TO: AARD Chairperson, 357 Armstrong Avenue, Minneapolis, MN 55418-1833

Please make ___2___ (No.) reservation(s) for the AARD on May 8.

A check for ___$36___ ($18 per person) is enclosed.

Meal choices are as follows:

Reservation No. 1: Chicken _____ Fish _____ Vegetarian __✓___

Reservation No. 2: Chicken _____ Fish _____ Vegetarian __✓___

Name:_____*Dorian Wu*_____

Address:_____*Route 3*_____

_____*Hudson, WI 54016-0329*_____

City, State, ZIP:_____

Exercise 3-12 • **E-mail**

Use the appropriate proofreaders' marks to show the corrections. Open 3-12 from the Chapter 3 folder on the student CD. Make corrections on the screen and print a hard copy.

FROM:	jcain@brown.com
TO:	aduecker@rlc.edu
Cc:	
SUBJECT:	Job Opening

I spoke with you today regarding posting an ad on you employment board. Please post the following positione.

General clerical position opening. Duties include filing, filing, reviewing and responding to messages, informatoin packet preparation, and special projects as assigned. Responsible for timely resolution off customer service issues that many involve detailed research.

Required Skills and Experience:

- Experience with QuickBooks.
- Proficiency with MS Word, Excel, and Outlook.
- Good communication skills including gramar, spelling, and punctuation.
- Keen attention todetail.

Exercise 3-12 • E-mail (*continued*)

Send resume and cover letter to:

Brown, Inc.

Attention: Jackie

P.O. Box 150

Vandalia, IL 62471

This is a full-time position with benefits. Brown employees work on a 9/80 work schedule, which compresses a two-week, 80-hour work period into nine normal workdays: Monday through Thursday are nine-hour workdays, with every other Friday an eight-hour workday. The alternate Friday is a day day off.

If you have any questions, please do not hesitate to e-mail me. We will consider a recent graduate.

Jackie Cain

Bookmark It!

Want more practice? Go to www.cengage.com/keyboarding/pagel for more proofreading activities.

Capitalization Errors

Spotlight on ACCURACY

Word power, the ability to use the correct word, is critical in business writing. Note these differences in the use and abuse of language:

- **Differ and disagree.** *Differ* refers to things that are unlike others. Her purse *differs* from mine. *Disagree* refers to people who have different opinions. He *disagreed* with me about the value of the class.

- **Appraise and apprise.** *Appraise* means "to assess," while *apprise* means "to inform." Kwame will have the house *appraised*. Keep me *apprised* of your progress.

- **Imply and infer.** *Imply* indicates that the speaker is suggesting something, though not making an explicit statement. Harry *implied* that the man was a thief. *Infer* indicates that something in the speaker's words enabled the listeners to deduce that the man was a thief. We *inferred* from his words that the man was a thief.

Objectives

- Understand the basic rules for capitalization.

- Recognize and mark errors in capitalization using the appropriate proofreaders' marks.

- Spell correctly 12 frequently misspelled words.

- Use correctly three sets of commonly confused and misused words.

>> Capitalization

Capital letters show the importance of words. For example, the first word in a sentence, proper nouns, names, and the pronoun *I* are always capitalized. Although the trend is to use fewer capital letters, several basic rules must be followed.

The proofreaders' marks that indicate the corrections for capitalization errors are shown here:

	MARKED COPY	CORRECTED COPY
Capitalize ≡	to <u>s</u>an Francisco	to San Francisco
Lowercase /	my new ¢lassmates	my new classmates

RULE 1   Capitalize the first word of every sentence and the first word after a colon if that word begins a complete sentence.

Example: The new semester will begin next week.

Example: The memorandum to parents included the following notation: the new bus schedule will begin the first Monday in October.

RULE 2   Capitalize the first word of every complete quotation. Do not capitalize the first word of an interrupted quote.

Example: "The team," said the coach, "will practice this afternoon."

Example: Miss Wakui announced, "all assignments are due on Friday."

RULE 3   Capitalize the first word of each item in a list when each item is a complete sentence. Capitalize the first word of each item in an outline.

Example: At the end of the class period, follow these steps:

1. Print and turn in a final copy of your assignment.

2. Turn off your computer.

3. Put away your textbook.

Example: I. Varieties of vegetation
   A. Western hill country

   B. northern plains area

Exercise 4-1 • Proofread and Mark

*Mark all capitalization errors using the correct proofreaders' marks. If the sentence is correct, write **C** to the left of the number.*

1. "We will have lunch," he said, "at the central high school cafeteria."

2. ms. Jordan said, "check your locker in the south hallway."

3. "When the team is on stage," the adviser said, "all of us should stand and cheer."

4. Each person should have the following items in a bag:

    1. sport Shirt

    2. Clean socks

    3. black tie

5. The special meeting is for the following students: freshmen, sophomores, and Juniors.

RULE 4 Capitalize all proper nouns (the names of specific persons, places, and things) and any adjective derived from a proper noun.

CATEGORY	PROPER NOUNS
Brand names	Ford, Kellogg's, Tide, Ore-Ida, Bic
Buildings	the Empire State Building, Trump Tower
Clubs	Boys and Girls Club
Company names	Midwest Express, Mobile, General Electric
Specific courses	English I, Advanced Chemistry
Geographic regions and places	Africa, Middle East, Wales, Frankfurt, the Missouri River, the Smoky Mountains, Lake Superior, Washington Avenue, Sixth Street
Governmental terms	Department of Health and Human Services, Federal Reserve Board, United Nations, Supreme Court, Detroit City Council (*but not* federal *or* state *unless part of an official agency name*)

CATEGORY	PROPER NOUNS
Historic events	VE Day, Battle of Gettysburg, the Great Depression
Organizations	National Honor Society, Business Professionals of America, Future Business Leaders of America
Organizational terms within one's own firm	the Economics Department, the Education Division, the Board of Trustees, the Safety Committee
Religious groups	Lutheran, Jewish, Catholic, Protestant
References to a deity	God, Allah, Yahweh, Holy Spirit

RULE 5   Capitalize days of the week, months of the year, and holidays. Do not capitalize seasons of the year. Use lowercase for a.m. and p.m.

Example: The exam is scheduled for November 29 at 8 a.m., the first Monday after Thanksgiving.

Example: We will have a new schedule for the W̸inter season by november 1.

Example: Our school will hold a special program on president's day.

RULE 6   Capitalize both parts of hyphenated words if they are proper nouns or proper adjectives. Do not capitalize prefixes or suffixes added to proper nouns.

Example: The name of the new student is Esteban Perez-Vadillo.

Example: The special film is for German-speaking students.

Example: The Mellville High School-north High School rivalry can be quite intense.

Example: The retirement party was for ex-principal Jefferson.

RULE 7   Capitalize words that show a family relationship when they appear alone or are followed by a personal name. Do not capitalize family relations preceded by a possessive pronoun.

Example: The class reunion was for Uncle George and Dad.

Example: The team manager is cousin Susan.

Example: My B̸rother got me the interview.

Exercise 4-2 • Proofread and Mark

*Mark all capitalization errors using the correct proofreaders' marks. If the sentence is correct, write **C** to the left of the number.*

1. The doctor called Aunt Phyllis about her test results.

2. The leader of the field trip is Judith A. Sutton-smith.

3. The first car in the homecoming parade will be a chevrolet.

4. Classes will Begin on the wednesday after labor day.

5. The federal Reserve Board will meet in the State of Washington.

RULE 8   Capitalize a title that comes before a name. However, do not capitalize a title that follows a name or is used in place of a name unless it is the title of a high-ranking national, state, or international official (such as the President, the Secretary of State, or the Governor).

Example: Dairy Princess Sherry Maki
Example: Ellery Preston, the president of Beacon Inc.
Example: Cameron Schmidt, Artist in Residence
Example: He was elected president of the United States.

RULE 9   Capitalize titles in letter addresses and closings. Capitalize the first word, all nouns, and titles in a salutation of a letter; but capitalize

The President lives in the White House.

only the first word of a complimentary close. Capitalize both letters of state abbreviations.

Example:

Ms. Clara Mendez, Head Counseling Center Northwest High School 321 North Lincoln Way Chicago, IL 60614-4321 Dear Ms. Mendez:	Yours truly, Bruce Karlstad Department Head

Example:

Mr. Philip Leron Student senate president Southwest College 337 East College Street Albuquerque, NM 87109-3233 Dear Mr. Leron:	Sincerely Yours, Marian Thomlinson Assistant principal

RULE 10   Capitalize the titles of officers in constitutions, bylaws, and minutes of meetings. Titles of company officials are not capitalized when they follow or replace a personal name.

Example: The constitution states that "the President shall appoint a three-person Credentials Committee."

Example: The minutes were taken by Bryan Victorson, Secretary.

Capitalize academic titles that precede or follow a name. However, do not capitalize academic degrees used as general classifications.

Example: She announced that Dean Antonio Gomez will speak on February 26.

Example: Each of the teachers has a Master's degree.

Exercise 4-3 • Proofread and Mark

*Mark all capitalization errors using the correct proofreaders' marks. If the sentence is correct, write **C** to the left of the number.*

1. The constitution states that "the treasurer shall be responsible for an annual report."

2. Ben has received his bachelor's degree in education.

3. The win was coach O'Neil's 150th victory.

4. The English IV class will be taught by professor Karjala.

5. The title in the closing of the letter should be "high school principal."

RULE 11   Capitalize points of the compass when they refer to specific regions or are used as proper nouns. Do not capitalize points of the compass to indicate directions or general locations.

> *Example:*   Next month the choir will tour the West.
>
> *Example:*   All 18 teams will compete in the Southern Region tournament.
>
> *Example:*   The summer school course includes visits to the m̲i̲dwest.
>
> *Example:*   The team will travel E̸ast on the first day of the trip.

RULE 12   Capitalize the first word and all important words in titles of literary and artistic works and in displayed headings. Do not capitalize articles (*a, an, the*), conjunctions (*and, as, but, or, nor*), and prepositions containing four or fewer letters (*at, by, for, in, of, on, to, with*) unless they are the first word of a title.

> *Example:*   The winning theme was entitled "Searching for the Lost Dream."
>
> *Example:*   Please purchase the paperback book *Your Guide to Correct Punctuation*.
>
> *Example:*   We are to study the chapter "The Era Ø̸f T̸he Ethnic Groups."
>
> *Example:*   The library subscribes to t̲h̲e̲ *Daily Mirror*.

RULE 13   Capitalize a noun that precedes a figure or letter *except* for common nouns such as *line, page, sentence,* and *size*.

> *Example:*   Place the instructions in Appendix G.
>
> *Example:*   The assignment begins on page 37.
>
> *Example:*   The sweatshirts should be S̸ize 14.

Exercise 4-4 • Proofread and Mark

*Mark all capitalization errors using the correct proofreaders' marks. If the sentence is correct, write **C** to the left of the number.*

1. The choir will sing "The Sweet Song of Spring" in the concert.

2. All saturday classes are scheduled for towns East of here.

3. Proofread the material starting on Line 8.

4. The new headline should read "Bond Issue Is defeated."

5. the new chapter begins on page 42.

CONFUSED AND MISUSED WORDS

allot   *v.* to allocate or distribute

a lot   *n.* (two words) a large amount; many

alot   incorrect spelling of *a lot*

Please **allot** two hours for our meeting.

Your help made the job **a lot** easier.

among   *prep.* comparison of three or more persons or things

between *prep.* comparison of only two persons or things

Distribute the work **among** your staff.

The goals will be divided **between** Paul and Christa.

assistance *n.* help

assistants *n.* helpers

Your **assistance** helped us meet our deadline.

The **assistants** are meeting at 3 p.m. to discuss the project.

Proofreading & Editing Tips

PEP Tip

* When checking for capitalization errors, skim the material to locate words with capital letters and decide if they are capitalized correctly.

* Check to ensure that each sentence begins with a capital letter.

* Review the word processing function that changes letters from upper- to lowercase and from lower- to uppercase.

PROOFREADING APPLICATIONS

Exercise 4-5 • Paragraph

Proofread the following material, and mark all errors using the appropriate proofreaders' marks.

Plans for the publication of the pamphlet entitled *Schools and the Future of our City* are complete. The draft copy was approved by the Citizens Committee for Future Plans. The Chairperson was principal Roosevelt-Grant. A meeting to discuss the pamphlet has been scheduled in the Northeast part of the district on Tuesday, October 1. Questions to be discussed include the following:

1. what are the plans for the new school buildings?
2. should school activities be curtailed?
3. Do taxes have to be increased?

The meeting will be in Room 102 of east High School. Arrangements for additional meetings will be made by Dr. Andrea glivem. The meetings must be concluded in November because voting on the school bond issue will take place a week after thanksgiving.

Exercise 4-6 • Spelling and Word Usage Check

*Compare the words in Column **A** with the corresponding words in Column **B**. Use the appropriate proofreaders' marks to correct the misspelled or misused words. If both columns are correct, write **C** to the left of the number.*

Column A	Column B
1. access	acess
2. resently	recently
3. schedual	schedule
4. committee	committtee
5. matterial	material
6. audet	audit
7. situation	sitaution
8. appropriate	apporpriate
9. analysis	analysis
10. communication	communiction
11. maxinum	maximum
12. spescial	special
13. They did not alot the money.	Please allot the quotas.
14. divide among Jo and me	between the two of us
15. Your assistance is required.	Kiko has two assistance.

Exercise 4-7 • International Vocabulary

*Compare the French and Spanish words in Column **A** with the corresponding words in Column **B**. If the word in Column **B** is different from the word in Column **A**, use the appropriate proofreaders' marks to correct Column **B**. If the words in both columns are the same, write **C** to the left of the number.*

Column A	Column B
1. comprender	comprender
2. comida	comidia
3. toujours	toujurs
4. depositar	depositer
5. projet	porjet

Exercise 4-8 • Letter

Proofread the following letter, and mark all capitalization and other mechanical errors using the appropriate proofreaders' marks.

CENTRAL COMMUNITY HIGH SCHOOL

372 North Street, St. Louis, MO 63122-2731
314-555-0138 • Fax 314-555-0148

october 1, 20--

Ms. Carlota Silva, President
Northern Fences Corporation
327 Witherspoon Drive
St. Louis, Mo 63138-4422

Dear Ms. Silva:

The Citizens Commitee for Future Plans recently published a booklet about planning for our future schools. This assistants was provided to help the Citizens of our community better understand the effect that our schools have on the life of the community.

As a member of the committee, I would be pleased to meet with your westside Business Culb to reveiw the contents of the pamphlet and to help the members understand the importance of the facts that the commitee has assembled. We would like to meet with you this Fall. Would there be time during your October 15 meeting for such a presention?

Sincerely Yours,

Marilyn Roosevelt-grant
Principal

tcm

Proofread the following memo, and mark all errors using the appropriate proofreaders' marks.

CENTRAL COLLEGE
MEMORANDUM

TO: Louise Hemker

FROM: Alisha Irwin-miller

DATE: April 22, 20--

SUBJECT: Learning Communities

Learning communities establish conditions that promote a cooperative spirit and a sense of common purpose. We are forming learning communities in Transitional Math and english this Fall.

These groups will provide students with the opportunity to develop their understanding of the important basic concepts presented in English 101, math 101, and math 102. Attending learning communities will assist students in reinforcing the information presented during regular class time. Facilitators will be working closely with Faculty to ensure students are grasping the concepts needed to be successful in their classes. Students can attend one of the following sessions:

- English 101 Learning Communities will be held Monday, Wednesday, and Friday in LB 100 from 11 A.M. to noon.

- Math 101 Learning Communities will be held on Tuesday and Thursday in LB 210 from 11:00 A.M. to noon.

- Math 102 Learning Communities will be held on Monday, Wednesday, and Friday in LB 102 from 11 A.M. to noon.

Please encourage your students to join one of the new learning communities.

jak

PROOFREADING AT THE COMPUTER

Exercise 4-10 • Letter

1. Open 4-10 from the Chapter 4 folder on the student CD. (This is a computer copy of Exercise 4-8.)

2. Proofread the letter on the screen. Correct all errors on the screen copy that you marked with proofreaders' marks in Exercise 4-8.

3. Format the letter using default left and right margins and a 2" top margin.

4. Save the letter as 4-10R, and print it. You can store the file in a variety of locations, such as in a folder on your hard drive, a flash drive, a CD, a disk, a shared drive on a network, or to other removable storage media. Check with your instructor if you have questions about where to store your file.

5. Proofread the printed document. If you find any additional mistakes, correct the errors on both the hard copy and the screen.

6. Save and print the revised document.

Exercise 4-11 • E-mail Message

1. Open 4-12 from the Chapter 4 folder on the student CD.

2. Proofread the e-mail message, and make all necessary corrections.

3. Save the document as 4-12R, and print it.

4. Proofread the printed document. If you find any additional mistakes, correct the errors on both the hard copy and the screen.

5. Save and print the revised document.

Exercise 4-12 • Minutes

1. Open 4-11 from the Chapter 4 folder on the student CD.

2. Proofread the copy on the screen by comparing it with the correct handwritten copy on pages 58 and 59.

3. Correct all mistakes.

4. Format the minutes using default left and right margins and a 2" top margin.

5. Save the minutes as 4-11R, and print it.

6. Proofread the printed document. If you find any additional mistakes, correct the errors on both the hard copy and the screen.

7. Save and print the revised document.

CENTRAL HIGH SCHOOL STUDENT COUNCIL

ST. LOUIS, MISSOURI

October 25, 20--

The regular meeting of the Central High School Student Council was held on Thursday, October 25, 20--, in Room 205. Members present:

Eric Ashcroft, Grade 10	Haru Tokuda, Treasurer
Marla Staloch, Grade 10	Carol Goudge, Secretary
Tony Tiese, Grade 11	Ken Baertsch, Vice President
Chih Liang, Grade 12	Colleen Seifer, President
Janice Ludwig, Grade 12	Ms. Adrian, Adviser
Steve Hovland, Grade 11	Mr. Levine, Adviser

Recorder of minutes: Carol Goudge

1. The meeting was called to order at 1:45 p.m. by President Seifer. All members were present for roll call.

2. The October 18 minutes were read by Secretary Goudge and approved as read.

3. Treasurer Tokuda reported the balance in the treasury as $405.12.

4. Janice Ludwig reported the following:

    A. The homecoming buttons have arrived and can be sold starting October 28. Each council member is to sell at least 25 buttons.

B. Seven floats plus the marching band have already signed up for the homecoming parade.

5. New business included the following:

A. Mr. Levine asked if the Student Council wanted to participate in the preparation of a booklet entitled <u>Student Guide for New Students</u>. After discussion, it was agreed that they did.

B. Chih Liang moved that the Student Council assist with fall cleanup activities on November 12. The motion was seconded and adopted.

6. Vice President Baertsch announced that the Homecoming Parade Planning Committee would meet during fourth period on Tuesday.

7. Tony Tiese moved to adjourn. The motion was seconded and adopted. The meeting was adjourned at 2:35 p.m.

CUMULATIVE APPLICATION

Exercise 4-13 • Report

Proofread and correct all errors using the appropriate proofreaders' marks.

Going Green

After the release of former Vice president Al Gore's *An Inconvient Truth*, more and more people are asking "What can I do to reduce my carbon footprint in this world?" Going green means conserving energe, creating less waste, recycling, and being aware of one's impact on the environment.

Recycle

An easy and free way to begin to reduce our carbon footprint is to recycle. The computer paper at home, the junk mail, the magazines and catalogs all can easily be recycled. The milk jugs, the soft drink cans that fill up our trash can be recycled. Cell Phones can be turned in to organizations that reprogram and give to those in need.

Reduce Waste

When asked, "Paper or plastic," choose paper or better yet, take a reusable cloth bag to the grocery store. Instead of drinking bottled water, drink tap water. Use On-Line Banking. You can also sign up to receive your bills via e-mail. No more bills in the mail, no more checks, and no more stamps. Sign up for a service such as Green Dimes, which is like a do not call for junk mail. They will even plant a tree for you. Return your grass clippings to your lawn with a mulching mower.

Conserve Energy

Instead of driving to work, take a bus, carpool, ride a bicycle, or walk to work. For energy efficient lighting, consider purchasing and using compact fluorescent lights (CFL) and light emitting diode (LED) bulbs. CFLs are readily available in hardware stores and

Exercise 4-13 • Report (*continued*)

general purpose stores. CFLs are more efficient and last longer than incandescent bulbs. LED lightin uses less electricity than incandescent or CFL bulbs. Unplug appliances that are not in use. When buying new appliances, pay attention to the energy they use. Turning your thermostat down in the Winter and up in the Summer can reduce your power bills and reduce your carbon footprint.

Conclusion

There are many ways to reduce your carbon footprint in the world. There are ways that are expensive and other ways that not only cost nothing, but can actually save you money. Educate yourself by reading and researching on the Internet new technologies that may reduce your carbon footprint. If everyone in the World did their part, what a difference it would make.

Bookmark It!

Want more practice? Go to www.cengage.com/keyboarding/pagel for more proofreading activities.

Abbreviation Errors and Rough Drafts

Spotlight on ACCURACY

To be effective, an abbreviation must have the same meaning for both the writer and the reader. If confusion results, the wrong message may be conveyed. Which word or phrase is correct for the following abbreviations?

- AA (administrative assistant, Alcoholics Anonymous, associate in arts)

- St. (street, saint)

- k (kilogram, thousand)

Objectives

- Apply common abbreviation rules.

- Proofread revisions made from rough drafts.

- Spell correctly 12 frequently misspelled words.

- Use correctly three sets of commonly confused and misused words.

>> Abbreviations

An **abbreviation** is a shortened form of a word or phrase. Only standard abbreviations should be used. Consult a dictionary if you are in doubt about the correctness of an abbreviation.

Abbreviations may be important space savers in business writing, especially in short documents. Because the reader may not be familiar with an abbreviation, spell it out the first time and place the abbreviation in parentheses; for example, *World Health Organization (WHO)*. Thereafter, use only the abbreviation. **Note:** Use an abbreviation only when you know the reader will understand it as you intended.

Some abbreviations are acceptable with or without periods (for example, *ft.* or *ft*; *mi.* or *mi*). Use one style consistently within a document. One space follows a period used after an abbreviation (*Mr. Luft*), and no space follows a period within an abbreviation (*p.m.*).

Use the following proofreaders' marks to make corrections in abbreviations.

	MARKED COPY	CORRECTED COPY
Spell out. *sp* ⬭	Send by (Dec.) 20.	Send by December 20.
Insert period. ⊙	Mrs⊙Pahl is here.	Mrs. Pahl is here.
Close up space. ⬭	U. S. Post Office	U.S. Post Office
Delete period.	Radio Station KⱯVⱯGⱯNⱯ	Radio Station KVGN

General Style

Some abbreviations may be used with formal and informal writing. The following guidelines are appropriate for most business communication (letters, memos, reports, and e-mail messages) as well as for general usage. Consult a reference manual for more detailed rules.

Personal and Professional Titles.   Personal titles are used as a mark of courtesy. Generally, they include *Mr., Mrs., Miss, Ms.,* or *Dr.* Professional titles may also indicate one's military, religious, or educational status. Apply the following rules for abbreviating titles:

RULE 1   Abbreviate personal and courtesy titles that come before personal names.

Examples:

Mr. Reider	Messrs. Reider and Wood (plural of *Mr.*)
Mrs. May	Mmes. May and Connor (plural of *Mrs.*)
Ms. Nault	Dr. Deven Wieland

Note: *Ms.* is appropriate when the marital status of a woman is unknown or when the woman prefers this title. *Miss* is not an abbreviation.

RULE 2   Abbreviate personal titles following names. Titles such as *Jr.*, *Sr.*, *2nd*, or *III* are generally not set off by commas; however, academic and professional titles are.

Examples:

Jarod LaPorte Jr.	Randall Markum 2nd
Elizabeth Arnneski, CPS	William Lin III
Andrew Kelm, Esp.	Emily Stinson, Ph.D.

RULE 3   Do not abbreviate titles appearing with surnames.

Example:

Doctor Karjala	*but*	Dr. Betty Karjala

RULE 4   Write out professional titles whenever possible.

Examples:

Professor Katie Cain	the Reverend Nathan Green

Company Names.   Words such as *Bros.* (Brothers), *Co.* (Company), *Inc.* (Incorporated), *Ltd.* (Limited), and *Mfg.* (Manufacturing) are often abbreviated in official company names. Check the company letterhead for the appropriate style.

Examples:

Wolfe Industries, Inc.
Canadian Coins, Ltd.
Rangers Mfg.

Exercise 5-1 • Proofread and Mark

*Use the appropriate proofreaders' marks to identify the corrections that should be made. If the sentence is correct, write **C** to the left of the number.*

1. The defendant is Mister Weier.

2. All we know is that someone named Dr. Ivory answered.

continued

3. Tell Miss. Goodney that her company is the first respondent.

4. Norman Bruot, Ph.D., will forward the signed contract.

5. Prof. Costello will be in charge of the session.

Organizations.   Abbreviate names of government and private agencies, organizations and associations, radio and television broadcasting stations, and other groups when appropriate. These abbreviations are generally written in all capital letters without periods.

Examples:

FBI	Federal Bureau of Investigation
NATO	North Atlantic Treaty Organization
KRBI	(Call letters for a radio station)
KMSP-TV	(Call letters for a television station)

Note: Government organizations often include the abbreviation *U.S.* No space follows the period within the abbreviation.

Addresses.

RULE 1   Words and directions within addresses should not be abbreviated. However, compound compass point directions, such as *NW, NE, SW,* and *SE, are* abbreviated when used after street addresses.

Examples:

Avenue	Drive	Road
Boulevard	Lane	Square
Building	Parkway	Street
Court	Place	

852 Appalachian Drive East

49627 Arizona Avenue NW

RULE 2   Two-letter state abbreviations are appropriate only when they appear with a ZIP Code in an address. The appendix lists the two-letter state abbreviations.

Examples:

800 College Avenue	She lives in
Saint Peter, MN 56082-1498	Saint Peter, Minnesota.

RULE 3   Do not abbreviate the name of a city, state, or country or pre-fixes to most geographic names except when space is a problem. Periods are used with these abbreviations.

Examples:

Saint Clair   *or*   St. Clair

Fort Madison   *or*   Ft. Madison

Mount Saint Helens   *or*   Mt. St. Helens

United States   *or*   U.S. (no space after the internal period)

South Africa   *or*   S. Africa

California   *not*   Calif.

Exercise 5-2 • Proofread and Mark

*Use the appropriate proofreaders' marks to identify the corrections that should be made. If the sentence is correct, write **C** to the left of the number.*

1. We cannot send the report to the U. S. Army Corps of Engineers.

2. The road crosses the corner of the state of MT.

3. The ABC Radio Network was able to achieve its goal.

4. Pine Bluff, Ark., will eliminate the surcharge.

5. Send the list of addresses to Tatiana Sonamaran at
4903 E. Alberta St.

Time.   Abbreviate the standard time zones and expressions of time. Note the use of periods in the following examples.

Examples:

CDT (Central Daylight Time)

PST (Pacific Standard Time)

a.m. and p.m. (no space after the internal period)

Note: The abbreviation *a.m.* stands for *ante meridiem* (before noon), while *p.m.* stands for *post meridiem* (after noon).

Informal or Technical Style

Some abbreviations are appropriate for use in technical documents such as lists, business forms, and informal documents or when space is a prob-lem. Such abbreviations are not appropriate in formal reports or business correspondence.

Days and Months

Sun.	Thurs.	Jan.	May	Sept.
Mon.	Fri.	Feb.	June	Oct.
Tues.	Sat.	Mar.	July	Nov.
Wed.		Apr.	Aug.	Dec.

Measurements

in *or* in.	yd *or* yd.	oz *or* oz.
ft *or* ft.	sq *or* sq.	lb *or* lb.

Expressions

acct.	*for*	account
bal.	*for*	balance
dept.	*for*	department
ea.	*for*	each
EOM	*for*	end of month
PO	*for*	purchase order
P.O.	*for*	post office
No.	*for*	number (used when a number follows the abbreviation; e.g., The new order is No. 4406.)
vs.	*for*	versus

Exercise 5-3 • Proofread and Mark

*Use the appropriate proofreaders' marks to identify the corrections that should be made. If the sentence is correct, write **C** to the left of the number. Use the "general style" (not the "informal" or "technical style") in proofreading this exercise and all exercises that follow.*

1. The wrestling meet will begin at 8 p. m.

2. This decision will benefit the people who register before the deadline on Fri.

3. The enthusiasm of employees in the Acctg. Dept. is appreciated.

4. You should arrive at 8:05 a. m. E.D.T. on Mon.

5. Please notify KXLM-TV that the reception on Feb. 28 will be held at the U. S. Department of the Interior.

6. Saint George, Ut., is where our consultant lives.

7. The lawsuit in general court will be titled *Good vs. Erickson.*

8. Gloves, Inc., has opened a branch store near the K.X.T.Y. transmitter.

continued

9. Have Prof. Stoney forward the survey results to the University of Notre Dame graduate school.

10. Will Ms. Anderson have the schedule ready by Aug. 1?

» Rough Drafts

Newly composed documents are usually not in final form. They may contain keying and formatting errors. Sometimes word originators simply jot down ideas and instruct a copy editor to finish composing, keying, formatting, and printing the document.

The copy editor, using a pen and proofreaders' marks, makes corrections and revisions to the printed document. The result is a rough draft. On the basis of this rough draft, the copy editor completes the final editing, formatting, and printing of the document. Both the word originator and the copy editor need to use proofreaders' marks correctly. Then revisions will be marked consistently, and fewer errors will result.

When revising text, originators may move copy, change spacing, or return copy to its original form. Proofreaders must learn to recognize and apply the following proofreaders' marks when revising text:

	MARKED COPY	CORRECTED COPY
Move.	your letter of May 1	your May 1 letter
Stet (keep as is). *stet* or	the spacious room *stet* the spacious room	the spacious room
Single-space. *SS*	products were ready *SS* to be sold through the	products were ready to be sold through the
Double-space. *DS*	$12,087 + 3,724 $15,811 *DS*	$12,087 + 3,724 $15,811

Both the writer and copy editor must use proofreaders' marks correctly. Revisions will be marked consistently, and fewer errors will occur.

Exercise 5-4 • Proofread and Mark

In the following sentences, mark the corrections according to the information given in the "Changes" line.

1. The benefits cannot be changed before the is approved.

Changes: Add "contract" between "the" and "is."

2. The bush should be planted by May 15.

Changes: Move "by May 15" to the beginning of the sentence; capitalize "by"; lowercase "The"; add "currant" between "the" and "bush."

3. Three youths the Council meeting on October 12.

Changes: Move "on October 12" to the beginning of the sentence; capitalize "on"; lowercase "Three"; add "spoke at" between "youths" and "the."

continued

4. By working extra hours and putting in more time, we will be able to achieve the goals set at teh beginning of the year.

   Changes: Move "By working extra hours and putting in more time" to the end of the sentence; delete the comma after the word "time"; lowercase "By"; capitalize "we"; spell "the" correctly.

5. the motion was seconded after a long discussion.

   Changes: Capitalize "the"; insert "and approved" between "seconded" and "after"; insert a period at the end of the sentence.

6. on February 28 the constitution was approved by members at our regular meeting.

   Changes: Move "on February 28" to the end of the sentence; capitalize "the"; add "revised" between "the" and "constitution."

7. Marlys celebrated her birthday by having lunch with friends at her favorite establishment.

   Changes: Add "eighteenth" between "her" and "birthday"; delete "lunch" and insert "dinner"; delete "establishment" and insert "restaurant."

CONFUSED AND MISUSED WORDS

all together   *adv.* (two words) gathered into a single unit or group; collected in one place

altogether   *adv.* entirely, completely, utterly

The reference books are **all together** on the shelf.

She is **altogether** too busy to take on another responsibility.

allude   *v.* to make an indirect reference to something

elude   *v.* to avoid or escape notice

He **alluded** to the fact that Mary Beth was correct.

The criminal **eluded** capture.

any one   *adj./pro.* (two words) certain person; use when the pronoun is followed by an *of* phrase

anyone   *pron.* anybody; any person at all

Any one of us can go.

Has **anyone** talked with Josey?

* Use only those abbreviations that your audience will understand.

* Be selective when using abbreviations in business letters, memos, reports, and e-mail messages.

* Depending on the software program you use, your spelling checker may recognize abbreviations differently. However, you can add commonly used abbreviations to your word processing dictionary so those abbreviations are not flagged as possible errors.

PROOFREADING APPLICATIONS

*Proofread the following sentences, and mark all abbreviation errors using the appropriate proofreaders' marks. If the sentence is correct, write **C** to the left of the number.*

1. Mrs Tappe volunteers time each week at the Community Center.

2. Radio Station K.N.M.U. went on the air in Jan. 1966.

3. James Edward Tanner, III married Caitlin Jane Rogers in Lansing, MI.

4. Her brother lived at 38893 Craig Ave.

5. We cannot meet on Tues. or Thurs.

6. I believe the best time to meet tomorrow is at 3:30 pm C.D.T.

7. Did you know that Thelma works for the FBI?

8. Send your resume to the manager of our Acct. Dept.

9. The U.S. Post Office in Muncie is located on Nelson Lane.

10. Doctor Kenneth Postma is the new consultant.

11. The new pastor at our church is Rev. Alice Nease.

12. Alice Carrasco was elected to the U. S. Senate by a wide margin.

13. What did they hope to achieve by driving to 39904 West Ave.?

14. We plan to arrive by 8:45 am on Sun.

15. Miss. Jacqlyn Arneson was hired by Wisconsin Energy.

16. Edward and Emma enjoy vacationing in Penn.

17. Professor Newsome will speak at our convention in Minneapolis in March.

18. What is the bal. for our dept.?

19. Mr Westman is very particular about what he eats.

20. Kenard Thieland, Ph.D., visited San Francisco, CA.

Exercise 5-6 • Spelling and Word Usage Check

*Compare the words in Column **A** with the corresponding words in Column **B**. Use the appropriate proofreaders' marks to correct the misspelled or misused words. If both columns are correct, write **C** to the left of the number.*

Column A	Column B
1. benefit	benefit
2. particular	particlar
3. committment	commitment
4. enthusiasm	enthusiasam
5. consultent	consultant
6. defendent	defendant
7. achieve	achieve
8. can not	cannot
9. believe	beleive
10. eliminate	elimanate
11. congratulations	congradulations
12. corporate	corporite
13. Derek is all together too successful.	We are in this all together.
14. Were you able to allude detection?	Jasmine alluded to her judicial appointment.
15. Is anyone able to attend?	Can any one of you participate?

Exercise 5-7 • Word Division List

*Proofread the words in each line. If one or more words are divided incorrectly, correct the word(s) using the appropriate proofreaders' marks. Then write the word(s) on the blank line using hyphen(s) to show **all preferred points of division**. If all three words in a line are correct, write **C** on the blank line.*

Ex. thought	liv- able	mark er	*thought marker*
1. e-lude	econ- o- my	glu- cose	_____
2. def- en- dant	doc- u- ment	book- keeper	_____
3. de- pen- dable	lei- sure	dis- tor- tion	_____
4. ex- po- nent	fel- o- ny	dis- pro- por- tion	_____
5. in- terr- upt	sit- u- a- tion	mac- ro- eco- nom- ics	_____
6. lieu- ten- ant	lim- it	con- scious- ness	_____
7. en- dorse- ment	for- tu- itous	ques- tion- naire	_____
8. ven- ge- ance	usu- al- ly	dis- pute	_____
9. in- dis- pens- able	but- ter- fly	con- troll- ing	_____
10. mag- ne- sium	pref- er- en- tial	pla- gia- rize	_____
11. per- tin- ent	pe- des- tri- an	expect	_____
12. cra- zy	psy- chic	dic- tio- nary	_____
13. cri- te- ri- on	in- dis- pens- able	res- i- due	_____
14. re- pub- lic	con- tem- por- ary	da- tum	_____
15. cha- rac- ter	cross- reference	dis- pute	_____

Exercise 5-8 • Memorandum

Proofread the following memo, and mark all errors using the appropriate proofreaders' marks.

ACME INSURANCE COMPANY, INC.
MEMORANDUM

TO:　　Jason Realstad, Editor Acme Notes

FROM:　Marguerite Lorenz, Chairperson Awards Committee

DATE:　Sep. 5, 20--

SUBJECT: ITEMS FOR NEWSLETTER

Here are two items for the Dec. issue of "Acme Notes." Please modify them to fit the available space.

Item 1. <u>Year End Awards Program Scheduled.</u> The annual Awards Program will be held in Swift Auditorium on January 11. The auditorium is located at 9550 Prince Blvd. here in Manhattan.

An important part of the program will be the presentation of special awards for outstanding achievement during the current year. In addition, recognition will be given to employees who have been with the company for 25, 30, 35, and 40 years.

The speaker for the program will be Antoine Paez, corporate consultent for Maxon Industries, Chicago, Ill. His enthusiasm in working with companies like ours will be of particular benefit to us as we embark upon next year's sales campaign. Mr Paez has shown a tremendously large no. of people how to achieve the goals they have set. His message will be currant and direct. He will give us many usable suggestions.

Please attend the annual Awards Program and extend your personal congradulations to the award winners. More information will be distributed in December.

Item 2. <u>Manager's Meeting Scheduled</u>. Juliana Keltgen, legal council, has asked to meet with supervisors on Thursday, January 10. The company was a defendent in a recent court case that we won. Ms. Keltgen believes that a meeting is needed to summarize the results of the case and to help eliminate misunderstandings in the company's hiring process. We believe you will find this meeting well worth your time.

Exercise 5-9 • Letter

Proofread the following letter, and mark all errors using the appropriate proofreaders' marks.

ACME INSURANCE COMPANY, INC.

3842 West Grand Avenue • St. Paul, MN 55110-2910
612-555-0155 • Fax: 612-555-0156

Dec. 3, 20--

Ms. Floragene Adams, President
Southern Armstrong, Ltd.
728 Imperial Drive South
Nashville, TN 37210-4217

Dear Ms. Adams:

It is a pleasure to confirm our invitation to you to be the speaker at our Apr. 22 seminar in Wichita. You were recommended to us by Candace Okano, president of Midwest Travel Company in Kansas City, Kans.

The in-service meeting will be held in Suite 332 in the Grand Central Ins. Bldg. The seminar will begin at 10 a. m.

Two other speakers who will also be meeting with our managers are Josefina Ramos, chairperson, Board of Directors, Littleton, Inc., and Arthur Proehl, legal counsel for Juniper County.

We have also invited Ray Symthe, president, Toledo Consulting. Unfortunately, he can not be with us for this meeting.

Additional information will be sent to you concerning travel and housing arrangements. If you have any questions, please let me know.

We look forward to your being with us in Apr.

Sincerely,

Louis Roe
Seminar Coordinator

tfd

PROOFREADING AT THE COMPUTER

Students, please note the following:

- Standard operating procedures for saving, printing, proofreading the hard copy, and reprinting the document were provided for you in Exercise 2-15 on page 24. Beginning with this chapter, those directions will not be repeated. Instead, you should continue to follow the standard operating procedures you have learned for the exercises listed in Proofreading at the Computer from this point forward.

- Also, formatting instructions will no longer be provided for most of the documents. If necessary, refer to your text-workbook for assistance.

Exercise 5-10 • Letter

1. Open 5-10 from the Chapter 5 folder on the student CD. (This is a computer copy of Exercise 5-9.)

2. Proofread the letter on the screen. Correct all errors on the screen copy that you indicated with proofreaders' marks in Exercise 5-9.

3. Produce the letter in correct format following the standard procedures described in the previous chapters.

Exercise 5-11 • Memorandum

1. On the handwritten memo on page 79, mark the changes requested (shown in the box on page 80) using the appropriate proofreaders' marks.

2. Open 5-11 from the Chapter 5 folder on the student CD.

3. Proofread the copy on the screen by comparing it with the corrected handwritten rough draft.

4. Produce the memo in correct format following the standard procedures described in the previous chapters.

MEMO

TO: Ramon Schroader, Manager
Human Resources Department

FROM: Marguerite Lorenz, Awards Cmte.

DATE: November 23, 20--

SUBJECT: PRELIMINARY LIST FOR AWARDS

As you know, our annual Awards Program will be held on Feb. 3 with the dinner starting at 6 pm. We anticipate that the program will last from 6:45 p.m. to 8:15 p.m.

A major part of the program will be the presentation of awards to various individuals and several departments. One category of individual awards is for those who have worked at the company for 25 or more years.

Please review the records of all employees and prepare a list according to the following categories:

1. employed for 25 years

2. employed for 30 years

3. employed for 35 or more years

Our plan is to give a wristwatch to those employees with 25 years. Those with 30 years will receive a piece of crystal glass, and those with 35 years will receive a miniature sculpture.

In addition to identifying ea. person, we need a brief biographical sketch that can be printed in the program. Please contact each awardee to help you prepare a brief paragraph or two about his or her years here at ACME.

Finally, will you arrange for the no. of awards to be given in each category? Each watch should be engraved with a suitable inscription.

Could I please have a preliminary report on the no. of awards and the names of the awardees by Dec. 15.

Exercise 5-11 • Memorandum (*continued*)

PARAGRAPH	CHANGES TO BE MADE IN MEMO
Paragraph 1	Delete "As you know." Capitalize "our."
Paragraph 2	Insert "major" between "one" and "category."
Paragraph 3	In Item 3, delete "or more."
Paragraph 4	Replace "piece" with the word "vase."
Paragraph 5	Delete "that can be printed."
Paragraph 5	Move "in the program" to appear after "person."
Paragraph 6	Replace "watch" with "award."
Paragraph 7	Change date to December 1.

Exercise 5-12 • E-mail Message

1. Open 5-12 from the Chapter 5 folder on the student CD.
2. Proofread the e-mail message on the screen. Correct all errors.
3. Produce the e-mail message following the standard procedures.

Exercise 5-13 • Letter

1. Open 5-13 from the Chapter 5 folder on the student CD.
2. Proofread the letter on the screen.
3. Produce the letter in correct format following the standard procedures described in the previous chapters.

CUMULATIVE EXERCISE

Exercise 5-14 • Editorial

Proofread and correct all errors using the appropriate proofreaders' marks.

Editorial for ACME Notes

As we approach the end of another year, in the spirit of the holiday season, we want to extend our appreciation to the many people who have made this a successful year. We sincerely appreciate your strong committment to our company.

First, to the members of the Sales Dept., we salute you for your tremendous effort and enthusiasm throughout the year. Even during the recent economic recession, you were able to help our customers meet their needs in a very positive way. We can not tell you how much we appreciate your efforts.

Second, to all employees, we salute you for your excellent community service activities. Because we have been a longtime member ofthe Central City community, it is important that we show our support as a company for Central City's many activities and projects. Improvements in our community will result in improvements for us.

Finally, we salute our U. S. and European customers for their loyalty and particularily for their response to our request for assistance in the product improvement program. Preliminary results from the midyear survey show that over 50 percent of our customers provided reactions to our line of products, many offering suggestions for expanding the products and service that we have available.

have a happy holiday season! Thanks again for helping us acheive great success during the year!

Bookmark It!

Want more practice? Go to www.cengage.com/keyboarding/pagel for more proofreading activities.

Number Expression Errors

Spotlight on ACCURACY

It should be obvious why the use of exact numbers is critical when working with business documents. Documents with incorrect numbers can cost a company thousands, even millions, of dollars. Imagine ordering 10,000 widgets with the specifications of 2″ × 12″. When the widgets arrive, you realize that each widget should have been 2″ × 21″ (not 2″ × 12″). These widgets are of no value to your company because they are not long enough for the product you make. If each widget cost your company $10, your company just paid $100,000 for 10,000 items it cannot use. Not only are you out that much money, you do not have the exact item needed to begin construction.

The frequent use of numbers in business correspondence has created an increased need for accurate proofreading. Financial reports, telephone/fax numbers, ZIP codes, and credit card identifications are just a few of the ways in which numbers are being used.

Objectives

- Recognize errors in the expression of numbers.
- Spell correctly 12 frequently misspelled words.
- Use correctly three sets of commonly confused and misused words.

Often numbers must be checked against a source document for accuracy. For example, amounts listed on an expense summary are checked against receipts. Many of the decisions you make regarding numbers, however, will be related to whether the numbers should be expressed as figures or as words. The guidelines presented in this chapter will apply to most of the situations you encounter.

When you locate an incorrectly expressed number, use the proofreaders' marks you have learned for identifying the errors.

	MARKED COPY	CORRECTED COPY
Spell out.	There were ③ cars in the holiday race.	There were three cars in the holiday race.
Express as figures.	Invite ~~eighteen~~ 18 colleagues to dinner.	Invite 18 colleagues to dinner.

≫ Numbers Expressed as Words

Follow these general guidelines for expressing numbers as words.

RULE 1   Spell out numbers from one to ten. Express numbers above ten in figures. When a sentence contains a series of numbers, some of which are over ten and some of which are under ten, use figures for consistency.

Example: Our agent will describe the terms of five different policies.

Example: The teacher brought 6 tablets, 20 diskettes, and 4 textbooks.

Example: This group insurance policy will cover all ~~fifteen~~ 15 employees.

Example: Please include 5 apples, 18 oranges, and ~~eight~~ 8 lemons on the list.

If numbers can be grouped into different categories within a sentence, examine each category separately. Use the same style for all numbers within a related category.

Example: From the new book list for the seven library branches, we have ordered 21 hard copy versions, 33 paperback copies, 5 cassette recordings, and 9 CDs.

Example: The Sports Complex, which is open eight hours on Sundays, has 8 tennis courts, ~~four~~ 4 weight rooms, and 16 racquetball courts.

RULE 2   Spell out numbers that begin a sentence even if figures are used later in the sentence. When numbers from 21 to 99 are spelled out, key them with a hyphen.

Example: Twenty-seven children went on the trip 11 months ago.

Example: ⑭ people were selected for the jury, even though only eight were needed.

When a large number begins a sentence, rewrite the sentence so that it does not begin with a number.

Example: Twenty-one thousand one hundred fifty-two people live in that town.

Rewritten: There are 21,152 people living in that town.

RULE 3   Spell out approximate amounts and isolated fractions. Mixed numbers (a figure and a fraction) are expressed as figures. (Use a hyphen to join the numerator and denominator of a fraction written in words, unless either element already contains a hyphen.)

Example: The group drank almost fifteen gallons of lemonade at the picnic.

Example: The builder will need pipe that is 2 1/8″ in diameter.

Example: The gasoline gauge showed the tank to be 3/4 full. *three-fourths*

Example: His shoe size is ~~nine and one-half~~. *9 1/2*

RULE 4   Spell out street numbers through ten as ordinals (first, second, etc.). Use figures for house and building numbers. An exception is house or building number One, which is written as a word.

Example: The business has moved to 297 Sixth Street.

Example: The tennis courts are located near the corner of Trent Avenue and ~~7th~~ Street. *Seventh*

Example: MFC National Bank is located at One Gateway Drive.

RULE 5   Spell out ages ten and under unless stated specifically in years, months, and days. Use figures for ages 11 and over.

Example: His daughter is six years old.

Example: On April 16, he will be ~~seven~~ years, ~~five~~ months, and ~~eight~~ days old. *7 5 8*

RULE 6   When two numbers are used together, spell out one of the two—preferably the one that is the shortest word.

Example: At the sale, she found 6 ten-gallon cans. *sp*

Example: The inventory includes ~~twenty-four~~ ② -roll packs of paper towels. *24 sp*

Exercise 6-1 • Proofread and Mark

*Use the appropriate proofreaders' marks to correct the errors in number expression. If the sentence is correct, write **C** to the left of the number.*

1. The colors of the copies in the 3 categories should be 30 red, ten white, and 36 blue.

2. 16 new windows will be sent to your address at 9054 6th Avenue.

3. For the program booklet to fit into the six and three-fourths envelope, the booklet must be one-eighth inch shorter.

4. We received five hundred eight-page brochures.

5. The instructor distributed almost fifty copies.

» Numbers Expressed as Figures

Follow these general guidelines for expressing numbers as figures.

RULE 7   Use figures to express time except when used alone or with the contraction *o'clock*. Use *a.m.* or *p.m.* with figures. Zeros are not required for on-the-hour times of day.

Example: The appointment has been scheduled for 5 p.m.
Example: The bus will depart at ⑤ o'clock.

RULE 8   Use figures *without* adding *nd*, *st*, or *th* after a month to express the day and the year. (Set the year off by commas when it follows the month and day.)

Example: The Declaration of Independence was signed on July 4, 1776.
Example: She will retire on August ~~Ninth~~ 9, 20--.

Express the day in ordinal figures (*1st*, *2nd*, *3rd*, *4th*, etc.) when the day precedes the month or when the month is omitted. (The preferred abbreviation of *second* and *third* is *2nd* and *3rd*, respectively.)

Example: The state conference will start on the 21st of November.
Example: The ~~fifth~~ 5th of this month will be a school holiday.

RULE 9   Express in figures dimensions, measurements, and weights.

Example: The rug measures 10 by 12 feet.
Example: The fish weighed ~~five~~ 5 pounds.

RULE 10   Express in figures street numbers over ten and all address numbers except *One*. Street numbers above ten may be expressed as either cardinal numbers (*22*) or ordinal numbers (*22nd*). However, be consistent and use one style.

Example: Please send the order to 607 South 38th Street.
Example: The art gallery will be located at One Park Drive. *sp*
Example: The parade will begin at the corner of Main and ⑨th Street.

RULE 11   Express as figures numbers following nouns such as *page*, *chapter*, *room*, *rule*, and *policy*.

Example: Our final statement begins at the bottom of page 41 in Chapter 4.
Example: According to Rule ~~six,~~ ⁶ the motion is not needed.

RULE 12   Express in figures amounts of money, decimal amounts, percentages, and interest periods that include the year, month, and day.

Example: The cost per person will be $9.97.
Example: Money that is deposited into the account will earn ~~five~~ ⁵ percent interest.

Spell out the word *cents* for amounts under a dollar (*15 cents*, not *$.15*).

Example: The small souvenirs can be sold for 47 cents each.
Example: Be sure to add ~~six~~ ⁶ cents to the total for the tax.

The necklace will cost $9 on sale.

Express even amounts of money without zeros or decimal points (*$10*).

Example: The special ticket price will be $8 per person through Friday.

Example: The necklace will cost ~~nine dollars~~ *$9* when it is on sale.

In legal documents, express amounts of money in both words and figures.

Example: In consideration of One Hundred Sixty Dollars ($160), the contract will be binding on both parties.

Example: Upon payment of Four Hundred Thirty-two Dollars and Twenty-one Cents, the loan will be considered paid in full. *($432.21)*

Exercise 6-2 • Proofread and Mark

*Use the appropriate proofreaders' marks to correct the errors in number expression. If the sentence is correct, write **C** to the left of the number.*

1. The candidates' meeting will be held at 876 East 5th Street.

2. She purchased 4 $100,000 policies for her business.

3. The council approved the start of construction of an office building at 976 South Sixteenth Street.

4. On the questionnaire, she stated her son's age as 6 years, 6 months, and 27 days.

5. He purchased thirty-six 9-inch dividers for the file cabinets.

>> Zip Codes

To assist the post office, addresses on all letters and envelopes should include the correct two-letter state abbreviation and ZIP code. Whenever possible, the ZIP code should contain nine digits.

The proofreader should be sure the ZIP code on the envelope is the same as the ZIP code in the letter address. Accuracy in ZIP codes is important because errors cause delays in delivery of correspondence. The appendix contains a list of the two-letter abbreviations for states and U.S. territories. When in doubt about a ZIP code, check the official ZIP code directory available from the U.S. Postal Service. You may also find ZIP code information on the Internet.

Note: The U.S. Postal Service requests that envelope addresses be single-spaced and keyed in all capital letters with no punctuation.

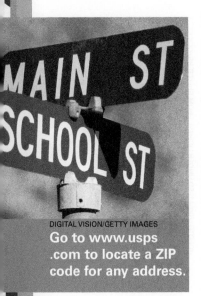

DIGITAL VISION/GETTY IMAGES
Go to www.usps .com to locate a ZIP code for any address.

Example: MS DEBBIE GONZALEZ
547 INDIANA AVENUE
CENTER POINT WV 26339-0487

Exercise 6-3 • Proofread and Mark

*Proofread the envelope addresses by comparing them to the correct letter addresses on the left. Correct the envelope addresses using the appropriate proofreaders' marks. If the envelope address is correct, write **C** to the left of the number.*

Letter Address	Envelope Address
1. Ms. Jana Morales	MS JANA MORALES
1135 Hiatt Way	1135 HIATT WAY
Phoenix, AZ 85024-1203	PHOENIX AZ 85024-1203
2. Mr. Joseph King	MR. JOSEPH KING
JWK Insurance Company	JWK INSURANCE COMPANY
P.O. Box 1923	P.O. BOX 1923
Garland, TX 75046-1923	GARLAND TX 70546-1923
3. Feather Duster, Inc.	FEATHER DUSTER INC.
Attention: Credit Department	ATTENTION CREDIT DEPARTMENT
807 Second Street South	870 SECOND SOUTH STREET
Kalamazoo, MI 49009-1208	KALAMAZOO MI. 49009-1208
4. Professor Anita Sandoval	PROF ANITA SANDOVAL
Marysville State College	MARYSVILLE STATE COLLEGE
546 South Cleveland Road	564 SOUTH CLEVELAND ROAD
Memphis, TN 38104-3232	MEMPHIS TENN 38104-3223
5. Dr. Lynwood Johnreit	DR LYNWOOD JOHNRIET
Vice President of Marketing	VICE PRESIDENT OF MARKETING
West Fisheries Company	WET FISHERIES COMPANY
901 Jefferson Boulevard	901 JEFFERSON BOULEVARD
Vancouver, WA 98660-3692	VANCOUVER Wa 98660-3692

CONFUSED AND MISUSED WORDS

can	*v.* to be able to do something
may	*v.* to be possible; to give permission

Can you type 50 words per minute?

Mrs. Colby, **may** I help you grade today's quiz?

cent	*n.* 1/100; penny
scent	*n.* a distinctive odor; perfume; a sense of smell
sent	*v.* past tense and past participle of *send*

Bank tellers must balance to the **cent** each day.

Your perfume has an unusual **scent.**

Miguel **sent** his resume to 15 companies.

complement	*n.* something that adds to or completes a whole; v. to complete or make perfect
compliment	*n.* an expression of praise; v. to praise

A black portfolio will **complement** most interview ensembles.

Mr. Tuttle did **compliment** me on my perfect attendance.

Proofreading & Editing Tips

PEP Tip

* Check the accuracy of all extensions, calculations, and totals of numbers.

* Verify the accuracy of numbers against their source document.

* Check the alignment of decimals that appear within a column.

* Although the style of expressing numbers as words or figures may vary depending on the formality of the document, follow one style consistently within a document.

PROOFREADING APPLICATIONS

Proofread the following paragraphs to locate errors in number expression as well as two additional errors. Use the appropriate proofreaders' marks to show the corrections.

CLASS RUNION TIME

You are cordially invited to attend the reunions for the Classes of 1980–1985. They will be held on Friday, January 15th, in Room fourteen of the Central Conference Center, 469 Grand Avenue East in Birmingham. Registration and the social hour will begin at 5:30 o'clock p.m. The dinner will begin at 6:30 p.m. and the program at 7:30 p.m.

We anticipate that the program will be over by 9:30. The rest of the evening will be available for remembering and listening to the music of THE ORANGE APPLES, an old-time music pep band from the high school.

2 copies of a questionnaire are enclosed for you to share with us your "personal history" since the big day in the early eighties. Please complete the questionnaire, and return it in the enclosed envelope to the high school secretary's office as soon as possible. We'll include a summary of the responses in the Early Eighties booklet you will get when you register. This booklet will be a wonderful compliment to your library.

Your friends and mine have done many things since they left the alma mater. Here's the chance to catch up in a hurry in 1 evening! See you there!

Enclosure

Exercise 6-5 • Spelling and Word Usage Check

*Compare the words in Column **A** with the corresponding words in Column **B**. Use the appropriate proofreaders' marks to correct the misspelled or misused words. If both columns are correct, write **C** to the left of the number.*

Column A	Column B
1. secrateries	secretaries
2. complience	compliance
3. emergency	emergency
4. questionaire	questionnaire
5. pryor	prior
6. categories	catagories
7. government	goverment
8. business	buisness
9. correspondance	correspondence
10. excellent	excellent
11. consensus	consensis
12. vendur	vendor
13. Can I leave now?	I may attend the conference.
14. He sent the letter yesterday.	The cent made me ill.
15. What a nice complement!	She paid the chef a nice compliment.

Exercise 6-6 • International Vocabulary

*Compare the French and Spanish words in Column **A** with the corresponding words in Column **B**. If the word in Column **B** is different from the word in Column **A**, use the appropriate proofreaders' marks to correct Column **B**. If the words in both columns are the same, write **C** to the left of the number.*

Column A	Column B
1. ejercicio	ejerciccio
2. empresa	empressa

Exercise 6-6 • International Vocabulary (*continued*)

3. Mademoiselle   mademoiselle

4. frijoles   friholes

5. bonsoir   bonsoir

Exercise 6-7 • Memorandum

Proofread the printed memo that follows by comparing it with the correct handwritten memo on page 94. Mark all errors using the appropriate proofreaders' marks.

TO: Colleen Branter
               Budget Office

FROM: Travis Neal, Manger
               Communication Center

DATE: October 10, 20--

SUBJECT: Budget Request for Next Year

Enclosed with this note is our completed budget request for next year. Please note several items:

29 reams of orange offset paper has been requested because next year we will be publishing and distributing the environmental promotion flyer each month.

The postage amount has been increased to $950.00 because of an expected rise in postal rates.

The MCK Company has informed us that the next version of its word proccesing software program will be available on the 6 of August; therefore, we will need at least $825.00 of the equipment budget to receive the appropriate software upgrade.

In addition, the literature for the newest model of MCK's computer should be scent on or shortly after August 31st. Finally, the miscellaneous amount has been increased by seven percent for use in an emergency situation.

Enclosure

TO: Colleen Branter
            Budget Office

FROM: Travis Neal, Manager
            Communication Center

DATE: October 10, 20--

SUBJECT: Budget Request for Next Year

Enclosed with this note is our completed budget request for next year. Please note several items:

Twenty-nine reams of orange offset paper have been requested because next year we will be publishing and distributing the environmental promotion flyer each month.

The postage amount has been increased to $950 because of an expected rise in postal rates.

The MCK Company has informed us that the next version of its word processing software program will be available on the 6th of August; therefore, we will need at least $825 of the equipment budget to receive the appropriate software upgrade.

In addition, the literature for the newest model of MCK's computer should be sent on or shortly after August 31. Finally, the miscellaneous amount has been increased by 7 percent for use in an emergency situation.

Enclosure

Exercise 6-8 • Letter

Proofread the printed letter that follows by comparing it with the correct handwritten letter on page 96. Mark all errors using the appropriate proofreaders' marks.

NATIONAL ACTIVITIES ASSOCIATION

632 Grandy Building
278 Balsam Avenue, Boise, ID 83701-1609
208-555-0162 • Fax 208-555-0163

April 13, 20--

Dr. Kalena Gilbrech, President
Emerald City Enterprises, Inc.
363 North Raintree Avenue
Honolulu, HI 96813-3084

Dear Dr. Gilbrech:

Thank you for your kind hospitality during my recent visit with you and the planning committee. I have reviewed the notes that Mr. Giles prepared, and I hasten to ask whether the following corrections might be made:

1. The business meeting should be scheduled for Room Seven rather than 17.
2. The 4 seminars on Friday morning should be planned to accommodate at least 40 people per session.
3. The banquet on Friday night will start at 7 p.m. rather than 8:00 p.m.
4. The shuttle buses will need to leave the main hotel every fifteen minutes.
5. The special V.I.P. reception on Saturday should be planned for thirty-one people.

If you have any questions, be sure to let me know.

Sincerely,

Anna Huang

tis

April 13, 20--

Dr. Kalena Gilbrech, President

Emerald City Enterprises, Inc.

363 North Raintree Avenue

Honolulu, HI 96813-3048

Dear Dr. Gilbrech:

Thank you for your kind hospitality during my recent visit with you and the planning committee. I have reviewed the notes that Mr. Giles prepared, and I hasten to ask whether the following corrections might be made:

1. The business meeting should be scheduled for Room 7 rather than 17.

2. The four seminars on Friday morning should be planned to accommodate at least 40 people per session.

3. The banquet on Friday night will start at 7 p.m. rather than 8 p.m.

4. The shuttle buses will need to leave the main hotel every 15 minutes.

5. The special VIP reception on Saturday should be planned for 31 people.

If you have any questions, be sure to let me know.

Sincerely,

Anna Huang

tis

PROOFREADING AT THE COMPUTER

Exercise 6-9 • Memorandum

1. Open 6-9 from the Chapter 6 folder on the student CD. (This is a computer copy of Exercise 6-7.)

2. Proofread the memo on the screen. Correct all errors on the screen copy that you indicated with proofreaders' marks in Exercise 6-7.

3. Produce the memo in correct format following the standard procedures described in the previous chapters.

Exercise 6-10 • E-mail Message

1. Open 6-10 from the Chapter 6 folder on the student CD.

2. Proofread the e-mail message, and make all necessary corrections.

3. Produce the e-mail message in correct format following the standard procedures described in the previous chapters.

Exercise 6-11 • Compare a Report to Expense Slips

1. Open 6-11 from the Chapter 6 folder on the student CD.

2. Proofread the report against the expense slips on page 98.

3. Correct all mistakes. Check the math. Apply proofreaders' marks to any errors you find in the expense report.

4. Produce the document following the standard procedures described in the previous chapters. (Make the amounts in the total column bold.)

Exercise 6-11 • Compare a Report to Expense Slips (*continued*)

Name _____ *John Jackson* _____
Employee I.D. _____ *12-0415* _____
Expense Report for Week Ending
_____ *3/19* _____
Destination _____ *San Jose* _____
Mileage _____
Meals __*$123*__ Hotel __*$280*__
Plane/Train _____ *$462* _____
Car Rental _*$171*_ Parking _*$35*_
Misc. Please List _____
Signed _____ *John Jackson*

Name _____ *Roger Norton* _____
Employee I.D. _____ *33-0821* _____
Expense Report for Week Ending
_____ *3/19* _____
Destination _____ *Salt Lake City* _____
Mileage _____
Meals __*$135*__ Hotel __*$277*__
Plane/Train _____ *$787* _____
Car Rental __*$158*__ Parking __*$40*__
Misc. Please List _____
Signed _____ *Roger Norton*

Name _____ *Nancy Cartwright* _____
Employee I.D. _____ *12-1419* _____
Expense Report for Week Ending
_____ *3/19* _____
Destination _____ *Chicago* _____
Mileage _____ *$178.20* _____
Meals _*$129.00*_ Hotel *$258.00*
Plane/Train _____
Car Rental _____ Parking __*$42*__
Misc. Please List _____
Signed _____ *Nancy Cartwright*

Name _____ *Imogene McDonal* _____
Employee I.D. _____ *22-8989* _____
Expense Report for Week Ending
_____ *3/19* _____
Destination _____ *Minneapolis* _____
Mileage _____
Meals __*$120*__ Hotel __*$269*__
Plane/Train _____ *$375* _____
Car Rental __*$153*__ Parking __*$30*__
Misc. Please List _____
Signed _____ *Imogene McDonal*

CUMULATIVE APPLICATION

Work with a partner to proofread this printed document. One of you should read from the correct handwritten document on page 100 while the other checks the announcement below, paying special attention to numbers. Mark all errors using the appropriate proofreaders' marks.

Announcement

Congratulations on your eligibility to attend the Outstanding Business Students Conference this year! Our goal is to provide information that will compliment the education of your emerging business leaders. We are looking forward to hosting students from the top 10 business schools in the country and are working dilagently to provide an attractive program.

Please indicate below the number of students you anticipate will be attending the various breakout sessions, and submit the information by September 21. My Associate, Kevin Crenshaw, will return your confirmation schedules by the 5 of October.

1 additional highlight will be the dinner banquet on Saturday from 5:30–9:30 p.m. This will include three enticing buffet lines and displays from 15 local employers. Let us know if we may assist you farther.

Breakout sessions:

Entreperneurship	BE-218	8:30–11:50	_____
Managerial Leadership	BE-129	8:00–9:50	_____
Free Enterprise	BE-219	10:00–11:50	_____
Globalization	BE-123	1:00–2:50	_____
Conflict Management	BE-215	1:00–4:30	_____
Resume/Interview	BE-217	3:00–4:30	_____

Exercise 6-12 • Announcement (*continued*)

ANNOUNCEMENT

Congratulations on your eligibility to attend the Outstanding Business Students Conference this year! Our goal is to provide information that will complement the education of your emerging business leaders. We are looking forward to hosting students from the top ten business schools in the country and are working diligently to provide an attractive program.

Please indicate below the number of students you anticipate will be attending the various breakout sessions, and submit the information by September 21. My associate, Kevin Crenshaw, will return your confirmation schedules by the 5th of October.

One additional highlight will be the dinner banquet on Saturday from 5:30-9:30 p.m. This will include three enticing buffet lines and displays from 15 local employers. Let us know if we may assist you further.

Breakout sessions:

Entrepreneurship	BE-218	8:30-11:50	_____
Managerial Leadership	BE-129	8:00-9:50	_____
Free Enterprise	BE-219	10:00-11:50	_____
Globalization	BE-123	1:00-2:50	_____
Conflict Management	BE-215	1:00-4:30	_____
Resume/Interview	BE-217	3:00-4:30	_____

Bookmark It!

Want more practice? Go to www.cengage.com/keyboarding/pagel for more proofreading activities.

Scholarship Search

Business and Professional Persons of America

Instructions: You have been hired as an intern for the Clarksville local chapter of Business and Professional Persons of America. The organization has given scholarships for postsecondary education for the past 20 years. Your job is outlined in the goals that Steve Meredith, Scholarship Chair, has submitted on the next page.

CLARKSVILLE BUSINESS AND PROFESSIONAL PERSONS OF AMERICA
Steve Meredith, Scholarship Chair
Goals

Goal Statement (Long-Range Goal)

In the spring of 20--, we will award scholarships to assist students financially as they pursue post-secondary education.

Mid-Range Goals (Steps to Reach Long-Range Goal)

Review last year's scholarship application forms to determine if the forms continue to meet our intentions.

Establish guidelines for the selection of awardees.

Send applications to Central High School Guidance Office and Boone County College Financial Aid Office.

Publicize the availability of the forms through local news media and through our membership, as well as any other methods determined during our initial steps of planning.

Run a news release in the *Clarksville Times* in January.

Meet as a committee and select the recipients of the scholarships.

Notify the winners and invite them to attend our Guest Night in April.

Steve Meredith

Steve Meredith, Scholarship Chair

Document 1 • News Release

Proofread the news release below and apply proofreaders' marks. Open P1 from the student CD and make corrections.

For Immediate Release

CONTACT:

Steve Meredith

Scholarship Chair, Clarksville BPPA

931-555-0152

smeredith@charter.net

Clarksville Business and Professional Persons of America to Award Scholarships

Clarksville business and professional persons of America is pleased to announce that their organization will be awarding a total of $3,500 in scholarships at its April 20-- Guest Night. The club is able to make these awards as the result of a highly successful National Business and Professional Persons of America Week Scholarship Luncheon in October, 20--.

Scholarships to be awarded are:

- 2 $750 scholarships to persons age twenty five and older as of February 28, 20--
- 2 $500 scholarships to members of the Central High School Class of 20--
- 2 $500 scholarships to upperclassmen (students who have already started college and are at any any level)

All applicants must provide an official academic transcript with the application and have and maintain a 3.0 GPA. Other qualifications are outliend in the application form.

Applications are available on our Web site at www.clarksvillebppa.org. Applications are also available at Central High School, Boone County College Office of Financial Aid, or be contacting committee chair Steve Meredith at 931-555-0152 or smeredith@charter.net and must be postmarked on or befor Feburary 28, 20--

Document 2 • Letter to Financial Aid Office

Proofread the following letter and apply proofreaders' marks. Open P2 from the student CD and make corrections.

CLARKSVILLE BUSINESS AND PROFESSIONAL PERSONS OF AMERICA

816 Cherry Lane

Clarksville, TN 37042-7812

Jan. 2, 20--

Mr. Patrick Wagoner

financial aid office

Boone County College

31820 College Road

Clarksville, TN 37042-7811

Dear Mr. Wagoner:

I am attaching a copy of the applications for the 3 scholarships which our organization will award at at our Guest Night on Apr. 11, 20--. We would greatly appreciate if you would make these scholarship applications available to your students or others who may contact you office. Please feel free to make all copies necessary.

The applications are also available on our Web site www.clarksvillebppa.org for download. They are available as pdf or rtf files on our Web site. Students must have a 3.0 GPA to be eligible for a scholarshp. Scholarship applications must be postmarked by Feb. 28, 20--. Other eligibility requirments are listed on each of the 3 applications.

If you or any applicant has questions about the scholarships, feel free to contact me at 931-555-0152 or smeredith@charter.net. Thank you for your help in making the applications available to your students.

Sincerely,

Steve Meredith

Steve Meredith, scholarship chair

Enclosures: Scholarship Applications

Document 3 • E-mail to Scholarship Committee

Proofread the following letter and apply proofreaders' marks. Open P3 from the student CD and make corrections.

FROM:	smeredith@charter.net
TO:	Scholarship Committee
DATE:	February 2, 20--
SUBJECT:	Scholarship Committee Meeting

There will bea Scholarship Committee meeting on Sat., March 2nd to review the applications and choose our recipients for scholarships. The meeting will be at my home at 816 Cherry Lane. To date, we have recieved seventy-one applications for scholarships. In light of the number of applications that we have received, the meeting will probably last until around 5 o'clock. Hopefully, this will be alright with everyone.

In review of our previous meeting, applicants must have a GPA of 3.0 or higher. We are looking at grade point average, extracurricular activities, community service, and need. We will choose 2 recipients and 1 alternate for each of our 3 scholarships. The 3 scholarship categories are Central High School graduate, 25 and older, and Upperclassman.

Thank you for serving on this very important committtee. Please let me know in advance if you cannot attend. If you know of any one that would like to apply, please refere them to our Web site at www.clarksvillebppa.org. Applications must be postmarked by Feb. 28.

Steve Meredith, Scholarship Chair

Document 4 • Scholarship Applicant Essay

Proofread the following essay received from a scholarship applicant. Apply proofreaders' marks. Open P4 from the student CD and make corrections.

My name is Samantha Kitchell. I am a thirty-four year old mother of 3 daughters. I have always wanted to attend college but put of my education to raise a family. I began classes last Fall and am enrolled in the Computer Application Specialist program at Boone County College. I am scheduled to receive that degree in the Spring of 20--. I would like to continue my education and attain my Bachelor's Degree in business or computer applications within the next few years. Eventually I would like to teach in those areas.

I am a member of phi theta kappa national honor society and have been on the President's List or Dean's List every semester. I have a 3.7 cumulative grade point average. My official transcript is attached. In edition to be a student, I am a student worker in the Success Center, where I do tutoring for computer application classes for fifteen hours a week. I love my job as a tutor and find it extremely rewarding to help other students learn how to use the computer. I am an active member of phi beta lambda at Boone County College. I have collected food for the food pantry, helped families in need at Christmas by participating in the giving tree, and rung bells for the salvation army. I am presently receiving no financial aid and my husband was recently laid off from his position at glacks manufacturing.

I sincerely appreciate your consideration of me for this scholarship. I would like to complement the club for all the good work you do in our cumminity.

Document 5 • Merged Letters to Scholarship Recipients

On the following page is the main document to merge for your scholarship recipients.

1. Open P5A and print your recipient list.

2. Open P5B and make corrections on the main document. Do not remove the words ADDRESS BLOCK, GREETING LINE or double scholarship SCHOLARSHIP, and amount AMOUNT. Save as P5 Form Letter.

3. Click the Mailings tab and then Start Mail Merge. Select Letters. Still on the Mailings tab, click Select Recipients. Select Type New List. Click Customize Columns at the bottom of the New Address List box.

4. From the list of Field Names, delete Company Name, Address Line 2, Country or Region, Home Phone, Work Phone, and E-mail Address. Then click Add and add columns for Scholarship and Amount. Click OK.

5. Type your data list beginning with Mr. Dan Cole, keying Mr. in the Title field then tabbing to go to the next field. Key all six scholarship recipients found in the printout of P5A. Click OK when you have finished typing your list. Save as P5 List.

6. In the letter, select the words ADDRESS BLOCK. Click the Mailings tab and then the Address Block button. Do not change anything in this box; click OK. Now delete ADDRESS BLOCK. In the letter, right-click «GreetingLine», Edit Greeting Line, and then change the colon to a comma. Click OK.

7. In the letter, select the word SCHOLARSHIP. Click the Mailings tab and then Insert Merge Field. Choose Scholarship and click the Insert button. Then select the word AMOUNT, Insert Merge Field, choose Amount, and click the Insert button.

8. On the Mailings tab, click Finish and Merge, Edit Individual documents, and OK. Save your merged letters as P5 Merged Letters. Print your merged letters.

CLARKSVILLE BUSINESS AND PROFESSIONAL PERSONS OF AMERICA

Mar. 11, 20--

ADDRESS BLOCK

GREETING LINE

Congradulations! I am pleased to notify you that you have been selected as one of the recipients for the BPPA SCHOLARSHIP Scholarship in the amount of AMOUNT for the Fall semester of 20--.

We will be introducing all of our recipients at our April 8th, 20-- Guest Night at the first Christian Church, 205 S. Elm, clarksville, Tennessee. The event will begin at 6 o'clock p.m. I would like to invite you to attend the dinner as our guest. Please let me know on or before March if you will be able to attend. If you would like to invite someone to attend with you as your guest, the cost of an editional meal is $10.00 and paid reservations must be made by March 30th.

At the meeting we will also give you information on how to provide your spring 20-- transcript and evidence that you are enroled for the Fall of 20-- semester so that we can issue the check to you and your college before your Fall tuition is do. You will also be introduced to the membership.
Again, congradulations on your selection as a scholarship winner, and I look forward to hearing from your about whether you will be able to join us on Guest Night.

Sincerely,

Steve Meredith, Scholarship Chair
Phone: 931-555-0152
Email: smeredith@charter.net

Document 6 • Final Scholarship Report

Proofread the following scholarship report. Apply proofreaders' marks.
Open P6 from the student CD and make corrections.

Clarksville Business and Professional Persons of America
Steve Meredith, Scholarship Chair
Report

Goal Statement (Long-Range Goal)

In the Spring of 20--, we will award scholarships to financially assist students as they pursue post-secondary education.

We selected 6 scholarship recipients announced at our April Guest Night. Those recipients included:

Dan Cole and Stephanie Kruse for the Central High School Scholarships for $500.00 each.
Sandra Swartz and Jeffrey Gebke for the Upperclassman Scholarships for $500.00 each
Nick Norton and Janet Miller for the 25 and Older Scholarships for $750.00 each.

Checks will be sent prior to the Fall semester after recieving transcripts showing a 3.0 GPA or higher and registration for Fall semester. Checks will be written to the recipient and the College they will be attending.

Mid-Range Goals (Steps to Reach Long-Range Goal)

We will review last year's scholarship application forms to determine if the forms continue to meet our intentions.

The committee of 6 met in early December to go over the applications from last year and decide whether we wanted to keep them the same as last year or recommend changes to the membership at large. We chose to keep them the same as last yer.

We will establish guidelines for the selection of awardees.

The committee made no changes in the guidlines from the previous year.

Send applications to Central High School Guidance Office and Boone County College Financial Aid Office.

We sent letters to Central High School Guidance Office and Boone County College Financial Aid Office with about 30 copies of the applications. They were told to feel free to make copies.

We will publicize the availability of the forms through local news media and through our membership, as well as any other methods determined during our initial steps of planning.

We emailed copies of the applications to all members of Clarksville bppa and send a campus-wide E-mail to employees at Boone County College. We also put the applications on our Web site for download. Many of our applicants used our Web site to download applications.

Scholarship Report
Page 2
May 10, 20–

Run a news release in the *Clarksville Times* in January.

We ran a news release in the *Clarksville Times* in Jan.

Meet as a committee and select the recipients of the scholarships.

We met on Saturday, March 2nd to go over the applications and select the recipients. We received eighty-six applications and the meeting lasted 4 hours.

Notify the winners and invite them to attend our Guest Night in April.

We sent letters to our 6 recipients and invited them to our Guest Night in April. 5 of the 6 attended the meeting.

Steve Meredith

Steve Meredith, Scholarship Chair

Subject-Verb Agreement

Spotlight on ACCURACY

In business communication, your writing style is important. Your mastery of a clear, concise writing style is essential to success because how you say something may be as important as what you say. A poor writing style can result in confusion to both your company and your customers. Think of the confusion that may have resulted from the following sentences written by people completing an accident report:

- The accident happened when the right back door of a car came around the corner without signaling.

- The other car hit my truck without giving warning of its intentions.

- He had been driving 45 years before falling asleep and having an accident.

- No one was to blame for the accident, but it would never have happened if the other person had been alert.

Objectives

- Recognize incomplete sentences (fragments).

- Find and mark errors in subject-verb agreement.

- Find and mark errors in singular/plural nouns.

- Identify intervening modifiers and indefinite pronouns.

- Find and mark errors in compound and collective nouns.

- Spell correctly 12 frequently misspelled words.

- Use correctly three sets of commonly confused and misused words.

Your instructor writes on your term paper, "You done a well job!" What is your reaction? Are you pleased? Yes, you are happy about the complimentary remark and the high grade you earned. But are you impressed with your instructor's use of English grammar? Not likely. In fact, you may react negatively and lose confidence in your instructor's ability to communicate correctly and effectively.

Businesspeople react the same way. A person is judged on his or her ability to communicate clearly and correctly—when speaking or writing. Your ability to communicate effectively in the business world is extremely important.

Proofreading for correct grammar requires patience and attention to detail. You must be alert and look for errors in grammar usage and sentence construction.

Chapters 7, 8, and 9 will discuss the most important principles of correct grammar. In this chapter, you will review and apply the rules of basic sentence structure. You will learn to recognize complete sentences and sentence fragments. You will learn to identify and use singular, plural, compound, and collective nouns. You will also learn how intervening modifiers and indefinite pronouns affect subject-verb agreement.

If you locate a grammar error when proofreading, draw a line through the error and write the correction above the error. If you are unsure of the correct grammatical structure or the writer's intended message, write a question mark in the right or left margin of the page. The question mark indicates to the writer that the meaning is not clear and that the sentence should be revised or rewritten.

	MARKED COPY	CORRECTED COPY
Change copy as indicated.	Ten resumes ~~was~~ *were* received.	Ten resumes were received.
Question the writer. ?	If I have a question. ?	If I have a question, I will ask her.

>> Sentence Structure

A **complete sentence** is a group of words that has a subject and a verb and expresses a complete thought. The **subject** is the person, place, or thing the sentence is about. It may be a noun or a personal pronoun (*I, you, he, she, it, we,* or *they*) that takes the place of the noun. The **verb** tells what the subject is or does. Verbs express either action or a state of being.

Action verbs often include **helping verbs** that indicate the **tense** (timing) of the verb. The main helping verbs are *is, are, be, am, was, were, has, have,* and *had.* Other helping verbs include *may, might, must, ought, can, could, would, should, shall, will, do, does,* and *did.* Helping verbs are easy to recognize; they help the main verb tell what the subject is doing.

ACTION VERBS	STATE-OF-BEING VERBS
Dexter *drives* a green Jaguar.	Juana *is* an actuary.
I *jog* five miles every day.	The food *looks* delicious.
The manager *uses* the computer.	I *am* the chairperson.

A **verb phrase** consists of the main verb plus any helping verbs. (A **phrase** is a group of words that does not contain both a subject and a verb.) In the following examples, the subjects are underscored once and the verb phrases are underscored twice.

Example: Lunch will be served in the Sunset Room.

Example: Cruise ships are designed for passenger comfort.

Example: How many cruises have you taken?

Linking verbs are state-of-being verbs. The most common linking verbs are forms of the verb *be* (*is, am, are, was, were, being, has been, have been,* and *had been*). Other linking verbs include *appear, become, feel, look, seem, taste,* and *sound.* Linking verbs answer the question *What?* and are followed by nouns, pronouns, or adjectives (called *complements*). **Complements** are words used after linking verbs to describe or rename the subject of the sentence.

The difference between a helping verb and a linking verb is that the helping verb is part of the verb phrase containing an action verb and helps to ask questions, give commands, or make statements. The linking verb "links" the subject of the sentence to the word (noun, pronoun, or adjective) that immediately follows the linking verb and completes the meaning of the subject by describing or renaming it.

In each of the following examples, the subject is underscored once and the linking verbs (or verb phrases) are underscored twice. Can you find the complements in the sentences?

Example: Gunther looks worried. (Gunther looks what?)

Example: Sarah is the cruise director. (Sarah is what?)

Example: Tuesday's activities were fun. (Activities were what?)

Example: Cruises are becoming favorite vacation choices. (Cruises are becoming what?)

Example: Liv celebrated by taking a yacht cruise. (Liv celebrated by what?)

Because cruise ships offer activities that appeal to people of all ages, they are quickly becoming favorite vacation choices.

Exercise 7-1 • Proofread and Mark

In each sentence, underline the subject once and the verb or verb phrase twice.

1. The president of the travel agency is Jennifer Evens.

2. The cruise ship was refurbished two years ago.

3. Long Beach seems like a popular port of call.

4. The barge cruise on the River Nile sounds exciting.

5. Luxury cruises have become very competitive.

» Sentence Fragments

A group of words that contains a subject and a verb is a complete sentence. If either the subject or the verb is missing, it is an incomplete sentence—more commonly known as a **sentence fragment**. When you locate a sentence fragment, write a question mark in the left or right margin of the page. This will alert the writer to explain the meaning of the sentence or to revise it. If the correction appears obvious, simply correct the fragment by changing it into a complete sentence.

SENTENCE FRAGMENT	COMPLETE SENTENCE
When you talk to travel agents. ?	When you talk to travel agents, they will explain all the options.

Exercise 7-2 • Proofread and Mark

*Write a question mark to the right of the sentence, as shown above, if the group of words is a fragment. Correct the copy if the error is obvious. If the group of words is a complete sentence, write **C** to the left of the number.*

1. My favorite vacation.

2. Choosing which cruise to take. One of life's most delectable dilemmas.

3. A wide variety of itineraries from which to choose.

4. The new addition to The Diamond Dining Room. Built by Contois Builders in 2009.

5. Accommodations range from inside cabins to penthouse suites.

≫ Singular and Plural Nouns

The subject and verb must agree in number (singular or plural) and in person (first person: *I, we, our/ours;* second person: *you, your/yours;* third person: *he, she, it, they, theirs*). A singular subject requires a singular verb. A plural subject requires a plural verb. Most singular present-tense verbs in the third person end with an *s.* Therefore, an *s* ending on most verbs indicates that the verb is singular. In the examples, the subjects are underscored once and the verbs are underscored twice.

Example: Cruising offers value that other kinds of travel do not offer.

Example: Rachel and Celia is fortunate to be able to travel in Europe.

Example: The cruise director's position require enthusiasm and stamina.

Note: When *there* or *here* introduces a sentence, the subject follows the verb. *There* and *here* are never used as subjects of sentences. In the following examples, the subjects are underscored once and the verbs are underscored twice.

Example: There are culinary artists preparing food fit for royalty.

Example: Here are the list of five-star cruise ships.

Example: There are cruise lines that offers special-interest programs.

Exercise 7-3 • Proofread and Mark

*In these sentences, correct the verb rather than the subject. Use the appropriate proofreaders' marks to correct the errors in subject-verb agreement. If the sentence is correct, write **C** to the left of the number.*

1. Purdy Cruise Line offer special group rates.

2. There was many shipboard activities to keep us busy.

3. Some passengers fears becoming seasick on a cruise ship.

4. Here are the list of ports on the Mexican Riviera cruise.

5. We highly recommend cancellation insurance.

>> Intervening Modifiers

The subject and verb must always agree in number, even if modifiers of a different number separate them. A **modifier** is a word or a word group that describes and is usually related to the subject of the sentence. Modifiers that occur between subjects and verbs are called **intervening modifiers**. When proofreading for errors in subject-verb agreement, disregard intervening modifiers. The intervening modifiers are italicized in the following examples. The subjects and verbs are also identified. (Remember, the verbs must agree with the subjects, not the modifiers.)

> *Example:* Proper <u>attire</u>, *as well as courtesy and civil behavior,* <u>is expected</u> on any cruise ship.

> *Example:* Travel <u>agents</u> *with training and experience* <u>are</u> very helpful.

> *Example:* The <u>ports</u> *of call* <u>~~is~~</u> *are* usually considered in selecting a cruise vacation.

> *Example:* Travel <u>counselors</u> *who assist people in selecting the right tour* <u>agrees</u> that satisfaction is based on attitude and flexibility.

Exercise 7-4 • Proofread and Mark

*Use the appropriate proofreaders' marks to correct the errors in subject-verb agreement. If the sentence is correct, write **C** to the left of the number.*

1. *Stardream*, like its partner ship *Stardust*, have a similar deck plan.

2. Active programs, as well as total relaxation, adds to your enjoyment.

3. The attendant who cleans and furnishes your cabin daily are responsible for your ultimate comfort during the cruise.

4. Everyone, from the captain to the assistant waiter, is devoted to treating you like a VIP.

5. Travel DVDs about every type of cruise imaginable is available for your viewing pleasure.

>> Compound Subjects

Sentences that contain two or more subjects are said to have **compound subjects**. Compound subjects, usually joined by the word *and*, require plural verbs. In the following examples, the compound subjects are underscored once and the verbs are underscored twice.

                   s   ***s***   ***v***

Example: Quality <u>food</u> and excellent <u>service</u> <u><u>are featured</u></u> on every cruise.

When a compound subject refers to one person or thing, use a singular verb.

                s   ***s***   ***v***

Example: My <u>friend</u> and <u>colleague</u> <u><u>is</u></u> an experienced world traveler.

When the compound subject is preceded by *each*, *every*, *many a*, or *many an*, use a singular verb.

                   s   ***s***   ***v***

Example: Many a <u>client</u> and travel <u>agent</u> <u><u>has wished</u></u> he or she could communicate more effectively.

               s   ***s***   ***v***

Example: Every <u>man</u> and <u>woman</u> who signed up <u><u>has been entered</u></u> in the mystery passenger contest.

When a compound subject is joined by *or* or *nor*, the verb may be either singular or plural. Use a singular verb when two or more singular subjects are joined by *or* or *nor*. Use a plural verb when both subjects are plural. If one of the subjects is singular and the other is plural, the verb should agree with the subject closest to the verb. In these examples, the subjects are underscored once and the verbs are underscored twice.

                 s   ***s***   ***v***

Example: The chief <u>purser</u> or the <u>assistant</u> <u><u>is</u></u> always ready to help.

                    s   ***s*** ***v***

Example: Neither the main <u>showroom</u> nor the <u>lounges</u> <u><u>are</u></u> large enough.

                 s   ***s***   ***v*** ₛ

Example: The dining room <u>captains</u> or the restaurant <u>manager</u> <u><u>accept</u></u>ₛ special requests.

Exercise 7-5 • Proofread and Mark

*Use the appropriate proofreaders' marks to correct the errors in subject-verb agreement. If the sentence is correct, write **C** to the left of the number.*

1. Sun bathing and jogging are two popular deck activities.

2. Destination and ports of call has always been considered important factors in selecting a cruise.

3. My associate and bridge partner, Natalia Suvarov, have decided to join me on the Rhine River cruise.

4. Evening dining or dancing do not always require formal dress.

5. The cruise director and entertainers has excellent voices.

» Collective Nouns

A noun that denotes a collection of persons or things regarded as one unit is called a **collective noun**. Examples of collective nouns are *team, choir, chorus, flock, herd, audience, staff, crowd, faculty, orchestra, committee, company, group,* and *people.*

When a collective noun refers to the collection as a whole, use a singular verb. When a collective noun refers to members of the collection as separate persons or things, use a plural verb. In the following examples, the collective nouns are underscored once and the verbs are underscored twice.

Example: The cruise <u>staff</u> <u>was</u> on duty day and night. (The staff is acting as a single unit.)

Example: The cruise <u>staff</u> <u>were introduced</u> at the welcome party. (Each member of the staff was introduced individually.)

Example: The <u>audience</u> ~~were~~ *was* <u>pleased</u> with the ship's entertainment.

Note: Do not treat a collective noun as both singular and plural in the same sentence.

Example: The <u>audience</u> <u>was</u> positive with ~~their~~ *its* praise.

The cruise ship's passengers danced all night in the lounge.

Exercise 7-6 • Proofread and Mark

*Use the appropriate proofreaders' marks to correct the errors in subject-verb agreement. If the sentence is correct, write **C** to the left of the number.*

1. The ship's entertainers rehearse at 3:15 p.m. daily.

2. The committee were undecided about which tour to give.

3. The deck staff has been assigned to different duties.

4. The game team consist of six people.

5. A flock of seagulls follow the ship everywhere.

» Indefinite Pronouns

An **indefinite pronoun** does not refer to or specify a particular noun. Some indefinite pronouns are always singular, others are always plural, and still others may be either singular or plural depending on their relationship to other words in the sentence. Study the following indefinite pronouns to become familiar with their number.

ALWAYS SINGULAR			ALWAYS PLURAL	SINGULAR OR PLURAL
anybody	everybody	neither	both	all
anyone	everyone	nobody	few	any
anything	everything	somebody	many	more
each	many a	someone	none	most
either	many an	something	several	
every			some	

Indefinite pronouns used as the subject of the sentence must agree in number with the verb. When a pronoun may be either singular or plural, check the noun to which the pronoun refers. The noun often occurs in a phrase beginning with *of*, as the following examples show. In the examples, the subjects (in some cases, indefinite pronouns) are underscored once and the verbs are underscored twice.

Note: Be careful when using the indefinite pronouns *most, some,* and *both*. Nouns immediately following these words are used as adjectives—not pronouns. When the phrase *of the* precedes a noun, *most, some,* and *both* are used as pronouns.

                            s   **v**

Example: Either of the two cabins is adequate for two people. (*Either* is singular and the subject of the sentence.)

Example: Both <u>cabins</u> <u>are</u> adequate for two people. (*Both* is used as an adjective.)

s *v*

Example: <u>Both</u> <u>are</u> adequate for two people. (*Both* is plural and the subject of the sentence.)

s *v*

Example: <u>Most</u> of the passengers <u>are</u> happy with the cruise. (*Most* refers to *passengers*, which is plural and the subject of the sentence.)

s *v*

Example: Most <u>passengers</u> <u>are</u> happy with the cruise. (*Most* is used as an adjective.)

Example: Most of the events <u>~~is~~</u> *are* designed for group participation.

Example: Everyone <u>seem</u> *s* to be enjoying the cruise.

Example: Everybody <u>~~are~~</u> *is* in a festive mood tonight.

Exercise 7-7 • Proofread and Mark

*Use the appropriate proofreaders' marks to correct the errors in subject-verb agreement. If the sentence is correct, write **C** to the left of the number.*

1. Most of the cruise staff also works as entertainers.

2. Many passengers considers entertainment and food more important than accommodations.

3. Nobody in our group have gained weight on this cruise.

4. Some of the duty-free items in the boutique is being offered at a 40 percent price reduction.

5. Everyone who performs in the passenger talent show receives a souvenir medal.

CONFUSED AND MISUSED WORDS

assure	*v.* to give confidence to; to feel sure; to convince
ensure	*v.* to make sure, certain
insure	*v.* to cover with insurance; to guarantee; to secure from harm

I want to **assure** you that you did the right thing.

Please **ensure** that the door is locked before you leave.

You will want to **insure** this building for $250,000.

capital	*n.* official seat of government; money to invest
capitol	*n.* a building in which a legislature meets

The **capital** of Iowa is Des Moines.

The U.S. Senate meets in Washington in the **Capitol**.

cite	*v.* to quote; to acknowledge
sight	*v.* a vision; *v.* to see or observe
site	*n.* a location

She was able to **cite** the Gettysburg Address.

You are a **sight** to behold!

Lawrence purchased a new **site** for our business.

✳ When proofreading for errors in subject-verb agreement, be alert for nouns whose singular and plural forms are spelled differently.

Singular	Plural
analysis	**analyses**
basis	**bases**
criterion	**criteria (or criterions)**
medium	**media**

✳ Use the team method of proofreading to improve accuracy, especially for longer documents.

Proofreading & Editing Tips

PEP Tip

Exercise 7-8 • Sentences

*Proofread the following sentences, and mark all sentence construction errors using the appropriate proofreaders' marks. If the sentence is correct, write **C** to the left of the number.*

1. Cape Lisburne in Alaska appears to be a beautiful city to visit.

2. All of your travel arrangements is to be completed by August 15.

3. Niki and Jaime was instrumental in designing the brochure.

4. Rated among the state's top ten attractions. Is the Arctic National Wildlife Refuge.

5. Holiday Travel Inc. are offering a trip to Germany.

6. There was more than a dozen daily activities in which we could participate.

7. Everyone, from the pilot to the flight attendant, were helpful.

8. Each man and woman have been participating in the contest.

9. The ship's bursar or the captain accept valuables for safekeeping.

10. The cruise director and the singers received our applause.

11. The group have signed up for another tour to South Africa.

12. Either of the two associates are eligible for the honor.

13. Most of the passengers were thrilled with their arrangements.

14. The captain assured us that we was about to see something extraordinary.

15. Is you as excited to visit this site as I am?

Exercise 7-9 • Spelling and Word Usage Check

*Compare the words in Column **A** with the corresponding words in Column **B**. Use the appropriate proofreaders' marks to correct the misspelled or misused words. If both columns are correct, write **C** to the left of the number.*

Column A	Column B
1. descriptive	discriptive
2. orientation	oriention
3. planing	planning
4. pursue	pursue
5. brochure	broshure
6. consistant	consistent
7. efficient	efficeint
8. impliment	implement
9. successful	successfull
10. responsibilities	responsabilities
11. arrangements	arrangments
12. internationl	international
13. I want to ensure this diamond ring.	I assure you nothing will go wrong.
14. You will need to raise some capitol.	Let's meet at the capital building.
15. Please meet me at the new work sight.	Were you able to cite your references?

Exercise 7-10 • International Vocabulary

*Compare the French and Spanish words in Column **A** with the corresponding words in Column **B**. If the word in Column **B** is different from the word in Column **A**, use the appropriate proofreaders' marks to correct Column **B**. If the words in both columns are the same, write **C** to the left of the number.*

Column A	Column B
1. ociosidad	ocoisidad
2. exagerar	exagarar

Exercise 7-10 • International Vocabulary (*continued*)

Column A	Column B
3. universitaire	universitaire
4. reluciente	reliciente
5. fournitures	fournatures

Exercise 7-11 • Travel Brochure

Proofread the following brochure, and correct all errors using the appropriate proofreaders' marks.

DISCOVER ALASKA'S INSIDE PASSAGE!

The pristine waters of the Inside Passage leads you to some of the friendliest little towns in the world. Each one of the towns are unique and rich in history and heritage. Totems depict the Indian spirits of the bald eagle, the whale, and the raven. Russian onion-domed churches gleams with gold icons. The many wonders of Alaska awaits your discovery. Let's visit two of Alaska's most popular sites.

Ketchikan. The Tongass Tribe of Tlingit call this historic "First City of Alaska" its home. Fishing along the Ketchikan Creek established this town as the "Salmon Capital of the World." Equally impressive are the large collection of totem poles. Fly over or cruise to Misty Fjords National Monument. Waterfalls cascades down sheer granite walls. Abundant wildlife is.

Wrangell. The Russians and the British flew their flags here before. The United States purchased Alaska in 1867. The bust of three gold rushes surely made this a flourishing timber industry town. Everything in this small but spirited town are within walking distance—shops, restaurants, galleries, and museums.

Exercise 7-12 • Business Letter

Proofread the following letter, and correct all errors using the appropriate proofreaders' marks.

DIAMOND CRUISE LINE

432 North Shore Avenue
San Francisco, CA 94114-1642
Phone: 415-555-0147 • Fax: 415-555-0149

January 16, 20--

Mr. and Mrs. Hector Romero
9067 Vista Avenue
Albuquerque, NM 87108-4631

Dear Mr. and Mrs. Romero

Captain Skytta and I was delighted that you enjoyed our recent Caribbean cruise aboard the *Royale Diamond*. The weather and scenery were fantastic, and everyone seemed to have a fantastic time.

The Diamond Cruise Line are already designing cruises for next year, and we believe we have a number of cruises that will be of interest to you. We recommend that you look at two of our new routes in particular because we believe these is the types which you prefer. The enclosed brochure highlights these two new routes to Honnisvag, Norway, in the Arctic, and Odessa, Ukraine, the "Pearl of the Black Sea." We are confident you will find these cruises to be exciting.

As a member of our Diamond Society, you are eligible for a number of benefits not provided to other people who go on our cruises. Our goal are to always provide you with consistent, top-quality accommodations, as well as fast, friendly service. As a Diamond Society member, you is also entitled to special members-only discounts of up to $750 on staterooms and up to $1,250 on penthouse suites for our 15- and 21-day cruises from September through November. All cruises includes a discounted flight from any of our gateway cities. And an on-board credit of $250 per person. However you look at it, you are a winner!

To receive our best deals, don't wait too long! We still have space available on the *White Diamond* and the *Silver Diamond*, both rated 10 stars by *Cruise Magazine*. But space are limited, and we expect to be sold out within the next 30 days. Please make your travel arrangements today!

We looks forward to welcoming you on board!

Sincerely

Eugene K. Patterson
Manager

rjs

Enclosure

PROOFREADING AT THE COMPUTER

Exercise 7-13 • Business Letter

1. Open 7-13 from the Chapter 7 folder on the student CD. (This is a computer copy of Exercise 7-12.)
2. Proofread the letter on the screen. Correct all errors on the screen copy that you indicated with proofreaders' marks in Exercise 7-12.
3. Produce the letter in correct format following the standard procedures described in the previous chapters.

Exercise 7-14 • Magazine Article

1. Open 7-14 from the Chapter 7 folder on the student CD.
2. Proofread the article on the screen, and make all necessary corrections.
3. Format the article using default left and right margins. Continue to produce the article in correct format following the standard procedures described in the previous chapters.

Exercise 7-15 • E-mail Message

1. Open 7-15 from the Chapter 7 folder on the student CD.
2. Proofread the e-mail message on the screen, and make all necessary corrections.
3. Produce the e-mail message in correct format following the standard procedures described in the previous chapters.

CUMULATIVE APPLICATION

Proofread the following announcement, and correct all errors using the appropriate proofreaders' marks.

Cruise Review

Diamond Cruise Line was delighted you selected our cruise line for your last vacation to Africa. The weather cooperated, and everyone agreed that the sites from our ship was fantastic.

One of our goals are to provide each person with an experience you will want to experience over and over again. Every cruise is different, and each trip provide you with an experience of a lifetime. One way you can help, however, is by completing the enclosed questionaire by July 15.

Your comments is important to us, and we promise you that each questionnaire is confidential and read carefully by our staff. By making suggested changes, we are showing our appreciation for your business. Please give us your honest evaluation. About every aspect of your last cruise with us. Please provide comments about what you enjoyed and what changes we might make.

Completion of this Cruise Review should take no more than 15 minutes of your time. Those who return a completed questionnaire within 2 weeks will be invited to a complimentary reception on their next cruise with us. Imagine being our guest of honor on your next cruise—just for taking time to complete this questionnaire! We ensure you that we will do our very best to make your next cruise with Diamond Cruise Line a trip you will never forget.

Danielle F. Schilla, President
Diamond Cruise Line

Enclosure

 ## Bookmark It!

Want more practice? Go to www.cengage.com/keyboarding/pagel for more proofreading activities.

Pronoun Problems

Spotlight on ACCURACY

Your writing style provides information about you as a writer. Did you mean what you wrote? Will other people interpret your message in the same way you meant it to be understood? How might a doctor interpret the following items found in patients' medical charts?

- Patient has chest pain when he lies on his right side for over a year.

- On the third day the knee was better, and on the fourth day it had completely disappeared.

- By the time she was admitted in the emergency room, her rapid heart had stopped and she was feeling great.

- Appears mentally alert but forgetful.

Like proofreading for other types of grammar errors, identifying errors in the proper use of pronouns requires reading the copy carefully and having a good understanding of the nature of pronouns. Because a pronoun acts as a substitute for a particular noun, the pronoun must give clear and correct reference to the noun. In addition,

Objectives

- Locate and correct errors in pronoun-antecedent agreement.

- Identify and correct errors in pronoun case.

- Spell correctly 12 frequently misspelled words.

- Use correctly three sets of commonly confused and misused words.

pronouns have various forms depending on their relationship to other words in the sentence. In this chapter you will learn to identify and correct misused pronouns.

›› Pronoun and Antecedent Agreement

A **pronoun** is a word used in place of a noun. The noun that the pronoun replaces is called the **antecedent**. In the sentence, "Roslyn was complimented for her professional attitude," the pronoun *her* refers to the antecedent *Roslyn*. To be correct, pronouns must agree with their antecedents in three ways:

1. **Person:** A *first-person* pronoun (*I, we*) refers to the person speaking, a *second-person* pronoun (*you*) refers to the person spoken to, and a *third-person* pronoun (*he, she, it, they*) refers to the person spoken about.

2. **Number:** A singular pronoun (*I, you, me, he, she, it*) refers to a singular noun. A plural pronoun (*we, you, ours, they, theirs*) refers to a plural noun.

3. **Gender:** A feminine pronoun (*she, her*) refers to a feminine noun (*Christina, woman, girl, lady*). A masculine pronoun (*he, him*) refers to a masculine noun (*Robert, man, boy, gentleman*). The neutral pronoun *it* may be used when no gender is designated.

	1ST PERSON	2ND PERSON	3RD PERSON
Singular	I, me, my, mine	you, your, yours	he, him, his, she, her, hers, it, its
Plural	we, us, our, ours	you, your, yours	they, them, their, theirs

In the following examples, the pronouns and antecedents are italicized.

Example: *Donald* paid *his* dues for the ski club. (The masculine, singular pronoun *his* agrees with the masculine, singular noun *Donald*.)

Example: Ten club *members* qualified for the tour, and *they* were all experienced players. (The plural pronoun *they* agrees with the plural noun *members*.)

Example: The *university* will send ~~their~~ *its* sports director to the tournament. (The singular pronoun *its* agrees with the singular noun *university*.)

Example: *Lori* was thrilled with ~~their~~ *her* sports trophy. (The feminine, singular pronoun *her* agrees with the feminine, singular noun *Lori*.)

Exercise 8-1 • Proofread and Mark

*Proofread the sentences, and correct the pronouns. If the sentence is correct, write **C** to the left of the number.*

1. The bus carrying the softball team lost their way to the field.

2. After making her speech, the coach was pleased to hear that the audience enjoyed their talk.

3. The rookies are habitually leaving their extra bats in the dugout.

4. The fans enjoyed the opportunity to have lunch with its softball team, and she had a good time.

5. Sun Beach, the Heat's winter training camp, is ideal because of their location and weather.

Collective Nouns as Antecedents

When proofreading for agreement of pronouns and antecedents, watch for collective nouns used as antecedents. Words such as *committee, team, audience,* and *jury* are called collective nouns because they refer to a collection of objects, people, or animals. (Refer to Chapter 7, page 118, for

The audience was pleased with the seminar.

other examples of collective nouns.) If the members of the collective noun act as a singular unit, use a singular pronoun. If the members of the collective noun act individually, use a plural pronoun. In the following examples, the pronouns and antecedents are italicized.

> *Example:*   The *team* made *its* decision after careful analysis of the alternatives. (The collective noun *team* is acting as one unit and agrees with the singular pronoun *its*.)
>
> *Example:*   The *audience* left ~~*its*~~ *their* seats immediately after the rally. (The plural pronoun *their* agrees with the collective noun *audience*. In this instance, the pronoun refers to individuals in the audience acting independently.)

Compound Antecedents

Just as the verb must agree in number with the compound subject, the pronoun must also agree in number with compound antecedents. A **compound antecedent** consists of two or more nouns. Apply the following rules for compound antecedents. The pronouns and antecedents are italicized in the examples.

RULE 1   Two or more nouns joined by *and* require a plural pronoun.

> *Example:*   *Claire*, *Paolo*, and *Tim* received *their* applications a week ago.
> *Example:*   The team *captain* and the *players* were honored for *their* success.

RULE 2   Two or more nouns joined by *or/nor* require a singular pronoun when both antecedents are singular.

> *Example:*   Neither the *board* of directors nor the *commission* is willing to change *its* position regarding the trading policy.

RULE 3   Two or more nouns joined by *or/nor* require a plural pronoun when both antecedents are plural.

> *Example:*   Neither the *coaches* nor the *players* have sent *their* lists of goals.

RULE 4   If one antecedent is singular and the other is plural, the pronoun must agree with the nearer antecedent.

> *Example:*   Neither the *captain* nor the *players* were ready for *their* speech.

Indefinite Pronoun Agreement

In Chapter 7, you learned that some indefinite pronouns are always singular, others are always plural, and still others may be either singular or plural. When the first pronoun is indefinite and is used as an antecedent, the second pronoun that follows the antecedent must agree in number with the first.

Example: *Each* of the men took *his* turn in demonstrating the techniques. (*His* agrees with the singular antecedent *each*.)

Example: *Both* of the players were sorry for *their* actions. (*Their* agrees with the plural antecedent *both*.)

Exercise 8-2 • Proofread and Mark

*Proofread the sentences, and correct the pronouns. If the sentence is correct, write **C** to the left of the number.*

1. The field hockey team's travel committee scheduled their monthly meeting for August 1.

2. Neither Tonya nor Janyce checked their itinerary before leaving.

3. Both Coach Palmer and Coach Kobe have made plans for his trip to watch the final game.

4. One of the women left her tennis rackets on the team bus.

5. The rowing team resolved to win their last three competitive events.

» The Case of the Pronoun

Incorrect usage of personal pronouns often occurs because pronouns have different forms known as cases. A personal pronoun case changes its form according to its relationship to other words in the sentence. Notice the two masculine pronouns in the sentence "When John called, he said not to wait for his reply." Even though *he* and *his* both refer to John, the cases are different because the two pronouns have separate functions in the sentence.

The three cases of pronouns are **nominative, objective**, and **possessive**. Study the three different pronoun cases, and learn to use them correctly. In the examples that follow, all of the pronouns are italicized.

Nominative Case

Nominative case pronouns include the singular pronouns *I, you, he, she,* and *it* and the plural pronouns *we, you,* and *they*. The nominative case is used in two ways.

RULE 1 **Subject pronoun.** Use the nominative case when the pronoun acts as the subject of the sentence (subject of the verb). The verb may be the main verb of the sentence or the verb within a clause. (Clauses will be discussed in Chapter 9.)

Example: *He* canceled the game because *we* had to work that week. (Both pronouns are the subjects of verbs—*canceled* and *had*, respectively.)

Example: Two players were hurt during the first quarter, but *they* were not injured seriously. (The pronoun is the subject of the verb phrase *were injured*.)

Example: William and Isabella will officiate while *you* and ~~her~~ *she* are away.

Example: Sumio and ~~me~~ *I* work well together as team members.

RULE 2   Predicate pronoun. Use the nominative case when the pronoun immediately follows a form of the linking verb *be* (*am, is, are, was, were, be, has been, have been, had been*). When a pronoun follows a linking verb, it is called a **predicate pronoun**. A predicate pronoun is used after a verb and refers to the same person or thing as the subject of the verb. A predicate pronoun is always in the nominative case.

Example: It was *I* who called about the schedule. (*I*, a predicate pronoun, follows *was*, a form of the linking verb *be*.)

Example: The star player for today's game is *she*. (*She*, a predicate pronoun, follows *is*, a form of the linking verb *be*.)

Example: The only students who complained were *you* and ~~him~~ *he*.

Example: The winner of the Satellite News 20-K run was ~~her~~ *she*.

Exercise 8-3 • Proofread and Mark

*Proofread the sentences, and correct the pronoun case errors. If the sentence is correct, write **C** to the left of the number.*

1. If the junior players were treated like the varsity players, would they do as well?

2. It was not me who requested that the tournament date be changed; it was Lee and her.

3. The senior track coach and him can meet with the press today.

4. The person in the photograph is her when she won the final match of the season.

5. The ticket office was recognized for its efforts because they have an experienced staff.

Objective Case

Objective case pronouns include the singular pronouns *me, you, him, her,* and *it* and the plural pronouns *us, you,* and *them.* Because objective case pronouns always function as objects, they are used with action verbs. Objective case pronouns are never used with linking verbs, such as *is, are, was, were, seem,* or *become.* The objective case pronoun is used in three ways.

RULE 1   Direct object of the verb. Use the objective case when the pronoun answers the question *what* or *whom* and the pronoun receives the action of the verb (called the object of the verb).

Example: When you call your brother, tell *him* to meet us at Gate 15. (You tell *whom?*)

Example: They selected *him* to be the team captain. (They selected *whom?*)

RULE 2   Indirect object. Use the objective case when the pronoun tells *to whom* or *for whom* something is done.

Example: Mother gave *me* the play-off tickets for my birthday. (tells that Mother gave to me the tickets—the preposition *to* is omitted)

Example: My niece bought *me* a sweater. (tells that my niece bought for me a sweater—the preposition *for* is omitted)

RULE 3   Object of the preposition. Use the objective case when the pronoun is used as the object of the preposition. **Prepositions** are words that relate a noun or pronoun to other words in the sentence. Some common prepositions are *about, after, at, before, between, by, for, from, in, of, on, over, since, to, until,* and *with.* A preposition and its object form a **prepositional phrase.** In the following examples, the prepositional phrases with the objective case pronouns are italicized.

Example: Caitlin discussed the gymnastics trials *with her*.

Example: Just *between you and me*, I won't be going to the game today.

Example: Are you saving this seat *for ~~he~~ him and ~~I~~ me*?

Example: You are assigned to work *with Lucio, Jeff, and ~~she~~ her*.

Note: When *to* is followed by a verb, the phrase is called an **infinitive phrase.** No other preposition can be used as an infinitive. Do not confuse the preposition *to* with the infinitive *to*.

Example: Auri mailed *to him* an Olympic souvenir program. (shown as a prepositional phrase)

Example: I plan *to take* the bus to Friday's championship game. (shown as an infinitive phrase)

Exercise 8-4 • Proofread and Mark

Proofread the sentences, and correct the pronouns. If the sentence is correct, write **C** *to the left of the number.*

1. The hockey coach sent Dennis and she copies of next week's practice schedule.

2. The sports public relations office will arrange interviews for you and I.

continued

3. I agreed to attend the game with Glenna and him.

4. The tournament director called the team managers and I to confirm the lineups for the game.

5. After the lacrosse team won, the coach surprised she with tickets to a concert.

Michael sold the car to her.

Who and Whom

The use of the pronouns *who* and *whom* is troublesome, even for experienced writers and speakers. Remember, the rules that apply when using nominative and objective pronouns also apply when using *who* and *whom*.

Who is a nominative case pronoun that may be used as the subject of the sentence or clause. *Who* must also follow a form of the linking verb *be* (predicate pronoun).

Whom is an objective case pronoun that is used as the direct object of the verb, indirect object, or object of the preposition.

To help you decide which pronoun is correct, mentally rearrange the sentence and substitute the pronoun *he*, *she*, or *they* in place of "who" and *him*, *her*, or *them* in place of "whom."

Example: Who signed up for the tour? (She signed up for the tour.)
Example: *Whom* did the agent call? (The agent called *him*.)
Example: To who did you sell the car? (You sold the car to *her*.)
Example: The boy in the photo is whom? (He is the boy in the photo.)

If *who* or *whom* appears within a clause, determine the pronoun's use within the clause, ignoring the rest of the sentence. Then substitute another pronoun in place of *who* or *whom*. In the following examples, the dependent clauses are italicized.

Example: Jeanette is the person *who will represent us.* (*Who* is the subject of the dependent clause. *She* will represent us.)

Example: The member *whom we elected* is most qualified for the position. (*Whom* is the direct object of the verb elected. We elected *him*.)

Example: Clyde, *whom we know* is ill, cannot attend the qualifying match. (*Who* is ill?)

Example: Sorphea is the person *who the league selected* as the sportsmanship award winner. (The league selected *whom*?)

Exercise 8-5 • Proofread and Mark

*Proofread the sentences, and correct the pronouns. If the sentence is correct, write **C** to the left of the number.*

1. Kelli, who you know well, always tries to win!

2. Whom was the last person to arrvive?

3. Whom did you ask to make our travel arrangements?

4. Is she the individual who you want to meet?

5. Who do you want for a roommate this year?

Possessive Case

The possessive case includes the singular pronouns *my, mine, your, yours, his, her, hers,* and *its* and the plural pronouns *our, ours, your, yours, their,* and *theirs.* Possessive pronouns show ownership, and they are always written without the apostrophe.

Note: Do not confuse the contractions *it's* (it is), *they're* (they are), *who's* (who is), and *you're* (you are) with the possessive pronouns *its, their, whose,* and *your.*

Example: All of the league teams mail *their* subscription season tickets.

Example: *Whose* racket case has the blue and red piping?

Example: The painting was restored because of *it's* deterioration.

Example: *Your's* were the best score predictions.

Possessive pronouns are also used immediately before a **verbal noun** or **gerund** (a verb ending in *ing* that is used as a noun). In the following examples, the gerunds are italicized.

Example: Travis takes his *jogging* very seriously.

Example: Their *complaining* has ruined the game for everyone.

Example: I appreciate your *working* late this week.

Example: She practices her *riding* every day.

Using Pronouns with *Than* or *As*

When using pronouns in comparing two persons or things, the pronoun that follows *than* or *as* can be nominative or objective, depending on the use of the pronoun. Because the clause has been deliberately omitted after the pronoun, mentally restate the clause to determine the correct use of the pronoun. Study these examples carefully.

Example: Mick is taller than *I.* (Mick is taller than I am tall.)

Example: Corrine knows him as well as *I.* (Corrine knows him as well as I know him.)

Example: Corrine knows him as well as *me.* (Corrine knows him as well as Corrine knows me.)

Example: My sister keys faster than *I.* (My sister keys faster than I key.)

Example: You helped them more than *I.* (You helped them more than I helped them.)

Example: You helped them more than *me.* (You helped them more than you helped me.)

Exercise 8-6 • Proofread and Mark

*Proofread the sentences, and correct the pronouns. If the sentence is correct, write **C** to the left of the number.*

1. The team's local ticket office offers the best prices for their home games.

2. The NFL announced their football schedule for the season.

3. You insisting on attending the May 28 game was a great decision.

4. She was allowed more time for practice than I.

5. Ask Joy and Lenny if she need more time to practice.

CONFUSED AND MISUSED WORDS

correspondence *n.* a communication by exchange of letters

correspondents *n.* those who write letters

They kept in touch through **correspondence**.

All volunteer **correspondents** write five letters a day.

currant *n.* small, seedless raisin

current *adj.* up-to-date; *n.* electricity

I have an easy recipe for **currant** jelly.

Marcy enjoys writing about **current** events.

device *n.* a machine or gadget

devise *v.* to invent or to plan

Arturo has a **device** that will automatically turn the lights on and off.

Can you **devise** a way to surprise them?

---

* Double-check the document. Read the copy the first time for content. Read the copy a second time for consistency and correct grammar.

* Use available references if you have questions about correct grammar.

PROOFREADING APPLICATIONS

*Proofread the following sentences, and mark all pronoun errors using the appropriate proofreaders' marks. If the sentence is correct, write **C** to the left of the number.*

1. Team owner Fay Sollenberger was pleased that the team was recognized at their awards banquet.

2. To whom did you write about reserving game tickets?

3. It was very noticeable that Jackson played better than me during yesterday's game.

4. The audience remained in their seats until the last inning.

5. The star player for the team is her.

6. The women's basketball team announced that anyone can attend their practices.

7. The meeting of the Whitland Athletic Club was disrupted by his arriving late.

8. Mail you're reply to our headquarters by November 1.

9. When the members of the International Olympic Committee meet, it is required to show their identification cards at the gate.

10. It is she whom we recommend for consideration on the hockey travel team.

11. Between you and I, the new Milwaukee Sports Arena is the most outstanding facility of its kind in the country.

12. To who should you address an inquiry about reserved parking?

13. Members of the golf team have its own ideas of how quality training helps.

14. My sister is a noticeably better baseball player than me.

15. The U.S. skating team will perform its exhibition program tonight.

Exercise 8-8 • Spelling and Word Usage Check

*Compare the words in Column **A** with the corresponding words in Column **B**. Use the appropriate proofreaders' marks to correct the misspelled or misused words. If both columns are correct, write **C** to the left of the number.*

Column A	Column B
1. acknowledge	acknowledge
2. noticeable	noticable
3. convenience	convinience
4. facilities	facilities
5. monitoring	monitering
6. occasionally	occassionally
7. reciept	receipt
8. particpation	participation
9. paralel	parallel
10. processing	proccessing
11. quality	guality
12. persevarance	perseverance
13. The correspondents are here.	The correspondence may use e-mail.
14. What is the currant year?	The current administration is busy.
15. The devise is interesting.	The new device works well.

Exercise 8-9 • Word Division List

Proofread the words in each line. If one or more words are divided incorrectly, correct the word(s) using the appropriate proofreaders' marks. Then write the word(s) on the blank line using hyphen(s) to show ***all preferred points of division****. If all three words in a line are correct, write* ***C*** *on the blank line.*

Ex. pow- er	pres- ent	prog- ress	power
1. ac- knowl- edge	com- pa- ny	li- a- bil- i- ty	__________
2. fa- cil- i- ty	lo- cal	com- pelled	__________
3. cos- tume	faith- ful	per- su- ade	__________
4. con- ven- ience	ga- ble	pho- nics	__________
5. no- tice- able	gad- fly	person- nel	__________
6. hi- ba- chi	flout	re- ceipt	__________
7. pic- ture- sque	mul- ti- ple	per- tin- ent	__________
8. des-pon- dence	oc- ca- sion- al	de- vel- op- ment	__________
9. hid- den	phan- tom	pro- cess- ion	__________
10. cus- tom	re- cip- i- ent	me- di- o- cre	__________
11. con- trad- ic- tion	qual- i- ty	nec- es- sary	__________
12. crack- ed	fam- i- ly	ex- trapo- late	__________
13. cross- bones	qui- et	pro- gramm- er	__________
14. reckon	suc- ceed	jea- lou- sy	__________
15. par- al- el	para- digm	ref- er- ence	__________

Exercise 8-10 • Business Letter

Proofread the following letter, and correct all errors using the appropriate proofreaders' marks.

SAN JOSE PANTHERS

Southern City Stadium
48322 Buckingham Avenue • San Jose, CA 95136-2382
408-555-0128 • Fax 408-555-0129

February 28, 20--

Ms. Helen G. Grays
480 Wallace Drive
Seattle, WA 98125-4130

Dear Ms. Grays:

As a loyal fan of the Los Angeles Angels of Anaheim, you have a once-in-a-lifetime opportunity to meet with the players of your favorite team. Imagine being able to meet with team members during its spring training!

Each year the Los Angeles Angles of Anaheim baseball team provides a limited number of fans the unprecedented opportunity to participate in spring training for ten days. During this time, you actually become a member of the team and attend their planning sessions, strategy meetings, and practice sessions. You will be able to visit the team's training facilitys and monitor any player's progress. And finally, you will have available to you the full services of the training staff and spend quallity time with your favorite players. This is an exciting time for everyone!

The enclosed brochure provides complete information about the three sessions we have planned this spring. We are confident you will enjoy your particpation in this event. The price for each session includes all expenses: food, lodging, transportation, and gratuities. We also plan to arrange for you to meet with the Public Relations Director and I during the first week.

As we anticipate a considerable response to this offer, we would appreciate you returning all forms and correspondents promptly in the enclosed envelope. You will be glad you took time to attend training camp and meet those whom participated with such intensity.

Just between you and I, you will be thankful you took advantage of this opportunity!

Yours truly,

David R. Collins
President

Enclosures

Exercise 8-11 • Memorandum

Proofread the following memo, and correct all errors using the appropriate proofreaders' marks.

TO: All Supervisors

FROM: David R. Collins, President

DATE: March 30, 20--

SUBJECT: Training Session for San Jose Panthers' Fans

We am attaching a copy of my letter of February 28, 20--, and the brochure entitled *Guidelines for Training Session*. These were sent to a select group of baseball fans who has indicated an interest in joining the San Jose Panthers for a limited time during spring training at the Marina facilities.

You will be contacted individually by Vice President Dawn Burnside in connection with logistics and related handling. However, I would like to take this opportunity to encourage you to extend yourself in making the participants in this program feel as though he is joining our family.

Remember, these people are more than guests; these people are sincere and dedicated fans of the Panthers whom have cheered the players when they were up and encouraged them when they were down. Its easy to acknowledge the applause and wave the pennants when "Lady Luck" is smiling. But it takes a special, dedicated fan to remain devoted to us team.

Please make use of the many convenient and exclusive touches we deviced to be used in this excellent program, such as the extensive menu that can be tailored to accommodate individual preferences as well as needs. Food is a most important part of this program, and we want to make sure that even those guests who have restricted diets enjoy his meals.

So I am asking for your assistance in monitoring this program to ensure that our guests enjoy their stay with us. When they return home, their happy memories will encourage them to join us again next year.

Thank you for you're continued support in making this an outstanding program.

Attachments

PROOFREADING AT THE COMPUTER

Exercise 8-12 • Memorandum

1. Open 8-12 from the Chapter 8 folder on the student CD. (This is a computer copy of Exercise 8-11.)

2. Proofread the letter on the screen. Correct all errors on the screen copy that you indicated with proofreaders' marks in Exercise 8-11.

3. Produce the memo in correct format following the standard procedures described in the previous chapters.

Exercise 8-13 • Enumerated List

1. Open 8-13 from the Chapter 8 folder on the student CD.

2. Proofread the list, and make all necessary corrections.

3. Format the list using default left and right margins and a 2" top margin.

4. Produce the list in correct format following the standard procedures described in the previous chapters.

Exercise 8-14 • E-mail Message

1. Open 8-14 from the Chapter 8 folder on the student CD.

2. Proofread the e-mail message on the screen, and make all necessary corrections.

3. Produce the e-mail message in correct format following the standard procedures described in the previous chapters.

CUMULATIVE APPLICATION

Exercise 8-15 • Letter

Proofread and correct all errors using the appropriate proofreaders' marks.

December 27, 20--

Mrs. Gloria Ayala
Health department
4300 North DeWolf Ave.
Clovis, CA 93611-0956

Dear Mrs. Ayala

We applaud the recent move by the Health Department to prohibit sales of soft drinks to middle school students. To help educate students about better nutritional choices, we are asking for you're assistants in distributing this information to all institutoins within California.

Since the benifits of a healthy diet includes increasing a student's ability to concentrate and improving one's overall learning experience, we believe this is a worthwhile effort. Perhaps among our two organizations we can help students device a plan for making healthier choices. We will hold a public forum in the cafeteria on February 10 for anyone who wishes to obtain more information.

Drink (8 oz.)	Carbs (g)	Calories	Sodium (mg)	Sugars	Calcium (g)
1% Milk	—	120	160	15	35%
Apple Juice	28	110	35	28	—
Soda	33	130	35	33	—
Orange Juice	27	110	25	24	2%
Frappuccino®	38	190	180	32	15%

We apreciate this opportunity to help us eliminite the selling of soft drinks in our middle schools.

Nutritionally yours,

Marcus Taylor, R.N.

rrh

 Bookmark It!

Want more practice? Go to www.cengage.com/keyboarding/pagel for more proofreading activities.

Sentence Construction

Spotlight on ACCURACY

Your writing style includes the six Cs of communication: courtesy, clarity, conciseness, correctness, completeness, and coherence. When you edit your documents, check that the message will be clear to your audience. How seriously do you think the principal took the following excuses when she received them?

- Please accuse Sam for being absent on February 29, 30, and 31.

- Sandy is under our doctor's care and should not take physical education. Please execute her.

- Rosangela has been absent because she had two teeth taken out of her face.

In Chapter 7, you learned that a sentence contains a subject and a verb and expresses a complete thought. Generally, sentences contain other elements that help to convey the writer's message. The alert proofreader must check that these elements are positioned correctly to ensure consistency and clarity. The proofreader must also check the language for any bias.

Objectives

- Understand the significance of phrases and clauses.

- Find and mark errors in parallel structure.

- Identify and correct dangling and misplaced modifiers.

- Use bias-free language.

- Spell correctly 12 frequently misspelled words.

- Use correctly three sets of commonly confused and misused words.

>> Sentence Elements

In addition to the words that act as subjects and verbs, most sentences also contain phrases and clauses. A **phrase** is a group of two or more related words without a subject and a verb. The entire phrase in a sentence may act as a noun, a verb, an adjective, or an adverb. Phrases may also modify nouns and verbs. Phrases that function as adjectives or adverbs are usually positioned near the words they modify. The phrases are italicized in the following examples.

Example: *The certified public accountant* audited their accounting records. (noun phrase acting as the subject)

Example: David *should work together* with Augustina on the assignment. (verb phrase)

Example: The book *lying on the table* belongs to Beatriz. (adjective phrase that modifies the noun *book*)

Example: My first class started *on time*. (adverb phrase that modifies the verb *started*)

Example: *Running late*, I forgot my 3 p.m. appointment. (participial phrase that modifies the subject *I*)

Example: Amelia will return *in the morning*. (prepositional phrase that is used as an adverb and modifies the verb phrase *will return*)

Example: The sweatshirt *with the gold stripes* is mine. (prepositional phrase that is used as an adjective and modifies the noun *sweatshirt*)

Example: Ellis wants *to retire*. (infinitive phrase that is used as a noun and is the direct object of the verb *wants*)

Clauses are groups of words that contain a subject and a verb. If the clause expresses a complete thought, it is a sentence and is called an **independent clause**. If the clause does not express a complete thought, it is called a **dependent clause**. In the following examples, the independent clauses appear in bold and the dependent clauses in italics. The subject and verb of both clauses are identified.

Example: **The representative returned my call.**
$\quad\quad\quad\quad\quad$ *s* $\quad\quad\quad\quad$ *v*

Example: *If you leave your number*, **I will call you tomorrow.**

Example: *When the package arrives*, **Helio will sign for it.**

Exercise 9-1 • Proofread and Mark

*In each of the sentences, identify the underlined group of words. To the left of the number, write **P** for phrase, **IC** for independent clause, or **DC** for dependent clause.*

1. <u>If we are to arrive on time</u>, we must follow their directions.

2. <u>You shouldn't leave the interview</u> without asking when they will contact you with a decision.

continued

3. <u>When you volunteer for the position</u>, consider the work hours and your ability to complete the necessary tasks.

4. <u>The grievance committee has total commitment</u> to further the work.

5. <u>For most people</u>, satisfaction is an important consideration.

» Parallel Structure in Sentences

Words, phrases, or clauses within a sentence that are related in meaning should be written in the same grammatical form. Using the same form makes the ideas **parallel**. When adjectives are parallel to adjectives, phrases are parallel to phrases, and clauses are parallel to clauses, the meaning of the sentence is clear and logical. When you find a sentence that sounds awkward, revise it so that related ideas are expressed in the same way.

Example: Michelle's career interests are *advertising* and *modeling*. (parallel noun forms, or gerunds)

Example: We are looking for someone who is *courteous*, *dependable*, and *considerate*. (parallel adjectives)

Example: Roland couldn't decide whether *to buy* a laptop computer or *to spend* the money on a trip to visit his brother. (infinitive phrases used as the objects of the verb *decide*)

Example: We will ski and ~~we will be~~ climbing mountains during our vacation. (unparallel verbs)

Example: Sharon is tall, ~~with~~ ^{has} brown eyes, and has a disposition ~~that is cheerful~~ ^{cheerful}. (unparallel adjectives) *Also correct*: Sharon is tall, brown-eyed, and cheerful.

Example: I have limited experience using desktop publishing, but word processing ~~is being used~~ ^{I use} extensively in my present job. (unparallel clauses)

Errors in parallelism occur frequently within enumerations. All related elements must be stated in the same grammatical structure. Additionally, the same grammatical structure must follow conjunctions that appear in pairs, such as *both … and, either … or, neither … nor,* and *not only … but also.* These pairs are called **correlative conjunctions**. The parallel elements are italicized in the examples. Note that all of the elements end in *ing*.

Example: Past job experience includes the following tasks:

1. *Keying* original copy and *proofreading* first drafts

2. *Saving* documents

3. *Printing* and *proofreading* hard copy

4. *Retrieving* and *revising* documents

Example: Daniel stated *that you had changed your mind* or *that you had canceled your reservation.*

Example: The topics to be covered include the following:

1. Identifying the purpose and audience
2. ~~To~~ plan ~~the~~ message *ning*
3. Writ~~e~~ ~~the~~ message *ing*
4. Editing the message
5. ~~Direct~~ and indirect messages *Writing*

Example: Suzette not only serves on the Personnel Committee but ~~she is~~ also on the Constitution Committee.

Exercise 9-2 • Proofread and Mark

*Correct errors in parallelism using the appropriate proofreaders' marks. If the sentence is correct, write **C** to the left of the number.*

1. We will hire only employees who are hardworking, ambitious, and who are trustworthy.

2. The guidelines were written for upgrading all employees, improving the morale, and to augment income.

3. A supervisor was hired to manage the new plant and that he would recommend changes in hiring practices.

4. The equipment now being installed can number the sections, rearrange the margins, and listing the corrections.

5. The editor called me about the manuscript draft and wanted more information about tomorrow's meeting.

>> Dangling and Misplaced Modifiers

A **modifier** is a word, a phrase, or a clause that describes another word in the sentence. To clarify the relationship between the modifier and the word it describes, the modifier must be placed in the correct position. If the modifier does not logically describe any word in the sentence, it is called a **dangling modifier**. If it is not close enough to the word it describes, it is called a **misplaced modifier**. You should place the modifier as close as possible to the word it modifies. Study the placement of the following modifiers:

DANGLING MODIFIER	CORRECTED
Keying very rapidly, the report had three errors.	Keying very rapidly, the operator made three errors.

MISPLACED MODIFIER	CORRECTED
Mara bought a canary for her friend that sings beautifully.	Mara bought her friend a canary that sings beautifully.

Errors frequently occur when introductory phrases and clauses do not modify the subject of the sentence. To correct a dangling or misplaced modifier, revise the sentence so that the subject completes the action described in the introductory phrase. If you are unsure about the subject of the sentence, ask the question who or what after the introductory phrase. The answer is the sentence's subject, which should immediately follow the introductory phrase. Compare the following sentences.

DANGLING MODIFIER	CORRECTED
Before deciding which van to buy, three agencies were visited by Christopher.	Before deciding which van to buy, Christopher visited three agencies. (Who visited three agencies?–Christopher)

MISPLACED MODIFIER	CORRECTED
While jogging on the sidewalk, a cyclist hit Donita.	While jogging on the sidewalk, Donita was hit by a cyclist. (Who was jogging?–Donita)

Exercise 9-3 • Proofread and Mark

*Revise the sentences that contain dangling or misplaced modifiers. If the sentence is correct, write **C** to the left of the number.*

1. Excelling in using Access, our manager hired Ella.

2. The report was proofread by Justin, lying on the desk.

continued

3. Constance learned how to use the new software. appearing somewhat doubtful it would increase efficiency.

4. Before leaving for an important meeting, an important telephone message for Leah was left by the administrative assistant.

5. Although all of the applicants were qualified for the position, they have little direct work experience in records management.

›› Bias-Free Language

A writer or speaker should never send a message that could alienate employees or potential customers. Instead, messages should be unbiased, ethical, and fair to all. **Bias-free language** avoids insensitive language regarding gender, race, ethnic group, age, religion, or disability.

Avoid Gender Bias

Traditionally, writers have used *he* or *man* to represent both genders. The practice of gender bias is outdated and no longer acceptable. It is inappropriate to use *he* or *his* to refer to both men and women. Likewise, it is incorrect to assume that certain jobs are "men's work" or "women's work." Today men and women are employed in all occupations; the *Dictionary of Occupational Titles* was rewritten to reflect job titles, not gender. To classify secretaries, elementary school teachers, or nurses as women and pilots, farmers, or police officers as men would be to stereotype occupations.

To treat men and women fairly, follow these general rules:

RULE 1   Use the plural pronouns *they, their, theirs,* or *them* or nouns such as *people* or *persons* when referring to a group that consists of both men and women.

Example: Salespersons must have their weekly reports completed by Monday.

RULE 2   Rewrite the sentence to avoid using pronouns if it is possible to do so without affecting the meaning.

Example: Sales reports are due on Monday.

RULE 3   Shift the sentence to second person.

Example: As an employee, you are responsible for reporting expenses correctly.

Firefighters proudly serve the public.

RULE 4   If you must use a singular pronoun, use both *he/she* and *his/her*. Do not overuse these expressions, for they can become annoying and sound repetitious.

> *Example:*   Each salesperson must have his or her report completed by Monday. (both genders used)

RULE 5   Use parallel phrasing if you must refer to people by gender. Use "women and men," "females and males," "boys and girls," or "ladies and gentlemen" for parallel structure. You would not say "men and girls" or "women and males."

> *Example:*   The boys and girls toured our offices.

RULE 6   Use business terms that do not imply the gender of a person.

OUTDATED (AVOID)	CURRENT (USE)
airline steward or stewardess	flight attendant
businessman	businessperson, executive, entrepreneur, professional
businessmen	businesspeople, people in business
chairman	chair, chairperson, group leader, moderator, president, presiding officer
coed	student
congressman	member of Congress, congressional representatives, representatives of Congress
foreman	supervisor, manager, executive
housewife	homemaker
mankind	persons, people, humanity, everyone, humankind
man-made	handmade, custom-made, custom-built
manpower	human resources, human power, human energy, workforce, personnel
repairman	repairer, repairperson, service technician

OUTDATED (AVOID)	CURRENT (USE)
salesman	salesperson, sales agent, sales representative
spokesman	speaker, spokesperson, advocate, proponent
statesman	politician, public official, political leader, public servant, government leader
waiter/waitress	server, waitperson, wait staff
workmen	workers, employees, personnel

Avoid placing the words *man, male, lady, female,* or *woman* before or after an occupational title. Compare the differences in these examples:

AVOID	USE
lady or female doctor	doctor
male nurse	nurse
policewoman, policeman	police officer
fireman, female firefighter	firefighter
male elementary school teacher	elementary school teacher

Exercise 9-4 • Proofread and Mark

*Revise the sentences that contain inappropriate language. If the sentence is correct, write **C** to the left of the number.*

1. A high school French teacher must demonstrate that he can spell French words correctly.
2. Rebecca Wentworth was elected chairman of the Marquette Economic Club.
3. Additional personnel are needed to build the Habitat for Humanity house by August.
4. Salesmen must be able to answer all questions asked by his customers.
5. The September meeting for foremen took place in Atlanta with more than 700 foremen attending.

Avoid Race and Ethnic Group, Age, Religion, and Disability Bias

The principle for writing messages that are sensitive to race and ethnic group, age, religion, or disability is as follows: *Avoid emphasizing race and ethnic group, age, religion, or disability when those categories have no relevance to your message.* The emphasis in business writing should be on competence and relevance, not on categories such as race, age, or religion.

Race and Ethnic Group Bias.   Mention race or ethnic group only when the race or ethnic group is relevant. Likewise, avoid language that suggests that all members of a certain racial or ethnic group have the same characteristics.

UNACCEPTABLE	ACCEPTABLE
Yens Weimer is an unusually fast German runner.	Yens Weimer is an unusually fast runner. (Being German is not relevant.)
Celine Casiano, the Spanish clerk, was selected for promotion.	Celine Casiano was selected for promotion. (Being Spanish is not relevant to her promotion.)

Age Bias.   Mention the age of a person only when age is relevant.

UNACCEPTABLE	ACCEPTABLE
Lu Chou, 29, was hired last month.	Lu Chou was hired last month. (His age, 29, was not relevant in being hired.)
Kay Aspen, the 51-year-old president of our company, has resigned.	Kay Aspen, president of our company, has resigned. (Her age, 51, was not relevant in her resignation.)

Religion Bias.   Religion usually has no relevance in a business setting and should not be mentioned.

UNACCEPTABLE	ACCEPTABLE
Mavis Mann, the Jewish account executive, gave a presentation on using laptop computers.	Mavis Mann gave a presentation on using laptop computers. (Being Jewish is not relevant.)

Disability Bias.   There is no polite way to label people with a physical, cognitive, or emotional disability. Eliminate mention of the disability if possible. If you must refer to people in terms of their disabilities, refer to the person first and the disability second. In addition, avoid using terms such as handicapped, crippled, afflicted, retarded, or victim.

UNACCEPTABLE	ACCEPTABLE
A diabetic, Everett is always the first person to arrive.	Everett is always the first person to arrive. (Being a *diabetic* has no bearing on when he arrives.)
The crippled worker, Kip, faces barriers on the job.	Kip, who is disabled, faces many barriers on the job. (Avoid using terms such as *crippled*, and refer to Kip by name prior to listing his disability.)

Exercise 9-5 • Proofread and Mark

*Revise the sentences that contain inappropriate language. If the sentence is correct, write **C** to the left of the number.*

1. Marco Galeone, former Italian-American mayor of our city, plans to run for U.S. senator.
2. Cedric's temper flared when he was questioned about his frequent tardiness.
3. Joachim, a member of the ELCA church, took the bus to Albuquerque.
4. Arianna, 22, will be joining our Accounting Department upon her graduation.
5. As a cancer victim, Janelle MacDonald is being treated for her disease.

IMAGE SOURCE/GETTY IMAGES

Janelle MacDonald is being treated for her disease.

CONFUSED AND MISUSED WORDS

cooperation	*n.* working together
corporation	*n.* a legal entity

Your **cooperation** is greatly appreciated.

This **corporation** is traded on the New York Stock Exchange.

council	*n.* an assembly of people
counsel	*v.* to give advice or guidance; *n.* a lawyer or group of lawyers; *n.* advice received

The **council** recommended that we approve the request for funding.

Your **counsel** was well received.

dairy	*n.* a commercial firm that processes and/or sells milk and milk products
diary	*n.* a daily personal record of events, experiences, and observations

She works at the **dairy** in Burnsville.

Have you read his **diary** for December 1?

---

* Select words carefully to eliminate insensitivity regarding gender, race, ethnic group, religion, age, or physical condition. Emphasis in business writing should be concerned with competence and relevance, not on categories such as gender, religion, or age.

* Read one word at a time—the opposite of speed-reading— especially for copy that contains specialized or highly technical vocabulary. Read unfamiliar words syllable by syllable or letter by letter.

* Check a dictionary to determine whether a compound word is written as one word, as two words, or as a hyphenated word.

Proofreading & Editing Tips

PEP Tip

PROOFREADING APPLICATIONS

*Proofread the following sentences, and mark all sentence construction errors using the appropriate proofreaders' marks. If the sentence is correct, write **C** to the left of the number.*

1. Jeffrey was required to take courses in management, computer information systems, and also in accounting.

2. Dustin and Wendy will visit relatives in Pittsburgh and then stop to visit relatives in Cleveland.

3. The most qualified candidate for the position in accounting had four years' work experience, a bachelor's degree in accounting, and he has great computer skills.

4. This desktop publishing software allows me to key text, insert tables, check for spelling errors, and I can insert graphics.

5. Before hiring a new account rep, four candidates were interviewed by Cylea.

6. Tawni purchased a new laptop computer for her son that weighs less than four pounds.

7. The lost keys were found by Ashley on the table.

8. Airline stewards are able to fly almost anywhere in the world.

9. Keith Prusi, the Polish executive, gave a presentation on his tour of Asian and African companies.

10. One of the mailmen will work next weekend.

11. The business luncheon was served by 24 male and female waiters.

12. Miranda was selected as president of her professional association.

13. In 2013 Dawn Ormiston, 27, completed her master's degree from the University of Kansas.

14. Gary meets with his supervisor each week at 9:30 a.m.

15. As a person who has multiple myeloma, Dawn Berube was selected as the salesman of the month for December.

Exercise 9-7 • Spelling and Word Usage Check

*Compare the words in Column **A** with the corresponding words in Column **B**. Use the appropriate proofreaders' marks to correct the misspelled or misused words. If both columns are correct, write **C** to the left of the number.*

Column A	Column B
1. acaddemic	academic
2. applicants	applicants
3. cleint	client
4. decision	decisoin
5. develope	develop
6. eligible	eligable
7. featured	faetured
8. installation	instalation
9. libary	library
10. percent	per cent
11. possibility	possability
12. recommendation	recomendation
13. Their cooperation was tremendous.	The cooperation declared bankruptcy.
14. The counsel meets on Wednesday.	I will accept your council.
15. I frequently visit the dairy.	The information in your dairy is fascinating!

Exercise 9-8 • International Vocabulary

*Compare the French and Spanish words in Column **A** with the corresponding words in Column **B**. If the word in Column **B** is different from the word in Column **A**, use the appropriate proofreaders' marks to correct Column **B**. If the words in both columns are the same, write **C** to the left of the number.*

Column A	Column B
1. embotellador	embotallador
2. alumbrado	alumbrado
3. proporcionar	proporcianar
4. visiteur	visituer
5. ophtalmologiste	ophtilmologiste

Proofread the following letter; and correct all errors in placement of phrases, parallel structure, misplaced or dangling modifiers, and gender stereotyping. Use the appropriate proofreaders' marks to make the corrections. Adjust margins as necessary to make this letter fit on one page.

THE GOURMET SOCIETY

143 Grant Plaza • 1621 West Market Avenue
San Francisco, CA 94105-1362
415-555-0173 • Fax 415-555-0177

July 24, 20--

Mr. Alton K. Ladene
4090 Strawberry Circle
Denver, CO 80123-4102

Dear Alton

I am excited about your decision to be spokesman at the fall meeting of The Gourmet Society.

This dinner meeting will be held in the Ruby Room of the Hotel Goldstrike, 9006 Mission Street, San Francisco, CA 94105-3428, at 7 p.m., Tuesday, September 6, 20--. Following the dinner meeting, we will have refreshments and also have dancing in the Diamond Room.

I enjoyed your recent article titled "The Many Faces of Pasta" in the June edition of *Cooking Western Style*. Our members would be pleased to have you speak on this subject. Topics you may want to develop in your presentation include the following:

1. Selecting the right pasta for the right dish
2. Pasta calories count
3. How to find the stores that offer the largest selection of pasta

You asked if I know any one-liners on the subject of food or dining that you can use in your presentation. I don't keep a library of jokes, but I'm enclosing some jokes that I've laughed at in the past. I am sure you will find these jokes to be tasteful, funny, and I think relevant for this dinner meeting.

All meeting arrangements will be handled by this office. You can be sure we will do everything possible to ensure a successful evening and that would be delightful.

Again, thank you for agreeing to be our spokesman. As your client, we look forward to your presentation. Just between us, I think the meeting is going to be a smash!

Sincerely,

Gretel Von Rotteck, Director
THE GOURMET SOCIETY

yha

Enclosure

Exercise 9-10 • Newspaper Article

Proofread the following article, and correct all errors using the appropriate proofreaders' marks.

Proven Grocery Shopping Tips

Grocery shopping may not be your favorite weekend activity, and it can be especially difficult if you aren't prepared for grocery shopping prior to setting foot in your local supermarket. Proven grocery shopping tips which will help you save money and time are as follows: (1) prepare a budget, (2) use coupons, (3) buy only what you need, (4) shop on a full stomach, and (5) you need to make a shopping list and stick to that list.

First, prepare a budget for what you anticipate will be his or her grocery shopping needs for the year. Break down your budget by months and weeks. Set a specific amount you can afford to spend each week. By setting a specific weekly amount. You will find yourself putting back items you don't need right now. Do you really need 10 pounds of sugar or 20 pounds of potatoes? Or can you wait for a better time or price?

Second, use coupons to purchase essential food items. Shoppers may think she can't save much money by clipping coupons. But they could be wrong! You don't need to spend hours each week. Cutting out coupons, but concentrate instead on those non-perishable items which are on sale. You may be surprised at how quickly the savings add up. If the sales item is out of stock, ask your stock girl for a rain check so you can buy the item later.

Third, buy only what you need. How many times have you overspent your food budget because you found items on sale that you just had to have—even though you didn't intend to cook that item this week? A shopping list is, after all, a list of what you need from the supermarket. The more perishable the item, the more you need to think about whether you actually need that item now. If you aren't sure about how perishable an item might be, ask the male store manager.

Four, shop only on a full stomach. This may, in fact. Be one of the most important points to remember. When you're hungry and go grocery shopping, you will often buy what you don't need. If you are hungry, you tend to purchase snack items you don't need. Even your German mother, 49, would agree on this point!

Five, you need to make a shopping list and stick to that list! Never buy what you don't need. A good deal is a good deal, right? Well, it's possible that buying in bulk isn't the best deal. Just remember that a larger size isn't necessarily the best deal or the least expensive. Any housewife will tell you that you need to check the unit price before selecting an item for purchase.

PROOFREADING AT THE COMPUTER

Exercise 9-11 • Newspaper Article

1. Open 9-11 from the Chapter 9 folder on the student CD. (This is a computer copy of Exercise 9-10.)

2. Proofread the newspaper article on the screen. Correct all errors on the screen copy that you indicated with proofreaders' marks in Exercise 9-10. Use the spelling checker.

3. Produce the newspaper article in correct format following the standard procedures described in previous chapters.

Exercise 9-12 • Notice

1. Open 9-12 from the Chapter 9 folder on the student CD.

2. Proofread the notice on the screen. Correct all errors.

3. Produce the notice following the standard procedures.

Exercise 9-13 • E-mail Message

1. Open 9-13 from the Chapter 9 folder on the student CD.

2. Proofread the e-mail message on the screen. Correct all errors.

3. Produce the e-mail message following the standard procedures.

CUMULATIVE APPLICATION

Exercise 9-14 • Notice

Proofread and correct all errors using the appropriate proofreaders' marks.

Crescent City Fire Department—Station 47

NOTICE

TO: ALL FIREMEN ASSIGNED TO STATION 47

EFFECTIVE AUG. 5, 20--

A time-honored tradition in the fire department is that all firefighters assigned to a given station participate, on a rotation basis, in meal preparation. This plan has work well for us.

In an effort to be more aware of different dietary requirements, I reccommend we use these herbs to prepare our meals.

1. <u>Basil</u>. Having a sweet flavor with an aromatic odor, basil is used whole or ground. It is good with lamb, ground beef, vegetables, dressing, and when you make omelets.

2. <u>Chives</u>. With a sweet mild flavor of onion, this herb are excellent in salads, fish, soups, and potatoes.

3. <u>Dill</u>. Both seeds and leaves of dill is flavorful. Leaves may be used to garnish or cook with fish, soup, and beans.

4. <u>Sage</u>. Sage may be used fresh or dried in tomatoe juice, fish, omelets, beef, poultry, and stuffing.

Use these herbs in small amounts, and taste before adding more. Our firemen are guaranteed to enjoy these refreshing tastes!

Jake Magnuson, Captain

Bookmark It!

Want more practice? Go to www.cengage.com/keyboarding/pagel for more proofreading activities.

Comma Errors

Spotlight on ACCURACY

Punctuation causes problems for many people. It appears that some people punctuate whenever they pause; others rarely punctuate. But when is punctuation necessary? The purpose of any punctuation mark should be to help the reader correctly interpret a written message. How does punctuation change your interpretation of the following sentences?

- We are going to eat Monte before we take another step.
  We are going to eat, Monte, before we take another step.

- The meeting ended, happily.
  The meeting ended happily.

- The Democrats, say the Republicans, are sure to lose.
  The Democrats say the Republicans are sure to lose.

≫ The Importance of Punctuation Marks

Why are punctuation marks so important in written communication? Why do you need to proofread for punctuation errors? If punctuation marks are used incorrectly or omitted, the meaning of the text may be unclear to the reader.

Punctuation marks are like traffic signals—they tell the reader when to stop, slow down, or proceed. *Terminal* (ending) punctuation marks appear at the end of a sentence and tell the reader to stop. *Internal* (within or inside) punctuation marks tell the reader when to pause and help the reader to interpret the sentence as the writer intended.

Terminal punctuation marks will be discussed in Chapter 11. In Chapter 10, you will review the rules pertaining to the use of the comma. Because the comma is the most frequently used punctuation mark, this entire chapter will be devoted to comma usage. Use the following proofreaders' marks to show comma corrections:

		MARKED COPY	CORRECTED COPY
Insert a comma.	⋏	The class had already started but I walked in anyway.	The class had already started, but I walked in anyway.
Delete a comma.	ℐ	Rob, and Bianca will graduate in May.	Rob and Bianca will graduate in May.

≫ The Comma

The comma is an important internal punctuation mark. When used correctly, commas make the relationship between elements (words, phrases, and clauses) in the sentence clear. You learned in Chapter 9 that a clause is a group of related words that contains a subject and a verb. A clause may be either a dependent clause, which does not express a complete thought, or an independent clause, which does.

Independent Clauses

A sentence may contain a combination of independent and dependent clauses separated by commas. A sentence that consists of two or more *independent* clauses is called a **compound sentence**. When the independent clauses are joined by the conjunction *and, but, or, nor, for,* or *yet,* separate the clauses with a comma. The word *independent* means "able to stand alone"; thus, independent clauses in a compound sentence may also be written as two separate sentences. The two clauses are joined with a conjunction simply because they are closely related in meaning. If the two independent clauses are very short, the comma can be omitted.

Example: I called and she answered.

In all of the examples that follow, the subject and the verb of each independent clause are identified. The conjunctions are italicized.

Example: Alicia's strength is her work ethic, *but* her weakness is her lack of time management skills.

Example: Secretaries are called administrative assistants, *and* they are knowledgeable in office management and computer technology.

Example: Garrett may work in the garden or he may attend the concert.

Note: When "you" is understood to be the subject in both clauses, a comma is still required.

Example: (You) Attend the annual meeting in person or (you) vote by proxy.

Note: The following sentence contains a compound verb (three verbs). It is still a simple sentence—not a compound sentence. Therefore, a comma is not required.

Example: He will hire a taxi or rent a car and drive to the meeting site.

Exercise 10-1 • Proofread and Mark

*Use the appropriate proofreaders' marks to correct the errors in comma usage. If the sentence is correct, write **C** to the left of the number.*

1. Shannon was late to the meeting and she had to leave early because of another appointment.

2. Tomoko was elected vice president and Ambrose was elected treasurer at the November meeting.

3. Oliver took minutes of the meeting and the minutes were approved the following month.

4. *Robert's Rules of Order Newly Revised* is the parliamentary authority for this organization.

5. Edward will chair the Elections Committee and Robbi will chair the Auditing Committee.

Insert a comma after most introductory words, phrases, or clauses that come before the independent clause.

Example: *Therefore,* I have decided to enroll in the computer class. (introductory word)

Example: *In other words,* the course is designed to develop basic skills on three application programs. (introductory phrase)

Example: *When you are ready to study,* I'll meet you at the library. (introductory clause)

Example: *No* you were not late for the first session.

Example: *As a rule* the chairperson's duty is to keep the meeting moving.

Example: *When the package arrives* check its contents to make sure nothing is broken.

Commas are generally not required after introductory words or restrictive, short phrases that answer the questions *when, how often, where,* or *why.*

Example: Tomorrow I will begin my diet. (I will begin my diet *when*?)

Example: In the margin you will find a short definition of new terms. (*Where* will you find a short definition of new terms?)

Commas do not set off noun phrases or noun clauses that function as the subjects of sentences (not introductory). The italicized phrases or clauses in the following examples function as subjects of the sentences and, therefore, are not set off by commas. Note that all of the italicized phrases in the following examples answer the question *what.*

Example: *Learning a new video game* can be both fun and frustrating.

Example: *To win this game* will require real team effort.

Example: *Whether we win or lose* will make no difference in our standing.

Exercise 10-2 • Proofread and Mark

*Use the appropriate proofreaders' marks to correct the errors in comma usage. If the sentence is correct, write **C** to the left of the number.*

1. After you send in your registration form you will receive a confirmation letter.

2. Learning the types of motions, will improve your leadership ability.

3. Today, I sent the revised agenda to all current members.

4. Yes the motion was approved by majority vote of the delegates.

5. Starting the meeting on time was my goal.

Series

Insert a comma after each item in a series (words, phrases, or clauses) except the last item.

Example: I invited Concepcion, Hunter, Wakako, and Reggie to the beach party. (series of words)

Example: Zach did not tell us where he would meet us, whom he would be with, or when his flight would arrive. (series of clauses)

Example: I scored 76, 94, and 85 on the last three science quizzes.

Example: Please read the chapter, complete the review, and study for the test.

Example: Felix and Myrna will be the game organizers, Teresita and Darwin will be the race timers, Noriko and Bernardo will be the scorekeepers, and I will be the official starter.

Note: Do not use commas when each item in the series is connected by *and*, *but*, *or*, or *nor*.

Example: We need Vince and Jorge and Sarit to watch the monitors.

Example: Neither Deon nor Sue nor Owen were available.

Exercise 10-3 • Proofread and Mark

*Use the appropriate proofreaders' marks to correct the errors in comma usage. If the sentence is correct, write **C** to the left of the number.*

1. My plan is to tour businesses in Madison, Milwaukee, Oshkosh, Eau Claire and Janesville.

2. The new digital television set gives you a clearer picture, provides access to more stations and makes it easier to record specific programs.

3. The prospective employer is looking for someone who can write well, meet new people easily and use both Access and Excel.

4. Jonathan completed courses in accounting, management, and statistics.

5. Dana and Marilyn will write out the invitations, Nathan and Ruth will address the envelopes, Cynthia and Jose will organize the games and Jackson and Tami will develop a menu.

Nonessential Elements

Nonessential elements consist of information that is not necessary to the meaning of the sentence. They include appositives, interrupting expressions, and nonrestrictive phrases or clauses. Set off nonessential elements with commas.

Appositives are words or phrases that rename a preceding noun or pronoun. Commas are used to set off appositives because they are not essential to the meaning of the sentence but provide further identification of the noun or pronoun. The appositives are in italics in the following examples.

Example: Suzanne Russo, *the president*, will preside at the annual meeting next month.

Example: San Francisco, *the City by the Bay*, is a popular vacation and convention site.

Example: Byron Canton, *a local real estate broker*, will respond to your question.

Example: Their first song, *written while they were teenagers*, was a tremendous success.

John Jackson, student teacher, arrived today.

Interrupting (also called *parenthetical*) **expressions** include such non-essential words or phrases as *furthermore, however, in addition*, and *of course*. Such expressions often indicate the writer's feelings.

Example: Ruth will, *of course*, accept your dinner invitation.

Example: Bennett, *however*, is an exceptionally talented pianist.

Example: Saturday's ballgame, *on the other hand*, may attract a large crowd of college students.

Example: We are determined, *nevertheless*, to finish today.

Nonrestrictive elements include phrases or clauses that further explain or describe the noun or pronoun they modify. However, the information is considered to be nonessential because it is not necessary in understanding the meaning of the sentence. Nonrestrictive clauses often begin with *which, who,* or *whom.* Analyze the following two examples. The nonrestrictive elements are italicized.

Example: Mr. Kline, *who works in the president's office*, will address the March meeting. (The nonrestrictive element does not affect the principal message in this sentence, which is that Mr. Kline will address the meeting in March.)

Example: We have been unable to complete the Jorgensen contract, *which you had negotiated so successfully.* (The nonrestrictive element has no bearing on the completion of the Jorgensen contract.)

Do not set off **restrictive phrases** or **clauses**, those that are essential to the meaning of the sentence. The restrictive clauses appear in italics in these examples:

Example: Those people *who are registered to vote* may cast their ballots in the school board election. (The restrictive clause identifies the people who may cast their ballots and is essential to the meaning of the sentence.)

Example: We have been unable to complete the contract *that you just negotiated.* (The restrictive clause identifies which contract is not yet completed.)

Example: The Lundgren bid arrived *after we had made our decision.* (The restrictive clause tells when the bid arrived.)

Example: The shops *that are located in Westwood Mall* are open on the Fourth of July. (The restrictive clause tells which shops are open.)

Exercise 10-4 • Proofread and Mark

*Use the appropriate proofreaders' marks to correct the errors in comma usage. If the sentence is correct, write **C** to the left of the number.*

1. Gloria Bastian, the local gardening expert, will respond to your question.

2. Jerald however will be expected to complete the project by the October 1 deadline.

3. The shops, that are located in the Westmire Mall, were open over the Memorial Day weekend.

4. Paul Metzger, vice president of the Economics Club will be our guest speaker next Tuesday.

5. Lou and Carl arrived, after the meeting had been called to order.

≫ Other Comma Uses

In addition to their very important role of setting off sentence elements, commas perform a variety of other roles.

Consecutive Adjectives

Use commas to separate consecutive adjectives that are parallel and not joined by a conjunction. Parallel adjectives describe the same noun to the same degree. To determine whether adjectives should be separated by commas, reverse the order of the adjectives and insert the word *and* between them.

Example: Joyce is a sincere, delightful person. (Joyce is a delightful *and* sincere person.)

Example: The student is faced with a difficult, frustrating decision. (The student is faced with a frustrating *and* difficult decision.)

Example: The tall‿handsome fellow in the photograph is my husband.

Example: They are looking for an intelligent‿enterprising young person.

Exercise 10-5 • Proofread and Mark

*Use the appropriate proofreaders' marks to correct the errors in comma usage. If the sentence is correct, write **C** to the left of the number.*

1. They enjoyed the sleek simple design.

2. Gentleness, and sincerity, are two personal traits that I look for in people I meet.

3. Fritz read the informative, entertaining articles.

4. Listening to soft soothing classical music is my favorite pastime.

5. She wants to purchase tough dependable tools to use around the house.

Direct Quotations

Use commas to set off the exact words of a speaker. Do not set off an indirect quotation. An indirect quotation is a rewording of the person's exact words and is usually introduced by *that* or *whether*.

Example: The director said, "You should return your music after the concert." (Direct quotation—a comma and quotation marks are required.)

Example: Jane asked the director whether we should return our music after the concert. (Indirect quotation—no comma or quotation marks are needed.)

When a direct quotation is broken up into two parts, such as in the next example, place a comma *after* the first part of the quotation (inside the quotation mark) and another comma *before* the second part.

Example: "The class colors," said Chuong, "are pink and green."

Example: Andrei stated, "I believe you made the right decision."

Example: I said that "the mail will be picked up at 3:10 p.m."

Example: "On the other hand," Savita remarked, "I may surprise you."

Note: Commas and periods at the end of a quotation are *always* placed inside the quotation marks. Other punctuation marks used with quotation marks will be discussed in Chapter 11.

Exercise 10-6 • Proofread and Mark

*Use the appropriate proofreaders' marks to correct the errors in comma usage. If the sentence is correct, write **C** to the left of the number.*

1. "In addition" Marlene said "you must pay the registration fee no later than February 15."

2. I thought you were going to say that "you will find the best deal possible."

3. Christi stated "This is the best possible solution to our problem."

4. "I believe the economy will improve" Larry said "beginning with the third quarter."

5. "The team's colors are blue and white," said Silvia.

Dates and Addresses

Use commas to set off the year when it follows the month and the day or to separate the weekday from the calendar date. Commas are not required when only the month and the year are given or when military style is used in expressing dates.

Example: August 31, 20--, is the deadline for filing applications for classes next semester.

Example: Our high school received its first laptop computers in May 20--.

Example: The letter from General Kraft dated 11 May 20-- was misplaced when the office was remodeled.

Example: The perishable supplies were shipped by air freight on Thursday June 30 20--.

Example: Clarissa graduated in June 20--.

Use commas to separate address parts when the address appears in text format. Do not use a comma to separate two-letter state abbreviations and ZIP Codes.

Example: The address is Majestic Records, 3090 Brookline Boulevard, Suite 254, Newark, NJ 07110-3201.

The perishable supplies were shipped by air freight on Thursday, June 30, 2011.

Direct Address and Titles

Use commas to set off a person's name or title when addressing the person directly.

Example: Please reserve a conference room, Noel, for October 14.

Example: Thanks for helping me with my homework ⌄ Dad.

Use commas after names of people when academic and professional titles are used. Do not separate personal titles, such as *Jr., Sr., II,* or *III,* unless you know that the individual prefers to do so.

Example: Professor Navara, Ph.D., is also a certified professional planner.

Example: Melissa Eby, CPA, will lead the panel discussion.

Example: Duane Simpson ⌄ Jr. will arrive tomorrow morning.

Example: Bridget Brostrom ⌄ Ed.D ⌄ is the coordinator of the seminars.

Setting Off *Inc.* and *Ltd.*

Use commas to set off the abbreviations or words for *Inc.* and *Ltd.* when they follow the name of the company, unless you know the official company name does not use a comma.

Example: We will notify United Movers, Inc., of the change of address.

Example: Braniff ⌄ Limited ⌄ has been awarded the contract for next year.

Exercise 10-7 • Proofread and Mark

*Use the appropriate proofreaders' marks to correct the errors in comma usage. If the sentence is correct, write **C** to the left of the number.*

1. My driver's license expires on Friday, December 28.

2. The return address on the envelope shows 218 South Front Avenue Liberty PA 12981-4825.

3. Can you help me Micha, in solving this difficult problem?

4. Aurelia be sure to call the airline to cancel the flight.

5. Afton Companies Inc. is located at 9770 Grandview Street Omaha NE 67115-0893.

CONFUSED AND MISUSED WORDS

farther   *adv.* more distant
further   *adj.* to a greater degree; additional
Ashley can run **farther** than Samantha.
Tremaine is **further** along in math than Chad.

its   *adj.* possessive form of *it*
it's   contraction of *it is* or *it has*
The bank will post **its** interest rates today.
It's my turn to drive.

lay   *v.* to place or set down an object
lie   *v.* to rest; to recline
Lay the pen on the desk, Francesco.
Tina, **lie** down and rest.

PEP Tip

  *   Punctuation marks are designed to add clarity. Check for errors in punctuation that may cause confusion or misunderstanding.

  *   When debating the placement of a comma, identify the rule or rules that apply.

  *   Keep a reference manual handy when proofreading; use it as needed.

  *   Proofread in a quiet place; noise can be distracting.

  *   Pay attention to important information, such as dates, names, addresses, and amounts. Do not assume they are correct.

PROOFREADING APPLICATIONS

*Proofread the following sentences, and correct all comma errors using the appropriate proofreaders' marks. If the sentence is correct, write **C** to the left of the number.*

1. Gary wrote the poem, "My Dream," and dedicated it to Isabella.

2. Ashton will revise her assignment or attend the concert, and eat dinner with her family on Wednesday.

3. When you are ready to leave you should send me a message by e-mail.

4. Yes, that was the correct answer on today's quiz.

5. My bowling scores were 189, 211 and 268.

6. I expect Bindu, and Joyce, and Gil to meet us for lunch.

7. Your new checking account requires a minimum balance of $2,000, provides free checks and provides a $2,500 line of credit.

8. Alford Sonnet our new secretary will attend to all the details for tomorrow's meeting.

9. Roslyn of course is prepared to attend the meeting in my place.

10. We were unable to answer the three questions, that you asked at the conference.

11. Everyone, listed on the program, will receive a complementary gift set.

12. Hanque is an interesting, articulate individual.

13. The personnel director asked "What are your qualifications for this position?"

14. "On the other hand" Ric remarked "you may be accepted for the leadership program based on your qualifications."

15. Can you attend a meeting at 8 a.m. Brandi and present your report?"

Exercise 10-9 • Spelling and Word Usage Check

*Compare the words in Column **A** with the corresponding words in Column **B**. Use the appropriate proofreaders' marks to correct the misspelled or misused words. If both columns are correct, write **C** to the left of the number.*

Column A	Column B
1. article	artical
2. assessment	assesment
3. custermer	customer
4. environment	enviroment
5. equipment	equipement
6. interupt	interrupt
7. maneger	manager
8. orientation	orientation
9. perposal	proposal
10. recognise	recognize
11. representative	representitive
12. session	session
13. Please respond further.	I ran further than Nel.
14. It's time to leave.	They say its going to rain.
15. May I lay on your couch?	Please lay the shirt on the bed.

Exercise 10-10 • International Vocabulary

*Compare the French and Spanish words in Column **A** with the corresponding words in Column **B**. If the word in Column **B** is different from the word in Column **A**, use the appropriate proofreaders' marks to correct Column **B**. If the words in both columns are the same, write **C** to the left of the number.*

Column A	Column B
1. motocicleta	motociclata
2. integrante	integrante
3. churrasco	churrisco
4. mappemonde	mappamonde
5. devancer	devencer

Exercise 10-11 • Editorial Letter

Proofread the following editorial letter, and correct all errors using the appropriate proofreaders' marks.

LETTER TO THE EDITOR, June 6, 20--

The Examiner, Loma Linda, California

Dear Editor:

I would like to offer an assessment of the latest trend in TV programming: reality-based television. On Friday May 13, 20--, I arrived home early and interrupted my six-year-old son, who was watching television. I said, "Brandon, what are you watching?" He replied, "Justice Agents." I asked what it was about and he said that "this program depicted the dispensing of justice by agents of a city swat-team-type organization." Yes, six-year-olds do talk like that today. I recognize that young children live in a fantasy world when they watch TV, but they often imitate what they see and hear. Sitting with Brandon for a few minutes, I was startled to see that the last part of the show was an uninterrupted, violent gun battle between the good guys and the bad guys.

My assessment is that it is not all right for a child to see this kind of realism on television. As a responsible parent and a customer of commercial television, I asked myself, "Is this a reality-based show and if so whose reality is it?" More importantly I wonder if this is a proper environment for a child.

I later asked myself whether such programs should be available at a time when young children can view them and the answer is that they shouldn't. We must recognize that a show of this kind has the potential for disaster. I don't believe it is necessary to show such an extreme negative environment in such detail. To a six-year-old, the actor is not just practicing a craft. The child, even an adult, is watching someone being brutalized or killed.

I have a proposal to make. Perhaps the corporation network would air an orientation session demonstrating the art of artifice and makeup so that the young, inexperienced and naive viewer can see the difference between make-believe and reality.

If any reader of this newspaper shares my views voice your opinion by writing to the network, Station KVRT, 408 South Bascom Avenue, Loma Linda, CA 90097-4213.

Curtis Bolt Jr.

Exercise 10-12 • Business Letter

Proofread the following business letter, and correct all errors using the appropriate proofreaders' marks.

June 10, 20--

Mr. Curtis Bolt, Jr.

14009 Van Ness Avenue

Loma Linda, CA, 90405-0332

Dear Mr. Bolt:

I appreciated your letter to the editor of *The Examiner* dated June 6, 20-- concerning reality-based television.

Having a son who is seven, I agree that this program is not suitable for viewing by primary school-age children. Since we are concerned, with children viewing inappropriate programs, scheduling is closely audited by Station KVRT. We did not anticipate that young children would be in the viewing audience at that time.

Reality-based television leaves much to be desired, and should not be used as a means of categorizing programs. We live in an age when people strongly believe in personal rights and they want to decide what programs to watch.

I like your idea, for a program that educates the young to be aware that what they see on television is playacting—that it has no application to real-life situations. So we invite your son and his classmates to tour Station KVRT. The tour will include sessions with various departments, such as costume, makeup and editing, and end with lunch at our cafeteria. Please limit the number of people in your group to no more than 30.

You may call Mrs. Loretta Huerta, a representative of our Public Relations Department to discuss final arrangements.

Sincerely,

Alfred P. McRay, President

c Mrs. Loretta Huerta Manager
  Public Relations Department

PROOFREADING AT THE COMPUTER

Exercise 10-13 • Business Letter

1. Open 10-13 from the Chapter 10 folder on the student CD. (This is a computer copy of Exercise 10-12.)

2. Proofread the letter on the screen. Correct all errors on the screen copy that you indicated with proofreaders' marks in Exercise 10-12.

3. Produce the letter in correct format following the standard procedures described in the previous chapters.

Exercise 10-14 • Magazine Article

1. Open 10-14 from the Chapter 10 folder on the student CD.

2. Proofread the article on the screen. Correct all errors.

3. Produce the article following the standard procedures.

Exercise 10-15 • E-mail Message

1. Open 10-15 from the Chapter 10 folder on the student CD.

2. Proofread the e-mail message on the screen. Correct all errors.

3. Produce the e-mail message following the standard procedures.

CUMULATIVE APPLICATION

Exercise 10-16 • Memo

Proofread and correct all errors using the appropriate proofreaders' marks.

TO: All Department Heads

FROM: Patrick E. O'Malley, Vice president, Marketing

DATE: July 14, 20--

SUBJECT: Letter to the Editor

On June 6, *The Examiner* published a letter to the editor from Mr. Curtis Bolt, Jr. about reality-based television. Mr. Bolt stated the need for caution in scheduling programs because of the negative affects programs may have on young children. As a result our president, Mr. Alfred P. McRay, invited the classmates of Mr. Bolt's son to visit our studio. This is how Mr. Bolt described the tour.

Like Dorothy in *The Wizard of Oz,* we had a feeling that we were no longer in Kansas when we past through the magic portals of Station KVRT. The maze of camera equipment, sets miniature cities, and sky-scrapers appeared to be twenty stories tall. Everyone's favorite department was makeup.

Lunch was especially enjoyable to the young enthusiastic visitors because many teenage stars was eating at the same time and didn't mind being asked for autographs.

Our tour also had a serious side. The children learned never to try the jumps, falls, or other stunts that they see on television because these actions are performed by professionals.

We thank Station KVRT for a fun, educational session.

rkt

Bookmark It!

Want more practice? Go to www.cengage.com/keyboarding/pagel for more proofreading activities.

Other Punctuation Errors

Spotlight on ACCURACY

An incorrectly placed comma in a sales contract once cost an American company $70 million. In Europe, commas are used instead of periods to mark decimal points. This American company misplaced a comma by one decimal point in an international contract. According to a company spokesperson, the customer held the American company to the price quoted, resulting in a loss of $70 million!

Objectives

- Identify and correct errors in end-of-sentence punctuation.

- Identify and correct errors in the use of semicolons and colons.

- Identify and correct errors in the use of apostrophes, underscores, and quotation marks.

- Identify and correct errors when using quotation marks with other punctuation marks.

- Spell correctly 12 frequently misspelled words.

- Use correctly three sets of commonly confused and misused words.

In addition to the comma, other punctuation marks appear in written material. In this chapter, you will review the use of end-of-sentence punctuation marks—the period, the question mark, and the exclamation mark. You will also learn to correctly use semicolons, colons, apostrophes, underscores, and quotation marks. Finally, you will learn to recognize errors when other punctuation marks are used with quotation marks.

When correcting errors for these punctuation marks, use the following proofreaders' marks:

G_STUDIO/ISTOCKPHOTO.COM

Carson started his new proofreading job two weeks after graduation.

	MARKED COPY	**CORRECTED COPY**
Insert a period. ⊙	Please send me your check⊙	Please send me your check.
Insert a question mark. ⌄? ?̂	How did you do on the test.̌	How did you do on the test?
Insert an exclamation mark. ⌄! !̂	Don't touch iť	Don't touch it!
Insert a semicolon. ⌄; ;̂	Please come to the fund-raiser,̌ we could use your help.	Please come to the fund-raiser; we could use your help.
Insert a colon. ⌄: :̂	Follow these steps^ 1. Revise copy. 2. Save copy.	Follow these steps: 1. Revise copy. 2. Save copy.
Insert an apostrophe. ⌄	the bikeřs helmet	the biker's helmet
Underscore or italicize. ___ or *ital.*	<u>Do not</u> be late to the meeting. *ital.* <u>Do not</u> be late to the meeting.	<u>Do not</u> be late to the meeting. *Do not* be late to the meeting.
Insert quotation marks. ⌄ʺ ʺ̌	King's new book is ǎʺmusťʺread.	King's new book is a "must" read.

» The Period, The Question Mark, and The Exclamation Mark

There are three **terminal punctuation marks**: the period, the question mark, and the exclamation mark. They are used at the ends of sentences and tell the reader when to stop.

RULE 1   Use a period after (1) a statement of fact, (2) an indirect question, or (3) a courteous request. A **statement of fact** is something declared or stated. An **indirect question** is a reworded question or another person's statement. A **courteous request** is not a question, but it is sometimes incorrectly punctuated as a question because it sounds like one. When deciding whether to use a period or a question mark, remember: If the person is expected to answer in words, use a question mark. If the person is expected to respond with action, use a period.

STATEMENT	INDIRECT QUESTION	COURTEOUS REQUEST
They delivered the new furniture on Wednesday.	Bea asked if you were available to help.	Would you please send this order today.

RULE 2   Use a question mark after a **direct question**—it requires an answer. When a sentence contains a series of short questions related to one idea, place a question mark at the end of each question in the series. (See example.) Within the series, only the first part is a full question; the rest are not. Therefore, capitalize only the first word of the first part; **do not** capitalize the first word of each remaining part.

QUESTION	INDIRECT QUESTION	SERIES OF QUESTIONS
Did you receive the report?	He asked if you received the report.	Do you wish to look better? feel healthy? lose weight? trim inches?

Example: Do you remember when the report was sent?
Example: I asked what the features on Model 72K15J were.
Example: After graduation, are you planning to do anything? to travel? to enter college? to work? Have you considered joining the military?

RULE 3   Use an exclamation mark after a sentence that expresses strong emotion, excitement, surprise, or urgency.

Example: Wow! What a game! But we lost!
Example: Congratulations! You got the job!
Example: Fantastic, Gary!

Exercise 11-1 • Proofread and Mark

*Use the appropriate proofreaders' marks to correct the errors in the use of the period, question mark, and exclamation mark. If the sentence is correct, write **C** to the left of the number.*

1. He asked whether we were expecting rain?

2. Did she arrive in time for her 2 p.m. meeting.

3. Congratulations. That was great.

4. How will we travel? by air? by rail? by bus?

5. Will you please return the book by Friday?

≫ The Semicolon

Within a sentence, the semicolon provides a stronger break than a comma, but a weaker break than a period.

RULE 4   Use a semicolon—not a comma—between two independent clauses of a compound sentence when the clauses are not joined by a coordinating conjunction (*and, but, or, nor, for, yet*).

Example: Wisdom is in knowing what to do next; virtue is in doing it.

Example: The package arrived; it was slightly damaged.

Example: The truths of life are not inborn, each generation must learn them through experience.

Example: I will accept the job if it is offered, I would enjoy working for the firm.

RULE 5   Use a semicolon between two independent clauses when they are joined by transitional expressions such as *however, moreover, consequently, namely, nevertheless, therefore, in addition, likewise, on the other hand, besides,* and *accordingly.* A comma is used after a transitional expression of more than one syllable or when a strong pause is needed after one-syllable words such as *hence, yet, thus,* and *then.* Remember, a semicolon comes *before* and a comma usually *follows* such expressions.

Example: The workshop will be held July 12–15; in addition, a second workshop is scheduled for August 9–12.

Example: I studied five months for this certification exam; consequently, I was confident that I would pass.

Example: We will meet five hours on Monday; then we are free to work on other projects.

Example: The presentation was scheduled for 9:30 a.m., unfortunately, the speaker missed her flight.

Example: The computer parts arrived this morning, therefore, we can proceed with the repairs.

RULE 6 Use a semicolon—not a comma—between two or more independent clauses of a compound sentence when the clauses are joined by a coordinating conjunction *and* when either or both of the independent clauses already contain commas.

Example: Hiking, boating, and camping are within easy driving distance from the city; but all of these activities require special permits.

Example: Claudine was interested in shopping, eating, and dancing, but Ethan was more interested in swimming, camping, and hunting.

RULE 7 Use a semicolon—not a comma—in a series when one or more of the items in the series already contain commas.

Example: The firm has branch offices located in Fort Lauderdale, Florida; Pueblo, Colorado; and Montgomery, Alabama.

Example: Interviews are scheduled for Friday, May 14, Monday, May 31, and Wednesday, June 16.

Exercise 11-2 • Proofread and Mark

*Use the appropriate proofreaders' marks to correct the errors in the use of the semicolon. If the sentence is correct, write **C** to the left of the number.*

1. Knowing the rules of the game is one thing; applying them is another.

2. The rules of business etiquette are not well known, it takes time to learn to apply the rules properly.

3. The jury, after six weeks of testimony, deliberated for nine days, but it did not reach a verdict until Friday.

4. The last order of the season was sent this morning, therefore, we will close an hour earlier today.

5. Next year we will vacation in Aspen, Colorado, Hilo, Hawaii, or Hartford, Connecticut.

» The Colon

A colon shows anticipation. It alerts the reader that what follows the colon will explain what came before it.

RULE 8   Use a colon before items such as a list, a series, or an explanation of what came before the colon.
Note: If the items appearing in a vertical list are not complete sentences, do not capitalize the first word in each item. Omit periods after the items unless one or more of the items is a complete sentence, a long phrase, or a dependent clause.

Example: Determine the following points for each career:
nature of the work
satisfaction from the job
advancement opportunities

Example: The job requirements are these: experience working in a medical office, ability to work independently, competence in using spreadsheets, and superior communication skills.

Example: Evaluate potential employers in terms of the following factors:

1. Are there opportunities for advancement?
2. Are the salary and fringe benefits attractive?
3. Does top management support the position?

In the following example, a colon is used after the first clause because the second and third independent clauses explain the first one.

Example: The representative says that the resort has it all. It has an excellent location, and it has outstanding food and entertainment.

Do not use a colon to introduce a list following a preposition or verb. Do not capitalize lists that are not in vertical form unless each item is a complete sentence.

Example: The secretary has the responsibilities of (1) keying the report, (2) sending a cover memo with the final results to the manager, and (3) filing the hard copy.

Example: The group includes Jessica, Pedro, Lani, and Herman.

RULE 9   Use a colon in the following situations: after the salutation of a letter that uses mixed punctuation, within ratios, and between hours and minutes. When time is expressed exactly on the hour, do not include the colon and the zeros.

Example: Dear Mr. Ybarra:
Example: The portions are 3:1 olive oil and water.
Example: The flight leaves at 1:49 p.m.

Example: Report to the principal's office at 3 p.m. sharp.
Example: Every dollar contributed will be matched 1:1.
Example: Set your alarm for 5:00 a.m.

Exercise 11-3 • Proofread and Mark

*Use the appropriate proofreaders' marks to correct the errors in the use of the colon. If the sentence is correct, write **C** to the left of the number.*

1. These are the required sections of your research paper.

   1. letter of transmittal.

   2. executive summary.

   3. body.

   4. bibliography.

2. Please include the following information on the form. full name, complete address, telephone number, and e-mail address.

3. My favorite colors include blue, green, orange, and black.

4. The meeting was called to order at 2 30 p.m.

5. The portions are 4-1 dry ingredients and water.

» The Apostrophe

The apostrophe is used to form contractions, the possessive case of nouns, and the plural forms of some words and letters. Watch for errors in the use of the apostrophe.

RULE 10   Add an apostrophe and *s* (*'s*) to form the possessive case of singular nouns not ending in an *s* sound.

Example: the committee's decision   (the decision of the committee)
Example: the manager's office   (the office of the manager)
Example: year's end   (the end of the year)
Example: Marcia's children   (the children of Marcia)
Example: The book's cover is torn.
Example: The company's warehouse is located in Milpitas.

RULE 11   Add an apostrophe and *s* (*'s*) when a new syllable is formed in the pronunciation of the possessive.

Example: Congress's vote (the vote of Congress)
Example: Tess's car (the car owned by Tess)
Example: Mr. Harris's report
Example: Mrs. Lopez's plans

Add only an apostrophe if an extra syllable would make a word ending in an *s* sound hard to pronounce.

Example: Mr. Osters' suit (the suit belonging to Mr. Osters)
Example: Ms. Hastings' proposal (the proposal submitted by Ms. Hastings)
Example: Mr. Marcos' doctor
Example: Miss Burroughs' investments

RULE 12   Add only an apostrophe to form the possessive case of plural nouns that end in an *s* sound.

Example: the girls' pep club (the pep club of the girls)
Example: the students' behavior (the behavior of the students)
Example: The candidates' names must be on file.
Example: Mr. Donohue announced the winners' names at yesterday's assembly.

RULE 13   Add an apostrophe and *s* (*'s*) to form the possessive of plural nouns that do not end in an *s* sound.

Example: women's organizations (organizations of women)
Example: the alumni's reunion (the reunion of the alumni)
Example: The sheep's wool was sheared.
Example: The children's favorite fruits are apples and bananas.

RULE 14   Add an apostrophe and *s* (*'s*) to only the final name when an item is jointly owned by more than one person.

Example: Dan and Carolyn's wedding (the wedding of Dan and Carolyn)
Example: Yoko and Magdalena's boutique (the boutique of Yoko and Magdalena)
Example: Hank's and Toby's ice cream is the best.
Example: For superior service, take your vehicle to Dom's, Rick's, and Mary's Auto Shop.

When two names indicate separate ownership, each name is possessive.

Example: Beau's and Donna's companies (two companies, separate ownership)
Example: Andrew's and Martha's signatures (each signature is separate)

RULE 15   Use the apostrophe to form the contraction of two words. Place the apostrophe at the point of the missing letter(s).

Example: don't   (do not)   haven't   (have not)
Example: it's   (it is)   you're   (you are)
Example: who's   (who is)   I'll   (I will)
Example: They're not here yet. But we're going to start because it's getting late.

RULE 16   Use an apostrophe to form the following: (1) the plurals of lowercase letters and the plurals of some abbreviations with two or more interior periods (to avoid misreading an expression for a word) and (2) acronyms. An **acronym** is a word formed from the initial letters of a series of words. Acronyms are usually written in all capital letters and without periods.

Example: dot your i's (*not* "is") all A's (*not* "As")
Example: x's and y's (*not* "xs" and "ys") M.A.'s and Ph.D.'s
Example: SADD's monthly meeting will be held May 3, 20–.

RULE 17   Use the apostrophe as a symbol for feet in measurements. (The quotation mark is the symbol for inches.)

Example: 4′ × 8′   (4 feet by 8 feet)
Example: 6′2″ tall   (6 feet 2 inches tall)

Exercise 11-4 • Proofread and Mark

*Use the appropriate proofreaders' marks to correct the errors in the use of the apostrophe. If the sentence is correct, write **C** to the left of the number.*

1. Ms. Lopez's intent was to complete the report by August 1.

2. The critique of Joes work habits will be completed by months end.

3. Janes and Bettys reactions were predictable to George.

4. Wont that affect your final recommendations?

5. The childrens' request was to play baseball.

» Underscoring and Italics

Both underscoring (underlining) and *italics* are marks of emphasis. Italic type is the preferred means of giving special emphasis to words and phrases and to literary titles and artistic works. The following examples show the use of italics and the underscore. With underscores any space between consecutive words should be underscored. However, a punctuation mark immediately following a word or phrase is not underscored (except periods within abbreviations).

RULE 18   Use italics or the underscore to set off titles of complete literary works, such as books, magazines, newspapers, movies, or plays.

Example: I subscribe to *TIME* and *The Wall Street Journal*.

Example: We have purchased the DVD of <u>The Sound of Music.</u>

Example: My subscription to <u>Quick Cooking</u> expires in November.

Example: I saw <u>The Lion King</u> on Broadway last summer.

RULE 19   Use italics or the underscore to emphasize or identify special words or phrases.

Example: Choose a computer that offers ease of use *and* compatibility.

Example: The word <u>site</u> means "a location."

Example: I said I was <u>not</u> going!

Example: Where were <u>you</u> going at that time of night?

» Quotation Marks

Quotation marks are used primarily to enclose direct quotations.

RULE 20   Use quotation marks to enclose all parts of direct quotations and words used in an unusual way.

Example: "The solution," announced the speaker, "is quite obvious."

Example: I heard Cindy tell Richie, "Get lost." So he did.

Example: "Bookworm" and "nerd" are not necessarily nice nicknames.

Example: "Come after school," Ronice said, "and we'll study for the exam."

RULE 21   Use quotation marks to set off parts of complete works, such as chapters within a book, titles of articles and feature columns, titles of essays, short poems, sermons, unpublished works, and songs.

Example: The most popular column in the *Recorder* is "Ask the Editor."

Example: Answer the questions from Chapter 1, "Office Ethics."

PHOTODISC/GETTY IMAGES
Carole is the finance editor of the Enquirer.

RULE 22   Use quotation marks with other punctuation marks in the following manner:

- Periods are placed *inside* quotation marks.

   Example: The editor said, "Please send all chapter drafts by Priority Mail."

- Commas are placed *inside* quotation marks.

   Example: "When I fly," I said, "I plan to fly first class."

- Exclamation marks and question marks are placed *inside* the quotation marks when the punctuation mark applies *only* to the quoted material.

   Example: Miles exclaimed, "Watch out!"

   Example: Marquetta replied, "What did you say?"

- Exclamation marks and question marks are placed *outside* the ending quotation mark when the exclamation or question applies to the entire sentence.

   Example: Why did you ignore Lauralee after she said, "Get out of here now!"?

- Semicolons and colons are placed *outside* the ending quotation mark.

   Example: I marked the package "fragile"; despite this fact, Morris handled the package carelessly.

   Example: Please send me the following items from the folder marked "Confidential": the proposal salary schedule, Bryce's evaluation, and the new employee contract.

Exercise 11-5 • Proofread and Mark

*Use the appropriate proofreaders' marks to correct the underscore and quotation mark errors. If the sentence is correct, write **C** to the left of the number.*

1. I enjoy reading BusinessWeek and Time magazines.

2. "Since today is the Fourth of July, Mary said, we are looking forward to the fireworks display."

3. Do we have to answer the questions on page 58 from Chapter 9, Computer Ethics?

4. My favorite column in the newspaper is Letters to the Editor.

5. The word *stitchery* means "needlework."

CONFUSED AND MISUSED WORDS

envelop   *v.* to cover with a wrapping
envelope   *n.* a paper container for correspondence

We will **envelop** the air conditioner with plastic before winter begins.
I will place your contract in this **envelope.**

foreword   *n.* an introduction; a preface
forward   *adj.* at or near the front; *v.* to send mail

Anne wrote the **foreword** for my new book.
Constantine **forwarded** the check to my new address.

later   *adv.* after
latter   *adj.* the second of two

They arrived **later** than Stephen and Brook arrived.
August and September are both excellent times to visit, but I prefer the **latter.**

Proofreading & Editing Tips

PEP Tip

＊   Train your eye to check the terminal punctuation of each sentence.

＊   Check that the punctuation mark conveys the proper meaning. If in doubt, ask the originator.

＊   Check that the closing quotation marks have not been omitted.

PROOFREADING APPLICATIONS

Exercise 11-6 • Sentences

*Proofread the following sentences, and mark all punctuation errors using the appropriate proofreaders' marks. If the sentence is correct, write **C** to the left of the number.*

1. We plan to leave no later than 1 p.m. on Thursday

2. Congratulations on receiving a promotion.

3. Would you please let me know when Danny arrives?

4. Spring is my favorite season of the year, I especially enjoy seeing the daffodils bloom.

5. The first exam is scheduled for September 27, however, it depends on whether we have discussed all the chapters.

6. We are scheduled to travel to the following cities in October, Fort Worth, Texas, Las Cruces, New Mexico, and Salt Lake City, Utah.

7. We are looking for people in these areas; accounting, marketing, and computer information systems.

8. Our team includes: Marcus, Heidi, and Mary Jean.

9. We were delighted to be invited to Jonathan's party.

10. The committees response was based on research.

11. We made reservations for Tony's and Debra's resort.

12. Erin reads Kiplinger's Personal Finance magazine every month as soon as the magazine arrives.

13. Its best that we decline their offer.

14. Autumn asked, When are they expected to arrive?

15. Charles enjoyed reading Harry Potter and the Deathly Hallows by J. K. Rowling.

Exercise 11-7 • Spelling and Word Usage Check

Compare the words in Column **A** with the corresponding words in Column **B**. Use the appropriate proofreaders' marks to correct the misspelled or misused words. If both columns are correct, write **C** to the left of the number.

Column A	Column B
1. cooperate	cooperite
2. criterea	criteria
3. curriculum	curriclum
4. development	developement
5. emphasis	emphasis
6. evaluate	evauluate
7. libility	liability
8. minamum	minimum
9. plaque	plaqeu
10. procedure	proceedure
11. reguard	regard
12. volumne	volume
13. The house was enveloped in snow.	He placed a first-class stamp on the envelop.
14. Your forward was well written!	Irene asked that nothing be forwarded to her.
15. Jamir arrived latter than I.	The later item is more popular than the first item.

Exercise 11-8 • Word Division List

*Proofread the words in each line. If one or more words are divided incorrectly, correct the word(s) using the appropriate proofreaders' marks. Then write the word(s) on the blank line using hyphen(s) to show all preferred points of division. If all three words in a line are correct, write **C** on the blank line.*

Ex. pi‿que	plati- tude	sub- stan- tial‿ly	*pique* *sub- stan- tially*
1. change- a- ble	call- ed	pla- gia- rism	_____
2. res- tau- rant	evalu- ation	congrat- u- la- tions	_____
3. priv- i- lege	cat- e- go- ries	success- ful	_____
4. com- pli- ance	pos- i- tive	de- ter- mine	_____
5. sit- u- a- tion	elimi- nate	hab- i- ta- tion	_____
6. pho- to- graph	checker	equip- ment	_____
7. fin- an- cial	pri- or	lan- guage	_____
8. pli- able	guar- an- tee	lo- cate	_____
9. poss- i- bly	quar- ter	im- pa- tient	_____
10. in- stalla- tion	sci- en- tific	hos- pice	_____
11. prin- ci- pally	knowl- edge- a- ble	par- a- digm	_____
12. schol- ar	ton- gue	man- age- able	_____
13. mis- cella- ne- ous	trans- fer- ring	par- a- chute	_____
14. ref- eree	oc- cur- rence	quo- ta- tion	_____
15. pri- or- i- ty	confess- ing	par- tic- u- lar	_____

Proofread the following letter, and correct all punctuation errors using the appropriate proofreaders' marks.

THE NEW CAPITOL THEATER

35 Central Avenue
West San Jose, CA 95128-1469
408-555-0109 • Fax: 408-555-0111

May 15, 20--

Mr. and Mrs. Frank Doolittle
3429 Oak Meadow Road
San Jose, CA 95134-3428

Dear Mr. and Mrs. Doolittle:

Do you remember those lean days in the twenties and thirties. Do you remember enjoying Saturday matinees at the local Bijou? the Orpheum or the Strand. Do you recall the anticipation as you walked to the theater and thought about the enticing smell of popcorn?

Well, this grand environment is not "gone with the wind". It's alive and well, and you can see it all at the New Capitol Theater, a once-popular landmark in San Jose.

Yes, the New Capitol has been rebuilt. The development of this replica of the original Capitol Theater, which opened in April 1926, took three years to complete, and due regard was given to restoring the luxurious ambiance that was so exciting in the heyday of the flapper era.

We also restored two pleasant amenities that were so much a part of attending a movie back then; (1) the usher who guided you to your seat with a pinpoint flashlight and (2) the washroom attendant who was always ready with a needle and thread to mend any clothing.

The enclosed flyer announces our opening double feature, "Footlight Parade" and "Gold Diggers of 1933," and includes a brief review of each movie.

If you know the way to San Jose, come join us for the joy of reminiscence. May we also suggest that you dress in appropriate costume of the twenties and thirties? You will find that the—good old days—were more than fodder for trivia games.

Rah. Rah. The—good old days—are here again.

Sincerely,

Desiree Van Wyke, Owner-Manager

wit

Enclosure

Exercise 11-10 • Announcement

Proofread the following announcement, and correct all punctuation errors using the appropriate proofreaders' marks.

MESSIAH LUTHERAN CHURCH

3456 State Street
San Jose, CA 93334-0278

TOP 50 MOVIE CONTEST

Sponsored by San Joses New Capitol Theater

Your challenge in this movie contest is to identify the ranking and the year in which each movie listed below was first shown. The rankings are based on the top 50 movies as selected by readers of the Mercury News in March 20--.

All of these movies meet the following criteria;

- among the top 50 movies selected by Mercury News readers

- shown between 1940 and today

- received a rating by the voters of 8.5 (on a scale of 10.0) or above

Would you please help our church by participating in this contest? For every vote received by the new Capitol Theater, our church will receive a donation to our endowment fund. This endowment fund will be used to send our youth to summer camp, to national meetings, or to attend special workshops sponsored by our congregation. The contest begins now, however, all votes must be received within 30 days from the beginning date of this contest.

The procedure for your participation is simple. Any church member can enter, however, there is a limit of two entries per family. Therefore, each familys participation is essential. Are you ready and willing to participate. Dennis Murray, Editor, Mercury News, says, "We are anxious to help area youth, and this is an excellent way our newspaper can help. Please make every effort to help us:

Please rank and identify the year of each of the following movies, as listed in alphabetic order.

American Beauty	Lawrence of Arabia
Apocalypse Now	Psycho
Casablanca	Schindler's List
Citizen Kane	Star Wars
Forrest Gump	The Silence of the Lambs

Send your vote to this address; Messiah Lutheran Church, 3456 State Street, San Jose, CA 93334-0278.

PROOFREADING AT THE COMPUTER

Exercise 11-11 • Announcement

1. Open 11-11 from the Chapter 11 folder on the student CD. (This is a computer copy of Exercise 11-10.)

2. Proofread the announcement on the screen. Correct all errors on the screen copy that you indicated with proofreaders' marks in Exercise 11-10. Use the spelling checker.

3. Produce the announcement in correct format following the standard procedures described in the previous chapters.

Exercise 11-12 • Manuscript Paragraphs

1. Open 11-12 from the Chapter 11 folder on the student CD.

2. Proofread the manuscript page on the screen. Correct all errors.

3. Produce the manuscript page following the standard procedures.

Exercise 11-13 • E-mail Message

1. Open 11-13 from the Chapter 11 folder on the student CD.

2. Proofread the e-mail message on the screen. Correct all errors.

3. Produce the e-mail message following the standard procedures.

CUMULATIVE APPLICATION

Proofread the following news release, and correct all errors using the appropriate proofreaders' marks. After you have proofread the news release, team up with one of your classmates to proofread a second time. Your partner will open 11-14 from the Chapter 11 folder on the student CD and read from the correct list of favorite movies. You should pay particular attention to the names of movies, the years, and the directors' names.

What excitement our ancestors had in the 1920s and 1930s. When films were first introduced. Up until then, they worked hard every day, and they had little time for leisure activities. however, films could now provide them with the opportunity to dream. and do things they could only imagine. Among the early films was romances, epics, comedies, and even dramas. Now, regardless of classification they could get away from his/her troubles for a few hours.

My favorite movies from the 1920s included these

- *The Four Horseman of the Apocalypse, 1921, Rex Ingram, Director*
- *Our Hospitality, 1923, Jack Blystone, Director*
- *The Iron Horse, 1924, John Ford, Director*
- *The Big Parade, 1926, King Vidor, Director*
- *The Circus, 1928, Charles Chaplin, Director*
- *The Broadway Melody, 1929, Harry Baeumont, Director*

Following is a list of my favorite movies from the 1930s

- *Animal Crackers, 1930, Victor Heeman, Director*
- *Frankenstein, 1931, James Whale, Director*
- *Farewell to Arms, 1932, Frank Borzag, Director*
- *The Merry Widow, 1934, Ernest Lubitsch, Director*
- *Modern Times, 1936, Charles Chapplin, Director*
- *Boys Town, 1939, Norman Taurag, Director*

As Marjorie Collins, movie critic for the New capitol Theater said "We have been fortunate to see major changes in the way

Exercise 11-14 • News Release (*continued*)

movies are made and distributed. What a difference a decade or two makes" Please let us know what favorites you have from the 1920s and 1930s and we will make every attempt to make those films available at our theater?

Bookmark It!

Want more practice? Go to www.cengage.com/keyboarding/pagel for more proofreading activities.

Format Errors: Letters and Memos

Spotlight on ACCURACY

It is estimated that approximately 20 percent of the adults in the United States are functionally illiterate; they cannot read, write, or calculate above the eighth-grade level. People who are illiterate are unable to read the daily newspaper; read a story to their children; or read the correspondence, memos, e-mail messages, and business reports that businesses need to operate.

Business calls illiteracy one of its most serious problems. An illiterate employee may cost a company thousands of dollars because he or she is unable to read a simple letter or manual. One such employee caused $250,000 worth of damage to an engine because he did not understand the repair manual that came with the machine. The problem of illiteracy costs business and industry billions of dollars every year!

Objectives

- Identify errors in block and modified block format.

- Identify format errors in interoffice memorandums.

- Use the appropriate proof-readers' marks to mark format error corrections.

- Spell correctly 12 frequently misspelled words.

- Use correctly three sets of commonly confused and misused words.

≫ Format

The layout of copy on a page is referred to as **format**. Some formatting considerations include margin settings, spacing between paragraphs, and the organization of document parts. It may also include underlining, capitalizing, and boldfacing letters or words.

Format is very important. The format of a document should enhance the message—not detract from it. The document presentation should reflect the competency of the sender. If a document has a sloppy appearance or if the format makes a document difficult to read, the document reflects negatively on the sender. On the other hand, a document that is formatted attractively and printed on high-quality stationery indicates quality and a professional attitude. It is an indication that the sender is a person you can work with and trust.

In this chapter, you will learn to recognize incorrectly formatted business letters and interoffice memorandums. Use the following proofreaders' marks to correct errors in format.

DIGITAL VISION/GETTY IMAGES
A well formatted letter creates a favorable impression.

	MARKED COPY	CORRECTED COPY
Begin new paragraph. ¶	Attendance was good. ¶ Next year's play will be a comedy.	Attendance was good. Next year's play will be a comedy.
Do not begin new paragraph. No ¶	Single-space them. No ¶ Memos should always be single-spaced.	Single-space them. Memos should always be single-spaced.
Center.] [	]BASIC OBJECTIVES[	BASIC OBJECTIVES
Align copy. ‖	‖Bring your pictures. We will design holiday ‖scrapbook pages.	Bring your pictures. We will design holiday scrapbook pages.
Make bold.	Use the new fax.	Use the **new** fax.
Move to the left.	[We can help you.	We can help you.
Move to the right.	The]crew will need it.	The crew will need it.
Move up.	They like to go. [would]	They would like to go.
Move down.	My trip provides [for] stops.	My trip provides for stops.

Exercise 12-1 • Proofread and Mark

Use the appropriate proofreaders' marks to revise the copy in the second column according to the instructions in the first column.

1. Center heading.	SUMMARY to be present.
2. Move down.	We plan
3. Move left.	Several people will volunteer.
4. Do not begin new paragraph.	I would like to attend. The presentation of the award will be held on Friday, June 12.
5. Move up.	Mr. Marcel Chapelin
	334 West Draxten Boulevard

≫ Letters

Letters are documents used to communicate with people, such as customers or clients, outside the organization. Therefore, proper format is especially important. Proofreading a letter for correct format includes checking three things: (1) the overall balanced appearance; (2) the correct placement, spacing, and sequence of letter parts; and (3) the consistency in the format of the letter style.

Balanced Appearance

A good proofreader judges whether the overall appearance of a letter creates a favorable or unfavorable impression. Overall balance is achieved when the left and right margins are approximately even and the top and bottom margins are balanced.

Proper balance may be attained by following these general guidelines: Letters are formatted with default 1-inch left and right margins, a 2-inch top margin, and a 1-inch bottom margin. Instead of a 2-inch top margin, letters may be centered vertically using the Center Page feature. To place a letter in reading position, insert two hard returns below the last keyed line.

Exercise 12-2 • Proofread and Mark

Proofread the following letters for their overall balanced appearance. Use brackets to show whether the copy should be moved right, left, up, or down.

1.

```
                              XXXXXXXXXX

     XXXXXXXXX
     XXXXXXX
     XXXXXXXXX

     XXXXXXXXXXXXX

     XXXXXXXXXXXXXXXXXXXXXXXXXXXXXXXXXXXX
     XXXXXXXXXXXXXXXXXXXXXXXXXXXXXXXXXXXX
     XXXXXXXXXXXXXX

     XXXXXXXXXXXXXXXXXXXXXXXXXXXXXXXXXXXX
     XXXXXXXXXXXXXXXXXXXXXXXXXXXXXXXXXXXX
     XXX

                         XXXXXXXXX

                         XXXXXXXX
                         XXXXXX

     XX
```

2.

```
                                   XXXXXXXXXX

          XXXXXXXXX
          XXXXXXX
          XXXXXXXXX

          XXXXXXXXXXXXX

          XXXXXXXXXXXXXXXXXXXXXXXXXXXXXXXXXXXX
          XXXXXXXXXXXXXXXXXXXXXXXXXXXXXXXXXXXX
          XXXXXXXXXXXXXX

          XXXXXXXXXXXXXXXXXXXXXXXXXXXXXXXXXXXX
          XXXXXXXXXXXXXXXXXXXXXXXXXXXXXXXXXXXX
          XXX

                              XXXXXXXXX

                              XXXXXXXX
                              XXXXXX

          XX
```

3.

```
                         XXXXXXXXXX

     XXXXXXXXX
     XXXXXXX
     XXXXXXXXX

     XXXXXXXXXXXXX

     XXXXXXXXXXXXXXXXXXXXXXXXXXXXXXXXXX
     XXXXXXXXXXXXXXXXXXXXXXXXXXXXXXXXXX
     XXXXXXXXXXXXXX

     XXXXXXXXXXXXXXXXXXXXXXXXXXXXXXXXXX
     XXXXXXXXXXXXXXXXXXXXXXXXXXXXXXXXXX
     XXX

                    XXXXXXXXX

                    XXXXXXXX
                    XXXXXX

     XX
```

4.

```
                              XXXXXXXXXX

     XXXXXXXXX
     XXXXXXX
     XXXXXXXXX

     XXXXXXXXXXXXX

     XXXXXXXXXXXXXXXXXXXXXXXXXXXXXXXXXX
     XXXXXXXXXXXXXXXXXXXXXXXXXXXXXXXXXX
     XXXXXXXXXXXXXX

     XXXXXXXXXXXXXXXXXXXXXXXXXXXXXXXXXX
     XXXXXXXXXXXXXXXXXXXXXXXXXXXXXXXXXX
     XXX

                         XXXXXXXXX

                         XXXXXXXX
                         XXXXXX

     XX
```

Letter Parts

Most letters are prepared using the same basic letter parts arranged in the same sequence. If any letter part is omitted, the sequence of the other parts should not be affected. When proofreading letters, check to make sure that all of the required letter parts are present and that they are in the correct sequence. Also check that the proper spacing has been used above and below each letter part. The eight basic letter parts include the following items:

1. Heading	**5.** Body
2. Date	**6.** Complimentary close
3. Letter address	**7.** Writer's name and title
4. Salutation	**8.** Reference initials

Other letter parts, such as the attention line, the subject line, and notations, may be added as needed.

Heading   In business letters, the heading is usually preprinted on letterhead stationery. The printed heading includes the name and address of the company. Additional information may include telephone number, fax number, e-mail address, and company logo. This heading is placed only on the first page of a multiple-page letter.

J & E COMPANY, INC.

279 Highland Park Court
Charlotte, NC 28208-4233
704-555-0131 • Fax: 704-555-0134
JECompany@email.com

If a letter is to be printed on plain paper, the sender's return address should be included on the lines immediately above the date.

279 High Park Court
Charlotte, NC 28208-4233
December 19, 20--

Date   The date includes the month, day, and year. Position it 2 inches from the top of the page or tap Enter one time below a letterhead that is more than 2 inches deep.

Office 2007 Defaults   In Office 2007, the line spacing is 1.15, and there are 10 points of white space after each paragraph. The extra white space between paragraphs makes text easier to read and saves the user time in tapping the Enter key only once between paragraphs. There are occasions, however, when it is necessary to remove the space added after a paragraph. You can do so in one of three ways:

1. Select the desired lines. From the Home tab, on the Paragraph group, click the down arrow on the Line Spacing button. Select Remove Space After Paragraph.

2. Select the desired lines. From the Home tab, select the No Spacing Style in the Styles group.

3. Hold down the Shift key and tap Enter after each line you do not want to have extra space instead of tapping Enter normally.

Office 2007 automatically removes the extra spacing for bulleted and enumerated items. The spacing information provided from this point forward in this chapter refers to Word 2007 spacing. For instance, when you would have double-spaced in a previous edition of Word, you tap Enter once instead in Word 2007. Likewise, when you would have tapped Enter four times in a previous edition of Word, you tap Enter only twice in Word 2007.

Letter Address   The letter address includes the personal title, name, and complete mailing address of the receiver. If the letter is addressed to an individual, the individual's personal title (*Mr., Mrs., Ms.*) or professional title (*Dr., Professor*) is included as a sign of courtesy. Use *Ms.* when a woman prefers that title or when her preferred title is unknown. The letter address is positioned at the left margin by tapping Enter two times below the date. Remove the extra spacing in the lines of the inside address with the exception of the last line, which includes the city, state, and ZIP code.

The letter address is used as the mailing address on the envelope. Should the letter be sent in a window envelope, the letter address may be keyed in all capital letters without punctuation. The alert proofreader should check that the city, state, and ZIP code are correct. (The appendix contains a list of two-letter state abbreviations.) Use one space between the two-letter state abbreviation and the ZIP code.

Ms. Lidia Ruiz	MS LIDIA RUIZ
Del Sol, Inc.	DEL SOL INC
379 North River Road	379 NORTH RIVER ROAD
Dallas, TX 75212-3682	DALLAS TX 75212-3682

Attention Line   An attention line is included in the letter address when the writer does not know the name of the receiver of the letter or is writing to an organization. The attention line is keyed as the first line of the letter address.

Attention Personnel Director
Del Sol, Inc.
379 North River Road
Dallas, TX 75212-3682

When an attention line is used, the salutation should read *Ladies and Gentlemen.*

Exercise 12-3 • Proofread and Mark

*Proofread the following list of cities and states by comparing the states in Column **A** with their two-letter state abbreviations in Column **B**. If the state abbreviation in Column **B** is not correct, use the appropriate proofreaders' mark to show what correction should be made. If the abbreviation is correct, write **C** to the left of the number.*

Column A	Column B
1. Cedar Falls, Iowa 50613-1822	Cedar Falls, IA, 50613-1822
2. Cincinnati, Ohio 45213-0733	Cincinnati, Oh 45213-0733
3. Bloomer, Wisconsin 54724-9125	Bloomer, WS 54724-9125
4. Minot, North Dakota 58701-8829	Minot, ND 58701-8829
5. Towanda, Illinois 61776-4931	Towanda, LI 61776-4931

Salutation   The salutation is the friendly "hello" of the letter. Depending on the relationship between the sender and the receiver, the salutation may be formal or informal. The salutation should agree with the first line of the letter address in number and gender. When the letter is addressed to a company, you should use the salutation "Ladies and Gentlemen." When the letter is addressed to an individual or position/title, the salutation should be that person's name or position/title.

Letter Address	**Salutation**
ABC Corporation 555 State Avenue Jamestown, MI 49427	Ladies and Gentlemen
Mr. Leonard Dreese 90 West Boulevard St. Ansgar, IA 50472	Dear Mr. Dreese

Personnel Director   Dear Persosnnel Director

ABC Corporation

555 State Street

Jamestown, MI 49427

The salutation is placed one line below the letter address (tap Enter once). A colon follows the salutation when *mixed punctuation* is used; the colon is omitted when *open punctuation* is used. The examples below illustrate various situations.

To an individual (open punctuation):	Dear Mr. Pham
To an organization (mixed punctuation):	Ladies and Gentlemen:
To an individual whose gender is unknown (mixed punctuation):	Dear Dale Komar:

Only when you know the receiver on a personal basis should you use the receiver's first name in the salutation.

Subject Line   The subject line, an optional letter part, states the main topic of the letter. It is positioned at the left margin one line (tap Enter once) below the salutation.

Dear Ms. Cohen:	Dear Mr. Dortch
April Madness Sale	Award Winners

Body   The body contains the message of the letter. It begins one line (tap Enter once) below the salutation (or subject line if one is included). Use the 1.15 default line spacing by tapping Enter at the end of paragraphs. This leaves 10 points of space between paragraphs.

In general, the body should include at least three paragraphs, which makes the letter look attractive. If the message is long, the body may extend to more than one page. In a multipage letter, maintain a 1-inch bottom margin on the first page. Use plain paper that is the same quality as the letterhead, and begin each succeeding page with a heading. Take out extra spacing in lines for the heading and include the receiver's name, the page number, and the date. Tap Enter once after the date before continuing the letter.

Mr. Genaro Ordonez

Page 2

November 12, 20--

Complimentary Close   The complimentary close is the social "goodbye" of the letter. Tap Enter once after the last line of the body for the complimentary close. Only the first word is capitalized. The style of punctuation used in the complimentary close must agree with the style of punctuation used in the salutation. A comma follows the complimentary close when *mixed punctuation* is used (meaning a colon was used after the salutation); the comma is omitted after the complimentary close when *open punctuation* is used (meaning no colon was used after the salutation).

Mixed punctuation: Dear Dr. Reed: **Open punctuation:**   Dear Dr. Reed
                          Sincerely,   Sincerely

While several forms of the complimentary close are used—Sincerely yours, Cordially, Truly yours, Very truly yours—the trend is to use only the word *Sincerely*.

Writer's Name and Official Title   The writer's keyed name and job title are positioned two lines (tap Enter twice) below the complimentary close. The job title may be positioned on the same line with the keyed name or immediately below. If it is below, remove extra spacing.

Sincerely,   Sincerely

Georgina Nascimento   Emi Mori, Treasurer
Conference Coordinator

Reference Initials   The initials of the keyboard operator are keyed in lowercase letters, no periods or spaces, at the left margin by tapping Enter below the writer's name, title, or department.

Georgina Nascimento
Conference Coordinator

tah

When the writer of a letter keys his or her own letter, reference initials are not needed.

Notations   When a document is included with a letter, an enclosure notation is keyed one line below the reference initials (tap Enter once). If a copy of the letter is to be sent to another person, a copy notation is included. The letter *c* is used, followed by the name(s) of the person(s) who will receive a copy. A postscript would be the last notation in a letter. As shown below, all of these letter parts are positioned at the left margin one line below (tap Enter once) the preceding part.

. . . are anxious to work with you.

Sincerely,

Theodore Klements, Manager

mri

Enclosure: Price List

c Andres Miranda

The deadline for the discount is . . .

The sender signs the letter in black ink above the typed signature.

Exercise 12-4 • Proofread and Mark

Proofread the following letter parts, and correct all format errors using the appropriate proofreaders' marks. If there are no format errors, write **C** *to the left of the number.*

1. . . . to discuss your proposal.

Sincerely,

Lorna Reinertson

c Jarod Sampson

tis

2. Ms. Gail Jaeckin
763 Jackson Street South
Anchorage, AK 99501-0942

Dear Ms. Jaeckin

    Holiday Shopping Plans

Yes, it is time to make your . . .

3. Pavement Prices Co.
9473 Chestnut Boulevard
New Orleans, LO 70118-3811

Dear Sir or Madam

4. MS. MIWAKU YOSHINO
SWEET SUGAR REFINERY
4715 OAHU AVENUE
HILO, HI 96720-4186

Ladies and Gentlemen

5. Mr. Larry Stelter, President
Comfort Homes, Inc.
257 Hampton Avenue
Wilmington, DE 19899-3169

Dear Mr. Stelter

continued

6. . . . and is enclosed for your use.

Sincerely,

Damon Wenisch
Sales Department
tbe

7. . . . and return the enclosed card by June 30.

Sincerely,

Nanette Jungers
National President

Enclosures

AK

8. August 11, 20--

Dr. Barbara Ericson
Hairs and Ribbons
7593 Bradley Circle
Nashua, NH 03063-0269

Award Winners

Letter Formats

Letters may be prepared in different formats and styles. Business letters are formatted in two basic styles: block and modified block. **Block format** is quick and easy to use because all letter parts begin at the left margin. This style is very popular because there are no paragraph or line indentations.

In **modified block format**, the date, complimentary close, and writer's name and official title *begin* near the horizontal center of the page. Paragraphs may be blocked at the left margin or indented 0.5 inch.

When proofreading letters, check that the letter format has been applied consistently. Also check that either open or mixed punctuation has been used consistently. Figures 12-1 and 12-2, which follow, illustrate the two letter formats.

Figure 12-1
Block Format with
Mixed Punctuation

GRAND WRITING INC.

39179 West Outer Drive • Knoxville, TN 37921-2648
Telephone: 865-555-0152 • FAX: 865-555-0153
writing@email.com

May 19, 20--

Ms. Myrtle Dallman
874 South Ash Avenue
Montgomery, AL 36117-1749

Dear Ms. Dallman:

Block Format, Mixed Punctuation

Block format arranges all of the parts of a business letter at the left margin.
Block format is efficient because no tabs are required.

This letter also illustrates mixed punctuation. The salutation is followed by
a colon, and the complimentary close is followed by a comma.

Block format appeals to firms that look for efficient ways to handle business
correspondence.

Sincerely,

Joan R. Zunder
Communications Specialist

tfd

GRAND WRITING INC.

39179 West Outer Drive • Knoxville, TN 37921-2648
Telephone: 865-555-0152 • FAX: 865-555-0153
writing@email.com

May 19, 20--

Ms. Myrtle Dallman
874 South Ash Avenue
Montgomery, AL 36117-1749

Dear Ms. Dallman

Modified Block Format, Open Punctuation

Modified block format is similar to block format except that the date, complimentary close, and closing lines begin near the center. This style has a more balanced appearance.

This letter also illustrates open punctuation. There is no colon after the salutation and no comma after the complimentary close.

Modified block format continues to be a favorite of mine. Do you prefer modified block or block format?

Sincerely

Joan R. Zunder
Communications Specialist

tfd

Figure 12-2
Modified Block
Format with Open
Punctuation

» Interoffice Memorandums (Memos)

Interoffice memorandums (memos) are informal documents used for communication within the same organization. Because they are internal, writers are generally not as concerned about enhancing the company image as they are with letters. However, employees are judged not only on their ability to compose clear and correct documents, but also on their ability to proofread carefully. Therefore, the proofreader must be sure the format is accurate.

Generally, memos address only one topic and include the following parts: receiver's name, sender's name, date, subject of the memo, body or actual message, and reference initials.

Memos are sent to personnel within the company. They are not sent to persons outside the company. Some companies have replaced interoffice memorandums with e-mail.

The memo includes four printed headings: TO, FROM, DATE, and SUBJECT.

Side margins are default settings of 1 inch. Tap Enter once below the subject line to begin the first line of the body. The paragraphs are blocked and use the default 1.15 spacing. Tap Enter once after the last line of the body to add the initials of the keyboard operator. Memos may be signed or initialed by the sender. Figure 12-3 illustrates the format of an interoffice memo.

Figure 12-3
Interoffice Memo

GRAND WRITING INC. Interoffice Memorandum

TO: Support Staff

FROM: Kyle Haack *KH*

DATE: April 12, 20--

SUBJECT: Format For Memos

This memo is designed for use on printed interoffice memorandum forms. If plain paper is used, the headings TO, FROM, DATE, and SUBJECT must be keyed and bolded.

Side margins are default. Tap Enter once below the printed headings to begin the message. Paragraphs are single-spaced and you tap Enter to end each paragraph. This puts 10 points between paragraphs. If someone other than the writer keys the memo, reference initials are keyed below the last paragraph.

The memo may be signed or initialed by the originator.

tbe

Exercise 12-5 • Proofread and Mark

Proofread the following memo, and correct all format errors using the appropriate proofreaders' marks.

GRAND UNION COLLEGE INTEROFFICE MEMO

TO: JoEllen Eustis, Head Librarian

FROM: Marv Eggersgluess, Management Department   *mE*

DATE: October 8, 20--

SUBJECT: Research Reports

Thank you for your interest in our Business

Communications class project. Each student was asked early in the semester to prepare a research report on a topic of his or her choice.

The reports that have been submitted are well done; and when we receive permission from the authors, we will place them on reserve in the library.

tos

CONFUSED AND MISUSED WORDS

loose   *adj.* not fastened; free
lose   *v.* unable to find; to fail to win
loss   *n.* a person or thing lost; a defeat
The rope is **loose.**
Please don't **lose** the keys.
Our win is their **loss.**

moral   *adj.* concerned with goodness or badness of human action and character; *n.* lesson contained in a story or an event
morale   *n.* attitude of an individual

He has a good **moral** character.
The **morale** of the staff was low after the recent layoffs.

precede   *v.* to come before in time or rank
proceed   *v.* to go forward

Babette will **precede** you in the graduation lineup.
You may **proceed** with your plans.

Proofreading & Editing Tips

PEP Tip

＊   In addition to the body, remember to proofread the special parts of a letter or memo. Also check to be sure that no parts have been omitted.

＊   When preparing more than one letter, be sure that each letter is inserted into the correctly addressed envelope. Check to be sure that all enclosures are, in fact, enclosed with the letter.

＊   When proofreading a letter for format, check that one letter style and one punctuation style have been used consistently throughout.

PROOFREADING APPLICATIONS

Exercise 12-6 • Business Letter Layout

*Place the letter parts in Column **A** in the correct order in Column **B**.*

Column A

Attention line

Body

Complimentary close

Date

Heading

Letter address

Reference initials

Salutation

Subject line

Writer's name and official title

Column B

1. _____

2. _____

3. _____

4. _____

5. _____

6. _____

7. _____

8. _____

9. _____

10. _____

Identify the punctuation style in each of the following:

1. _____   2. _____

Dear Mr. Wong:

. . . to thank you for your help.

Sincerely,

Roscoe Long

Dear Ms. Perea

. . . was most appreciated.

Yours truly

Lavonne Lahammer

Exercise 12-7 • Spelling and Word Usage Check

*Compare the words in Column **A** with the corresponding words in Column **B**. Use the appropriate proofreaders' marks to correct the misspelled or misused words. If both columns are correct, write **C** to the left of the number.*

Column A	Column B
1. beginning	begining
2. priviledge	privilege
3. salary	salery
4. pertinent	pertnent
5. similar	similiar
6. safety	safety
7. technical	technicle
8. especialy	especially
9. transferred	transfered
10. submited	submitted
11. accomodate	accommodate
12. established	establishd
13. We'll loose the game.	Don't lose your homework.
14. You will face moral issues.	The pay increase boosted employee moral.
15. The meeting will proceed.	Payment must proceed shipment.

Exercise 12-8 • International Vocabulary

*Compare the French and Spanish words in Column **A** with the corresponding words in Column **B**. If the word in Column **B** is different from the word in Column **A**, use the appropriate proofreaders' marks to correct Column **B**. If the words in both columns are the same, write **C** to the left of the number.*

Column A	Column B
1. Nos vemos	Nos vemos
2. orenada	orendada
3. chapeau	chapaeu
4. profesora	professora
5. accoutrement	acoutrement

Exercise 12-9 • Letter in Block Format

Proofread the following letter formatted in block style with mixed punctuation. Correct all errors using the appropriate proofreaders' marks.

JACY'S
Providing a Full Range of Investing Services
One Main Street
Houston, TX 77002-1015
Phone: 713-555-0177 • Fax: 713-555-0175

January 5, 20--

Ms. Samantha Theiu

Healthy Ways Fitness Center

228 Apple Way Street

Houston, TX 77002-10158

Dear Sam,

The Health and Wellness Committee of Jacy's is considering offering our employees either free or reduced memberships at a gym or gyms. Healthy Ways Fitness Center was a suggestion by one of our employees. We have about five hundred employees that live in the surrounding area. We would like to meet with you and discuss the possibility of offering this service to our employees.

In preparation for the meeting, can you answer the following questions?

1. What are the hours of operation of your gym during the year? Does it vary from season to season or is it the same in the fall as the summer, etc.?
2. What is your normal fee for joining? What are your monthly fees? Is there a minimum time that one has to join, like a year? Is this negotiable for a large group such as ours.
3. What specific equipment does your gym have? Do you have any nutritional programs that would complement the workout programs in your gym?

We at Jacy's are committed to wellness for our employees. We feel this could be a mutually rewarding relationship between Jacy's and Healthy Way Fitness Center.

Thank you for your consideration in this matter, and I look forward to hearing from you.

Sincerely,

Donald Igenstein, CFA
Senior Research Analyst

taf

Exercise 12-10 • Memorandum

Proofread the following memo for all format errors. Mark the corrections using the appropriate proofreaders' marks.

GENERAL MANUFACTURING, INC.
Interoffice Memorandum

TO: Faustino Colon

FROM: Antoinette Davies

DATE: November 30, 20--

SUBJECT: Recognition of Staff

President Yuan has received several letters of commendation on the excellent job you did at the national convention last week. We have submitted copies of your letters to Personnel to be placed in your employee file. Congratulations!

Please complete the enclosed form by Friday so that we can include the information in the next issue of General Notes. This newsletter will be published at the end of next week. Don't lose out on this opportunity to highlight the excellent work that you did!

Also, please send us a photograph that we can use with the article.

tih

Enclosure

PROOFREADING AT THE COMPUTER

Exercise 12-11 • Letter in Block Format

1. Open 12-11 from the Chapter 12 folder on the student CD. (This is a computer copy of Exercise 12-9.)
2. Proofread and correct all errors on the screen copy that you indicated with proofreaders' marks in Exercise 12-9.
3. Save the letter following the standard procedures.

Exercise 12-12 • Memorandum

1. Open 12-12 from the Chapter 12 folder on the student CD.
2. Proofread the memo on the screen. Correct all errors.
3. Produce the memo following the standard procedures.

Exercise 12-13 • Personal Letter Without Letterhead

1. Open 12-13 from the Chapter 12 folder on the student CD.
2. Proofread the letter on the screen. Correct all errors.
3. Produce the letter using mixed punctuation and following the standard procedures.

CUMULATIVE APPLICATION

Exercise 12-14 • Business Letter

Proofread the following letter formatted in block style with open punctuation. Correct all errors using the appropriate proofreaders' marks.

CORNSBURG DISTRIBUTING COMPANY
976 Oak Lane NE
Salt Lake City, UT 84115-3199
801-555-0166 • Fax 801-555-0167

Mr. Girard Heitner
Mountain View Advertising
15 S. Jackson Way
Albuquerque, MN 87108-2713

Dear Mr. Heitner;

Our marketing staff recently decided to contact your company about advertising rates for our campaign in New Mexico. Late this summer we will be introducing our new line of packing boxes at outlets throughout the western UnitedStates.

In each state we will ask an ad agency to be responsible for promotion. You are one agency we are considering for the state of New Mexico. We were especially impressed with the ad campaign your developed for the Geneva Company last year.

Please send us your response within the next fourteen days so we can finalize our advertising plans.

Sincerely

Luisa Diaz, Manager
Marketing Department
be

 Bookmark It!

Want more practice? Go to www.cengage.com/keyboarding/pagel for more proofreading activities.

Format Errors: Reports and Job Search Documents

Spotlight on ACCURACY

Your letter of application in a job search is similar to a sales letter. The purpose of this letter is to match your qualifications with the employer's needs in the best way possible. Because of its importance, your letter must be perfect—no errors. Consider the impression you might make on a potential employer if these errors were found in your letter:

- I have worked in sales since 1098.

- I am enclosing my resume, along with other important parts of me.

- I have taken the following curses in my studies: keyboarding, business law, communications, and entrepreneurship.

Objectives

- Recognize format errors in reports.

- Recognize format errors in job search documents.

- Use the appropriate proof-readers' marks to indicate corrections in format.

- Spell correctly 12 frequently misspelled words.

- Use correctly three sets of commonly confused and misused words.

❯❯ Reports

Reports are used to provide or analyze information and to communicate within a company or with other companies. Business reports can be used for financial, managerial, operational, sales, planning, forecast, and other informational reporting. There is a standard format for most reports, just as there is for letters and resumes. School reports, such as themes, book reports, and term papers, are usually prepared in the standard report format as well.

Reports may be formatted as unbound, leftbound, or topbound documents. The most common format is the unbound report. Although the spacing and arrangement of report parts may vary somewhat from writer to writer, you will review the basic unbound format in this chapter.

Report Parts

When proofreading a report, check closely for consistency and correctness among report parts. For example, check that the spacing above and below similar headings is the same throughout the report. Report parts vary depending on the length and formality of the report. The basic parts, however, include the title or cover page, the body, and the references pages.

Cover Page   Word offers the Cover Page feature, which inserts a fully formatted cover page. You may choose from a variety of attractively formatted covers. The cover page usually includes the title of the report, a subtitle if needed, the date, and the writer's name. Figure 13-1 illustrates the format and spacing of a cover page in an unbound report.

Body   The body, the message of the report, begins with the **main heading**—placed approximately 2 inches from the top. You should capitalize the first letter of all main words, tap Enter after the title, and apply the Title style. The Title style is 26-point Cambria font with a bottom border. The main heading is the title of the report, also found on the title page. So the information is easy to read, the body is organized under one or more levels of headings. The first level of headings is called a **side heading**. Key side headings at the left margin. Capitalize the first letter of all main words. Apply Heading 1 style to side headings; this style is a 14-point Cambria font. Tap Enter once after the heading.

Enumerations are often used to emphasize certain facts or to present information in an easy-to-read format. Use the default .25 inch indentation for numbers and bullets. Tap Enter after each item.

Margins and spacing should be consistent throughout the report. For an unbound report, the side margins and bottom margins are the default of 1 inch. The top margin for the first page is 2 inches; on all other pages, it is 1 inch. Generally, reports use the default 1.15 line spacing. Pages are numbered beginning with the second page, where the page number is positioned at the top using right alignment.

Figure 13-1   Unbound Report with Cover Page

KASKASKIA COLLEGE

Format for Unbound Reports

Randy Rolfingsmeyer

April 23, 20--

This is Word's Built-In Conservative cover page.

This is a report on preparing an unbound report.

---

2 inches
Page number at right margin → 2

FORMAT FOR UNBOUND REPORTS   *Title style*

A report is started with the normal style. We enter three times to give the first page of the report a 2-inch top margin. We use the default 11point Calibri font with 1.15 line spacing. This gives the report more white space between lines, which makes it easier to read. We also have 10 points after each paragraph, which is the default in Word 2007. In prior years, academic reports used double spacing and businesses traditionally used single spacing in reports. The title is typed with capital letters for the first letter of all main words and the Title style is applied. The title style is 26 point Cambria font with a bottom border.

Headings   *Heading 1 style*
Side headings are keyed at the left margin with capital letters for the first letter of all main words. The Heading 1 style is applied to side headings. This style is a 14 point Cambria font. The Heading 1 style applies the appropriate white space above the heading.

Enumerated Items
Use the default .25 inch indentation for numbers and bullets and tap Enter after each item. This gives the enumerated items or bulleted items 10 points of white space between each item.

Page Numbers
The first page is not numbered. Second and succeeding pages are numbered in the upper-right corner in the header position, which is .5. You can insert page numbers with Word's Page Numbering feature.

Guidelines for Dividing Copy
Use the Wordwrap feature when you key a document. Words are rarely divided at the end of a line. If it is necessary to divide a paragraph between two pages, at least two lines of the paragraph should appear on each page.

Documenting with References
All ideas of others should be cited so that credit is given. Word allows you to do so with its Citations and Bibliography feature. This feature allows you to choose from many styles including the MLA, APA, and Turabian styles. (VanHuss, 2008) ← *Textual citation*

Page number at right margin → 3

Summary
Use the defaults when typing a report in Word 2007. You will want to apply the Title style to the main title and Heading 1 style to the side headings. Word will apply appropriate white space and formatting in your document. Once you have completed the document, you have several paragraph styles you may choose from. The styles can be found by clicking the Change Styles button in Word 2007. The office or business that you work for may have a style that they always use or a style of their own that is required by that particular business. One must give credit to ideas or words by other authors or publications. Word has provided a Citation and Bibliography feature to use for this purpose. There are several styles to choose from including MLA, APA, and Turabian.

Bibliography
VanHuss, S. H. (2008). *Keyboarding and Formatting*. Cincinnati: Cengage.

Bibliography at end of report

References   If references have been used in writing the report, they are listed at the end. The references are listed under the heading REFERENCES, WORKS CITED, or BIBLIOGRAPHY. You can use the Bibliography feature to insert your WORKS CITED, BIBLIOGRAPY, or REFERENCES page. You may put it at the end or as a separate page.

Because of the increased use of electronic sources as references, you should also know how to document electronic citations. An electronic citation includes the following reference components: Author. "Title of Work." URL (Date you accessed this site).

> Powell, Jim. "The Education of Thomas Edison."
> http://www.self-gov.org/freeman (27 April 20--).

Documentation

When using another person's ideas or quoting statistics or other specific information, the writer must indicate the sources from which the information was taken. Reference to the originator adds credibility to the report and gives credit to the originator. The most common means of documentation for business writers include textual citations, footnotes, and endnotes. More formal documentation styles include the MLA and APA styles of notation.

BLEND IMAGES/JUPITER IMAGES

Lee arrived promptly for his job interview.

Textual Citation   Textual citations have grown in popularity. They usually include the last name of the author(s) and the year of publication. Textual citations are placed in parentheses within the body of the report. The complete references are then listed in alphabetical order by author surnames under the heading REFERENCES or BIBLIOGRAPHY at the end of the report (See Figure 13-1).

The Modern Language Association (MLA) and the American Psychological Association (APA) styles of citation are used in formal reports. The MLA style is used primarily in preparing scholarly manuscripts and lists in parentheses the author's last name and page number (*Author, 14*). The APA style is used primarily by writers in the social and behavioral sciences and lists in parentheses the last name of the author and the year of publication (*Author, 2012*).

Footnotes   Footnotes are numbered consecutively throughout the report. They appear at the bottom of the page on which the references are cited. Superscripts are used to number footnotes.

If you are using the Footnote and Endnote feature of your word processing program, the feature will automatically insert a superscript number and position your footnotes correctly at the bottom of the page.

Endnotes   Endnotes are essentially the same as footnotes. But unlike footnotes, endnotes are listed together on a separate page at the end of the report.

If you are using the Footnote and Endnote feature of your word processing program, it will automatically insert a superscript number and place the endnote at the end of your document.

Exercise 13-1 • Proofread and Mark

*Proofread the following paragraph from a bound report. Use the appropriate proofreaders' marks to correct the errors. If the line is correct, write **C** to the left of the number.*

1.   Deere & Company, with Headquarters in Moline Illinois is

2. one of the worlds oldest and respected most companis. Deere

3.   & Com. manufactures, distributes and finance a full line of

4. agriculturel equipment, as well as a braod range of

5. construction and forestry equipment.

» Job Search Documents

Three documents are crucial to a person's application for employment: a resume (also called a data sheet or vita), an application (cover) letter, and (following an interview) a follow-up letter. Because of the importance of these documents in the employment process, each should show the employer the highest standard of work of which the applicant is capable. Since each document should be submitted without error, careful proofreading is crucial.

Resume

Prospective employers use resumes to screen individuals for an interview. As such, the resume should summarize a person's background in several important sections—personal, education, work experience, and related activities. Other sections might include your career objective, summary of qualifications, computer experience, and references. There is not one set way to format a resume. However, you should include certain information and the formatting should be appealing and consistent.

The most common resume formats are chronological, functional, and combination. The **chronological format** lists your employment history in reverse chronological order, with your most recent employment first. This resume emphasizes your work stability and experience.

The **functional resume** focuses attention on your qualifications or skills rather than on your past employment history. Applicable skills may include areas such as communication, management, human relations, and computer software. The functional resume is appropriate for applicants who lack related work experience or who have gaps in their employment history.

The **combination resume** takes advantage of the best features of both the chronological and the functional resume. The combination resume emphasizes the applicant's skills or qualifications and includes a job history.

Personal This section is at the top of the page and includes your name, home address, e-mail address, and telephone number(s). Do not include a telephone number or an e-mail address from your current place of employment.

Education This section should include the name and address of the schools attended—the most recent one listed first (reverse chronological order). Only the city and state are needed as the address. It is also appropriate to include the dates you attended each school, your GPA, and those courses that have provided special preparation for the desired position.

Work Experience In this section, you should list any previously held jobs, even though they may not directly relate to the desired job. Whether you have worked in agriculture, a service industry, or an office position, a prospective employer is interested in your experience in working with people, your attitude toward work, and your values. Work experience shows the prospective employer that you know how to take initiative and responsibility for your actions.

Related Activities This section shows your involvement in organizations and athletics during your years in school, as well as any awards, honors, or scholarships you may have received. Include the name of the organization, as well as the period of time that you were a member, and indicate any officer positions you may have held.

Optional Sections Try to limit your resume to one page. What differentiates you from all other applicants? If the information is not important to an employer, it should not be included on your resume.

Because many jobs today require specific computer experience, consider having a separate section that identifies your background in computers. You might also include this information under "education."

While a separate "references" section was important in the past, most employers today are not interested in a list of references until later in the interview process. For example, an employer might request a list of references from the top candidates. Instead of listing references on your resume, take a separate list with you to the interview. Each entry on this list should include the name and courtesy title of the person; his or her official title (coach, teacher, principal, supervisor, etc.); complete mailing address; telephone number(s); and e-mail address. Always ask for permission before listing someone as a reference.

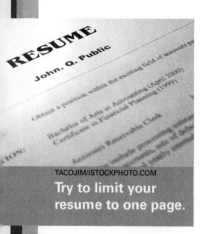

TACOJIM/ISTOCKPHOTO.COM
Try to limit your resume to one page.

Many companies now request a resume as an electronic submission. The computer looks for key words and phrases during the scanning process and selects only those resumes that included those key words. Information on your resume should be formatted so that the reader can understand it easily. Figure 13-2 illustrates a correctly formatted resume.

Figure 13-2   Sample Resume

JANEEN K. GENTRY

218 South Andrew
Whitewater, WI 53190-1118
608-555-0168
janeen.gentry@auburn.net

EDUCATION

Northview Public Schools, Whitewater, Wisconsin, 2010–2014
(Will receive high school diploma, 2014)
Graduated with High Honors (3.65 on a 4.00 scale)

Special Preparation:
Completed courses in English, math, science, and business
Key 65 words per minute

COMPUTER SOFTWARE EXPERIENCE

Experienced in using the following software applications:
Word, PowerPoint, Microsoft Excel, Microsoft Access, and PageMaker

WORK EXPERIENCE

Administrative Assistant, Dayton Office Supplies, Inc., Fort Atkinson,
Wisconsin, May 2012–December 2013
Worked 15 hours each week after school and on weekends

Responsibilities:
- Answered telephones
- Deposited cash
- Stocked and ordered supplies
- Trained employees in using Word and PowerPoint

RELATED ACTIVITIES

National Honor Society, 2014
Student Council Senior Class Representative, 2014
Future Business Leaders of America
President, 2011, and Publicity Committee Chair, 2012
Volleyball and Soccer, 2012

Application (Cover) Letter

The application (cover) letter should be keyed on plain paper with a return address, as described in Chapter 12. An alternate to beginning with the return address is to create your own personal letterhead with name, address, phone, and e-mail address. The body of the letter should include three to five paragraphs.

You should begin the first paragraph by identifying the position; telling the reader where you heard of the position (placement office, newspaper ad, counselor, teacher, etc.); explaining what you understand the title of the position to be; and saying that you are a candidate for the job.

In the middle paragraphs of the letter, you should briefly tell the reader about your interest in and background for the job. Discuss your key qualifications, education, and work experience as they relate to this position; do not repeat everything listed on your resume. In this section you should also state that you are enclosing your resume.

Because an interview is a crucial aspect of any employer's decision process, in the last paragraph you should ask for an interview at the reader's convenience. Be sure to sign your letter of application above the typed signature line in black ink. Figure 13-3 (pages 233–234) shows a sample application letter.

Follow-up Letter

After you have had an interview, you should send a short thank-you note to the interviewer, expressing your appreciation and explaining again your interest in the job. Your thank-you note should be sent within 24 hours after the interview. Figure 13-4 (page 235) illustrates a sample follow-up letter.

Figure 13-3a   Sample Application (Cover) Letter

218 South Andrew
Whitewater, WI 53190-1118
May 23, 20--

Ms. Rita Joseph
Human Resources Department
Hummel Manufacturing
37 Main Street
Whitewater, WI 53190-4498

Dear Ms. Joseph:

Mr. Timothy Tabin, my business teacher at Northview High School, told me about the opening you have at Hummel Manufacturing for a technical assistant. Please consider me an applicant for this position.

As you will see from the enclosed resume, I will graduate next week from Northview High School. In addition to taking advanced courses in English, math, and science, I worked with Mr. Tabin in training students in word processing and desktop publishing. I am comfortable working with most software applications, and I am a quick learner.

I have worked part time at Dayton Office Supplies, Inc. During my time there, I have been given increased responsibilities. I was also commended by my supervisor for my human relations skills and technical competence in using software applications.

I would appreciate the opportunity to discuss with you my qualifications for this position. I may be contacted at 608-555-0168 to set up an interview.

Sincerely,

Janeen K. Gentry

Enclosure

Alternately, you can create your own personal letterhead.

Figure 13-3b   Sample Application (Cover) Letter

JANEEN K. GENTRY
218 South Andrew
Whitewater, WI 53190-1118
608-555-0168
jentry@yahoo.com

May 23, 20--

Ms. Rita Joseph
Human Resources Department
Hummel Manufacturing
37 Main Street
Whitewater, WI 53190-4498

Dear Ms. Joseph:

Mr. Timothy Tabin, my business teacher at Northview High School, told me about the opening you have at Hummel Manufacturing for a technical assistant. Please consider me an applicant for this position.

As you will see from the enclosed resume, I will graduate next week from Northview High School. In addition to taking advanced courses in English, math, and science, I worked with Mr. Tabin in training students in word processing and desktop publishing. I am comfortable working with most software applications, and I am a quick learner.

I have worked part time at Dayton Office Supplies, Inc. During my time there, I have been given increased responsibilities. I was also commended by my supervisor for my human relations skills and technical competence in using software applications.

I would appreciate the opportunity to discuss with you my qualifications for this position. I may be contacted at 608-555-0168 to set up an interview.

Sincerely,

Janeen K. Gentry

Enclosure

Figure 13-4   Sample Follow-Up Letter

218 South Andrew
Whitewater, WI 53190-1118
June 2, 20--

Ms. Rita Joseph
Human Resources Department
Hummel Manufacturing
37 Main Street
Whitewater, WI 53190-4498

Dear Ms. Joseph:

Thank you for meeting with me yesterday about the technical assistant position at your company. Your description of what the job requires was very helpful in learning what would be expected of me. I particularly liked the opportunity to tour the company and to meet with members of your technical team.

As a result of our meeting and the tour, I am even more interested in being a part of the "Systems Team" and helping Hummel Manufacturing meet its objectives.

If you need additional information, please let me know. I'm excited about the possibility of working for your company.

Sincerely,

Janeen K. Gentry

CONFUSED AND MISUSED WORDS

lean   *adj.* thin; not fat; meager; *v.* to slant away from a vertical position

lien   *n.* the right to sell property of a debtor

Ted is a very **lean** person.

The mortgage company has a **lien** on their house.

may be   *v.* to be allowed or permitted to

maybe   *adv.* perhaps; possibly

We **may be** able to tour downtown Chicago tomorrow.

Maybe we should send her an e-mail.

personal   *adj.* private; pertaining to a particular person

personnel   *n.* people employed; staff of a company

They made a **personal** choice not to attend.

All **personnel** arrived at 9:30 a.m.

Proofreading & Editing Tips

PEP Tip

* Proofread technical material and legal descriptions in pairs.

* When proofreading a lengthy report, proofread all similar parts as a separate step. For example, check the format of all side headings; then check all paragraph headings. Check separately the continuity and sequence of all numbered pages, tables, and figures.

* When preparing a multipage document, prepare a style sheet to show how unusual features, such as names, titles, or terminology, will be handled.

PROOFREADING APPLICATIONS

Exercise 13-2 • Paragraphs from a Report

*Proofread the following paragraphs from a report, and mark all format errors using the appropriate proofreaders' marks. If the line is correct, write **C** to the left of the number.*

1.	**Germany**
2.	History
3.	Germany was immersed in two devastating World Wars in the first half of the
4.	twentieth century and was occupied by the victorious Allied powers of the
5.	United States, the United Kingdom, France, and the Soviet Union in 1945.
6.	With the start of the Cold War, two German states were formed in 1949:
7.	the Federal Republic of Germany (FRG) and the German Democratic
8.	Republic (GDR).
9.	Geography
10.	Germany is located in Central Europe and borders the Baltic Sea and
11.	North Sea. The total land area is 349,223 square kilometers.
12.	Government
13.	Germany is a federal republic with its capital located in Berlin. Germany
14.	Has 16 states. Unification of East Germany and West Germany took
15.	Place on October 3, 1990.

Exercise 13-3 • Spelling and Word Usage Check

*Compare the words in Column **A** with the corresponding words in Column **B**. Use the appropriate proofreaders' marks to correct the misspelled or misused words. If both columns are correct, write **C** to the left of the number.*

Column A	Column B
1. commission	comission
2. quantity	quanity
3. tomorrow	tomorrow
4. financial	finantial
5. preperation	preparation
6. offerred	offered
7. permissable	permissible
8. approximately	approximatly
9. disatisfied	dissatisfied
10. guarantee	guarentee
11. knowledgeable	knowledgeable
12. counselor	counseler
13. Dodd Associates has experienced some lien years.	The marker leans to the south.
14. Josh maybe able to help us.	May be the time is right!
15. Let's not make this personal.	Our company has hired personal for the new Macon plant.

Exercise 13-4 • International Vocabulary

*Compare the French and Spanish words in Column **A** with the corresponding words in Column **B**. If the word in Column **B** is different from the word in Column **A**, use the appropriate proofreaders' marks to correct Column **B**. If the words in both columns are the same, write **C** to the left of the number.*

Column A	Column B
1. acantilado	acantilado
2. coleccionista	colecionitsa
3. ressentiment	resessentiment
4. llamamiento	llamemiento
5. froideur	froideur

Exercise 13-5 • Report

Proofread the following report; and correct all formatting, grammar, and spelling errors using the appropriate proofreaders' marks.

Wales

One part of Great Britain that is not too well known is the country of Wales. Wales is located on a peninsula directly across the Irish Sea from Ireland. The peninsula is approximately 130 miles long from north to south and approximitely from east to west at its widest point. Wales is part of Great Britain, as is Scotland and England. England lies to the east of Wales, and Scotland lies to the northeast of Wales (and to the north of England).

Geography

Wales is a very mountainous country, with Mount Snowdon at 3,500 feet in northern Wales being the highest point in England and Wales. Slate quarrying was a major source of employment in northern Wales for many years. In recent years other types of building materials has replaced slate, and it is no longer as prominent in the Welsh economy.

Some of the world's finest coalfields for steam coal are located in the mountainous part of southern Wales. Many people have gained an impression of Welsh coal minors and their way of life from scenes in the movie *How Green Was My Valley*. The movie, based on the book by the same name by Richard Llewellyn, was set in the Rhondda Valley of southern Wales. Over the years, as alternate forms of energy were developed, the demand for steam coal decreased. Today very few mines are still open.

Language

One of the distinctive features of Wales is its language—Welsh. Many people consider it to be a difficult language to learn until they find out that *w* and *y* are considered vowels. Some of the sounds of Welsh letters are different from those in English. For example, an *f* is pronounced like a *v*. The word *Gymanfa* is pronounced "gih-MAHN-vah."

Exercise 13-5 • Report (*continued*)

Some other unique sounds in the Welsh language is the ones for *dd* and *ll*. The *dd* is pronounced like "th" in the English word *the.* Therefore, in the Welsh word *Eisteddfod,* the middle syllable is pronounced "teth" rather than "ted."

The *ll* sound requires that the speaker place the tip of his or her tongue at the top of the back side of the front teeth and then carefully blow out each side. This technique is used twice in pronounceing the name of the city Llangollen and the author Llewellyn.

Conclusion

Much more could be written about this small country and its contribution to music, the arts, politics, the economy, etc. It is a "region of great . . . beauty."[1]

----

[1]The Encyclopedia Americana, International Edition, S.V. "Wales."

Exercise 13-6 • Application Letter

Proofread the following letter; and correct all formatting, grammar, and spelling errors using the appropriate proofreaders' marks.

10 Divot Court
St. Peters, MO 63376
July 10, 20--

Jill Brown, Executive Director
Around-the-World Travel Club
2710 W. Clay

St. Charles, MO 63301-2553

Dear Ms. Brown

My professor, Susan Kauling, informed me about the opening you have for a student intern. I hope, after reviewing my resume, you will consider me for the position.

I will be in my last year of college at St. Charles Community College pursing an assoiciate degree in Office Technology. I feel that I would bring the skills you are looking for and more. I would love to be involve in world travel at any level. I am also local and could arrange the hours with my school schedule.

I have a good background for the job. I have gained knowledge in Office 2007, accounting, business math, and business communications while at St. Charles Community College. I am proficient with Microsoft Office and am a Microsoft Certified Application Specialist in Word 2007 and Excel 2007. I believe I have the skills you are looking for ina student intern.

Although I do not have an abundance of work experience, I gained valueable skills working with students from diverse backgrounds and ages through my summer job at the Recreation Center in St. Charles. I am detail oriented. If a student was on a special diet, I knew it was up to me to see that wherever we went, the appropriate menus must be available or brought along. I understood that if a family wanted 2 double beds and got one queen size beds, there would be much unhappiness. I would make sure to take care of all the details. Above all, I bring eagerness and the ability to learn quickly to a position. I have an excellent academic record and work ethic. I would very much like a career in the travel industry. I also had two years of Spanish in high school.

I am available for a personal interview at you convenience. My phone is 636-555-0155 or you may contact me by email at samstudent@sibae.net. Enclosed with this letter, you will find my resume. I look forward to hearing from you and meeting you in person.

Sincerely

Sam Student

Enclosure: Resume

Proofread the following resume; and correct all formatting, abbreviation, capitalization, and spelling errors using the appropriate proofreaders' marks.

SAM STUDENT
10 Divot Court St. Peters, MO 63376
636-555-0155 • samstudent@sibae.net

PROFESSIONAL OBJECTIVE

A position in the travel industry providing the opportunity to make a strong contribution by utilizing and expanding upon related education, skills, education, and capabilities.

QUALIFICATIONS PROFILE

Experience/ Skills:	**General Bussiness:**
	• Cultural sensitivity and awareness
	• Office management skills
	• Business math skills
	Computers:
	• Microsoft Certified Application Specialist in Word, Excel
	• Proficient with PowerPoint and Access
	Communication:
	• Excellent written comunications skills including editing and proofreading
	• Writing and submitting technical reports
	• Making public speaking and PowerPoint presentations
	• Beginning Spanish skills
Education:	**Associate in Applied Science, Office Technology, Anticipated August 20--**
	St. Charles Community College, St. Charles, Missouri, GPA 3.4/4.0
	• Missouri Merit Recognition Scholarship
	• Pi Omega Business Society
	• National Society of Collegiate Scholars
Strengths:	➢ Always ready to try new things and go new places
	➢ Ability to communicate with diverse groups of people
	➢ A people person
	➢ Detail oriented

WORK EXPERIENCE

20010 to Present	St. Charles Recreation Department

Summer Camp Guide
I served as a summer camp guide for the City of St. Charles Recreation Department. Clientele included students from 6-14 years of age. Organized, planned and executed many daily programs for youth. Activitys included planning trips to various points of interest in the City of St. Charles and the City of St. Louis. Effectively guided and led students in activities making it interesting and making it fun for the students.

PROOFREADING AT THE COMPUTER

Exercise 13-8 • Application Letter

1. Open 13-8 from the Chapter 13 folder on the student CD. (This is a computer copy of Exercise 13-6.)

2. Proofread and correct all errors on the screen copy that you indicated with proofreaders' marks in Exercise 13-6. Use the spelling checker.

3. Produce the letter in block format following the standard procedures described in the previous chapters.

Exercise 13-9 • Resume

1. Open 13-9 from the Chapter 13 folder on the student CD.

2. Proofread the resume on the screen. Correct all errors.

3. Produce the resume following the standard procedures.

Exercise 13-10 • Follow-Up Letter with Personal Letterhead

1. Open 13-10 from the Chapter 13 folder on the student CD.

2. Proofread the follow-up letter on the screen. Correct all errors.

3. Produce the letter following the standard procedures.

CUMULATIVE APPLICATION

Exercise 13-11 • **Unbound Report**

Proofread the following two-page unbound report, and correct all errors using the appropriate proofreaders' marks.

Business Communication Skills

The world in which we work has seen an explosion of changes in the ways we communicate in a global society. No longer must we rely entirely on a hard copy of a business document to be sent by mail from one location to another. Instead, information may be send electronically by satellite, by computer, by electronic mail, etc. Depending on the channel used, messages that are critical in making a decision may be received within seconds of the time they are sent.

Regardless of the channel used to send a business message, the writer of a message must have a basic understanding of language skills. These basic skill include excellent grammar, spelling, and punctuation skills. They include the ability to analyze an audience an to determine the purpose of a message. They also include the ability to edit and revise a document. Without basic language skills, the technology used in preparing a business document is of little value.

A business writer must also be an excellent proofreaders and catch errors in format, word use, spelling, and punctuation. Perhaps an even more important concept is that the writer must understand some of the complexities of writing business documents. "Quantity" in writing is not important, but "quality is important.

Sequence of Ideas

One basic fact that writers must understand is the importance of using the right sequence of ideas in a business document to provide the the greatest impact on the reader. When a person decides to write a business document, one of the first questions to be answered are "What will be the impact on the reader? Will he or she be pleased with the content? Will he or she be disappointed? Will he or she be neutral in his or her reaction?" The answers to those questions provide a clue as to the sequence the writer should use in creating the communication.

If the writer assumes that the readers reaction will be neutral or pleasant, the correct sequence of ideas is to use a deductive approach. With a deductive approach, the writer starts with the main idea in the first sentence. This is then followed with details that elaborate on the main idea.

Exercise 13-11 • Unbound Report (*continued*)

If the writer assumes that the reader will be disappointed with the message or must be persuaded to do something he or she may not ordinarily do, the writer should use an indirect approach. The direct approach starts with a neutral beginning and is followed by a detailed explanation of details. To further lesson the impact on the reader, the negative answer should be placed somewhere in the middle paragraphs.

Careful attention to the sequence of ideas in a business document will make the message even more effective, and the communication will have it's maximum impact. As Guffey states, "The most successful players in this new world of work will be those with highly developed communication skills."[1]

Do you have what it takes to be a successful player? Let's hope so!

---

[1]Mary Ellen Guffey, <u>Essentials of Business Communications,</u> 6th Edition (Cincinnati: Cengage/Southwestern, 2004), 4.

Bookmark It!

Want more practice? Go to www.cengage.com/keyboarding/pagel for more proofreading activities.

Editing for Content, Clarity, and Conciseness

Spotlight on ACCURACY

Like the letter of application in the job search, a resume briefly summarizes your qualifications for the job for which you are applying. This document, too, must be perfect—without *any* errors. How do you think a prospective employer might react to the following statements in your resume?

- Attended University of Ohio from 1892–1997.

- Graduated Magna Cum Loud.

- A position that allows me to use my superior commuter skills.

- My GPA at night is 3.2 (4.0).

Objectives

- Edit a message for completeness, correctness, and consistency in content.

- Edit a message for conciseness by avoiding redundancy and eliminating unnecessary modifiers.

- Edit a message for clarity by using simple words; avoiding trite, overused expressions; and presenting ideas logically.

- Distinguish between active and passive voice.

- Spell correctly 12 frequently misspelled words.

- Use correctly three sets of commonly confused and misused words.

» What Is Editing?

As you know, **proofreading** is the process of locating mechanical errors that may occur because of incorrect keying, spelling, capitalization, grammar, punctuation, abbreviation, word division, number usage, and formatting. **Editing** involves checking copy to see that every aspect of the content is correct and that the message is clear, concise, and complete. Editing may also require changing words, correcting errors, and rewriting parts of the document.

Editing and proofreading are two distinct procedures that must be performed separately. The objectives of both, however, are the same—to improve the quality of the final copy and to make the intended message clear so that no possibility of misunderstanding or misinterpretation exists. Once copy is edited, however, it must be proofread a second time for accuracy. It is impossible to edit the content of a message and proofread for mechanical errors at the same time.

» Editing for Content

Editing for content involves checking to see that the message is accurate. All facts, figures, and calculations must be correct. If errors in content exist, the reader may lose confidence in the writer. Correctness shows competence and regard for the reader.

The best way to locate content errors is to read the document carefully, at a natural, unhurried rate, and concentrate on what you are reading. As you read, be alert for:

- Incomplete information (omission of essential information)

- Incorrect facts (names, dates, addresses, numbers, etc.)

- Inconsistency in the way material is written (style and format)

- Incorrect usage of words, especially **homophones** (words that sound alike but differ in spelling and meaning). Examples: cite, site, sight; right, rite, wright, write; sell, cell; sail, sale.

It is important to realize that the editing changes may vary due to the proofreader's understanding and interpretation of the material. Therefore, the proofreader must make sure that the editing changes retain the message the writer intended to convey.

Complete Information

Editing a message for completeness means checking to see that all necessary information is included. It would be puzzling to discover that the enclosures mentioned in a letter have not been included. It would be frustrating to be unable to make a business decision because important information has been omitted. When possible, answer the "who, what, when, where, and why" information in bulleted items rather than in long, drawn-out sentences.

To assure completeness, reread the message and check to see that dates, addresses, times, and other factual information are included. Make sure that any enclosures mentioned in the letter are indeed enclosed.

Check for omissions of copy by comparing the final copy with the rough draft or the original document source. Reading the wrong column or the wrong line results in material being omitted, especially in long or complex documents. Skipping a word or a whole line also leads to omissions. Likewise, if information has been transferred from one document to another, double-check to make sure that nothing has been omitted.

To avoid omissions in tables and lists, use a helpful device such as a card, a ruler, or a piece of paper. Laying the straight edge of the card, the ruler, or the paper under the line you are reading helps focus your attention.

Correct Facts

"The meeting will be held from Wednesday through Friday, September 15–18." This statement is confusing. Because *Wednesday* is *September 15*, *Friday* is definitely not *September 18*. Did the writer intend to say *Wednesday through Saturday*, *Tuesday through Friday*, *September 15–17*, or *September 16–18*?

Incorrect facts may appear in numerical data (dates, amounts, ZIP codes, social security numbers, serial numbers, identification numbers, stock numbers, and addresses).

Unusual, unfamiliar, and foreign names (*Papadopulos, Teutschel, Shimabukuro*) as well as similar sounding names (*Johnson/Johnston*) must be checked for accuracy. Names are easily misspelled, especially because they can be spelled in so many different ways. Note the various ways the following names can be spelled:

Andersen, Anderson

Brown, Browne, Broune, Braun

Cain, Caine, Cayne, Kane, Kaine, Kayne

Carol, Carole, Carrol, Carroll

Hernandes, Hernandez

Smith, Smithe, Smythe

Schmid, Schmidt, Schmit, Schmitt

Schneider, Schneiter, Snider, Snyder

Tomson, Thomson, Thompson

Never assume you know how to spell a name; always check to see that the spelling used in the original document source is correct. In a business letter, for example, check the addressee's name in the letter address, in the salutation, within the body, and on the mailing envelope.

Locating incorrect facts requires concentration and attention to detail. Whenever possible, you should check the document against the rough draft or the source document. If you are not sure about the accuracy of a statement, write a question mark next to the copy to alert the writer that the message is unclear and that the statement should be revised.

Consistency

Consistency means that all similar ideas are handled the same way. Related ideas should be expressed in the same grammatical form (parallel structure). Likewise, format within a document should be consistent. Although enumerations may be blocked at the left margin or indented, all enumerations within a document should be formatted in one style.

Correct Word Usage

The proficient proofreader should be able to determine whether the correct words are used so that the reader will understand the writer's message. **Word usage** refers to how language is used to best convey the intended meaning. Words that sound alike but are spelled differently and have different meanings (homophones) must be checked carefully. Study these sentences, and notice how the italicized words are used.

> There is no solution in *sight*.
>
> The *sights* of London are breathtaking.
>
> The *site* of the new building is convenient to public transportation.
>
> He was *cited* for speeding.

Note: Answers to the exercises in this chapter will vary, because there is often more than one acceptable answer. Remember that you must retain the meaning intended by the writer.

Exercise 14-1 • Proofread and Mark

Using the factual information in the table as a reference, edit the message on the next page for content errors. Correct the message using the appropriate proofreaders' marks. Write the revised message on the blank lines.

Speaker	Dr. Elayne Rachut, Pembroke Graduate School of Business
Topic	"Preparing for Global Literacy"
Location	Foust College, Johnston City
Date	Thursday–Friday, March 21–22, 20--
Time	2:30 p.m. to 5:30 p.m., Thursday 4 p.m. to 6:30 p.m., Friday
Completion	Certificate awarded for two-day attendance
Fee	$25 for one day; $40 for two days

continued

The three-day conference, "Preparing for Global Literacy," is scheduled for Friday–Saturday, March 14–15, at Foust College in Johnson City. Friday's session will be from 4:30 to 6:30 p.m.; Saturday's session, from 3:00 to 5:30 p.m. The workshop will be conducted by Miss Elayne Rachute, noted professor at Pembroke Business School.

_____

_____

_____

_____

_____

_____

_____

_____

Exercise 14-2 • Proofread and Mark

Analyze the following message for completeness. On the blank lines, list any important but missing information that you believe would make the message clearer.

Here are your travel arrangements for the three-day meeting at Foust College on March 21–22. You will fly Liberty Airlines and earn frequent flyer miles. I know you like to stay at the Royal Court Hotel. Let me know if these arrangements are satisfactory.

_____

_____

_____

» Editing for Clarity

It is important to check that the words used to write messages do not confuse the reader and that ideas are presented in a clear, logical manner.

When writing to a person, use the same words that you would use when talking to that person face-to-face.

Clear and Simple Words

Clear and simple words are not only easier to write, but also easier to read. Such words help the writer say exactly what he or she means. When writing, use the same words that you would use when talking to that person face-to-face. Clear messages are more likely to be understood as they were intended. When proofreading a document, follow these guidelines to correct unclear messages.

Use Familiar Words   Familiar words increase understanding. Difficult words annoy the reader and distract him or her from concentrating on the message. To achieve clarity, substitute a simpler word for a more difficult one. Compare the more difficult words in the first column with the simpler words in the second column.

DIFFICULT WORDS	SIMPLER WORDS
alternative	choice
germane	appropriate, fitting
optimum	best
oblivious	unaware
provincial	unsophisticated, narrow
remuneration	pay
sagacious	keen, shrewd
substantiate	prove
verbose	wordy

Use Precise Words   Words have different meanings for different people. For example, to one person, *average* may mean "mediocre"; to another person, it may mean "normal." To a customer waiting to receive an order, the word *soon* may mean "tomorrow"; to the retailer who must first obtain the merchandise from a supplier, *soon* may mean "within ten days." When editing a message for clarity, use words that help convey the exact meaning.

Appropriate Words

Some words and expressions are outdated or overused. Inappropriate words and expressions do not impress a reader. They imply that the writer did not try hard enough to express ideas in a simple-to-understand manner. Apply the following guidelines to help make a message clear.

Avoid Cliches   Cliches are ready-made expressions. They are dull, overused, sometimes old-fashioned, and trite. Avoid cliches and use language that is more appropriate. Cliches are especially confusing to people whose first language is not English. Following are some examples of cliches:

- a stick-in-the-mud
- barking up the wrong tree
- bite off more than you can chew
- jump on the bandwagon
- keep your head above water
- keep your nose to the grindstone
- the bottom line
- the head honcho or the big enchilada
- the tip of the iceberg
- throw in the towel
- turn over a new leaf
- a day late and a dollar short

Eliminate Overused Words and Expressions   Replace overused words and expressions with exact words. In the following examples, notice that the words in the second column are more direct and clearer than the words in the first column.

OVERUSED EXPRESSIONS	EXACT EXPRESSIONS
acknowledge receipt of	received
at your earliest convenience	immediately, tomorrow, Friday
due to the fact that	because
enclosed herewith	here is
enclosed please find	enclosed is
in spite of the fact that	although
in the near future	within __ days
in the event that	should, if
pursuant to your request	as requested, you asked
thanking you in advance	thank you
under separate cover	in another package, separately
would like to recommend	recommend

Logical Organization

Well-organized messages are easy to read and understand. All ideas within a business letter, for example, should generally support one primary purpose. Likewise, each sentence within a paragraph should focus on one central idea or concept. When editing for clarity, ask yourself these questions:

- Is the main idea or purpose of the message clear to the reader?

- Does each paragraph express one idea?

- Do all of the paragraphs support the main idea of the message?

- Is there a logical relationship that binds all of the parts of the message together?

- Does one idea flow easily into another?

Exercise 14-3 • Proofread and Mark

Edit the following message for clarity using the appropriate proofreaders' marks. Write the revised message on the blank lines.

Enclosed herewith is the information pursuant to your request of February 10. In the event that you find these accommodations germane for your business trip next month, I would like to recommend the optimum hotels in the city.

_____

_____

_____

_____

_____

_____

Exercise 14-4 • Proofread and Mark

Edit the following message for clarity using the appropriate proofreaders' marks. Write the revised message on the blank lines.

So that you won't be barking up the wrong tree, I have listed two lodging alternatives where you will be comfortable. Remember to obtain receipts for your expenses to substantiate business expenses to the head honcho so that you can be remunerated for out-of-pocket expenses.

_____

_____

_____

_____

_____

_____

Exercise 14-5 • Proofread and Mark

Edit the following message for clarity using the appropriate proofreaders' marks. Write the revised message on the blank lines.

Due to the fact that fiscal budget preparations will begin in the near future, the bottom line is that we must have all of the essential facts regarding operations before the first meeting.

_____

_____

_____

_____

_____

_____

≫ Editing for Conciseness

Conciseness means saying only what is necessary to send the intended message to a reader. Conciseness requires eliminating unnecessary words or repetitious ideas. Businesspeople appreciate messages that make each word count. Concise messages have impact.

Unnecessary Words and Modifiers

Follow these guidelines to achieve conciseness:

- Delete phrases such as *I believe* or *in my opinion*. Generally, what is stated is the writer's belief; however, such expressions can serve the purpose of conciliation or diplomacy. They can soften criticism, too.

- Revise sentences that begin with *There is/are* or *Here is/are* whenever possible.

- Avoid using unnecessary modifiers; say *unique*, not absolutely unique, or *perfect* instead of almost perfect or nearly perfect.

Note in the table on the next page how the words in the right column have greater impact than those in the left column.

WORDY	CONCISE
as a matter of fact	in fact, indeed
at the present time	now
basic fundamentals	basics
come to the conclusion	conclude
consensus of opinion	consensus
during the time that	while
each and every	each, every (do not use both)
end result	result
feel free to	please
for the amount of $250	for $250
free gift	gift
in spite of the fact that	even though
in the amount of	for (give exact amount)
in the near future	soon, on (exact date)
past history	history
true facts	facts

Active Versus Passive Voice

Voice indicates whether the subject is performing the action or receiving the action of the verb. The **active voice** portrays the subject as performing the action and assigns responsibility to someone or something. For example, in the sentence, "The accountant wrote the report," the subject *accountant* is performing the action of the verb.

The **passive voice** portrays the subject as receiving the action of the verb. "The report was written by the accountant" is expressed in the passive voice and shows the subject *report* receiving the action of the verb. The passive voice is also used to de-emphasize a negative message. Generally, business messages are written in the active voice. As the examples shown below illustrate, the active voice is forceful and concise.

ACTIVE VOICE	PASSIVE VOICE
The instructor selected the software for the course.	The software for the course has been selected by the instructor.
Verify the facts before writing the report.	The facts should be verified before the report is written.
You did not submit your report on time.	Your report was not submitted on time. (de-emphasizes the negative message)

DIGITAL VISION/GETTY IMAGES

Active voice: The senior team reached an agreement on Tuesday.

Passive voice: An agreement was reached by the senior team on Tuesday.

Exercise 14-6 • Proofread and Mark

Edit the following sentences to make them more concise. Rewrite each sentence on the blank lines. Convert sentences written in the passive voice to the active voice.

1. There are several ideas that I would very much like to introduce at the staff meeting.

   _____

   _____

   _____

2. In my opinion, this report lacks the basic fundamentals needed to come to the conclusion that the budget be increased.

   _____

   _____

   _____

3. As a result of last week's increase in sales, all sales staff may anticipate receiving bonuses in the near future.

   _____

   _____

   _____

4. The past history indicates that the agents are always late whenever they must submit their reports.

   _____

   _____

   _____

5. It is my personal opinion that we should continue on with the project.

   _____

   _____

   _____

CONFUSED AND MISUSED WORDS

quiet   *adj.* calm; opposite of noisy

quit   *v.* to stop; to resign

quite   *adv.* completely; considerably

You must be **quiet** when working in the library.

I may **quit** my job.

Kirk didn't **quite** understand your directions.

recent   *adj.* occurring at a time immediately prior to the present; modern or new

resent   *v.* to feel anger from a sense of being injured or offended

re-sent   *v.* (past tense of *resend*) sent again

Jolene's **recent** haircut looks great!

Will you **resent** not being asked to run the meeting?

Dell **re-sent** the statement last week.

seas   *n. pl.* continuous bodies of salt water

sees   *v.* (third-person form of *see*) to perceive with the eye; to observe; to view

seize   *v.* to grasp suddenly and forcibly; to take or grab

Cruise ships sail the seven **seas**.

Lynda always **sees** the best in people.

The government can **seize** your assets if you don't pay your taxes.

---

*   Read the document at a normal, unhurried pace when editing so that you can concentrate on what you are reading.

*   Wait a few minutes before you edit your own writing. You may find mistakes that you would have otherwise overlooked.

*   Edit the document for one specific purpose at a time. For example, first check the accuracy of facts. Then check for completeness, conciseness, and clarity.

*   Proofread for mechanical errors after you have edited the document.

Proofreading & Editing Tips

PEP Tip

PROOFREADING APPLICATIONS

Analyze the following messages for completeness and clarity using the appropriate proofreaders' marks. On the blank lines, list details that are missing from the original message. Convert sentences in the passive voice to the active voice.

1. Enclosed please find your travel arrangements for the two-day conference at Reedley College on October 20–22. Attendees will be staying in the campus dorms. I would like to recommend that you take time to visit the Gourmet Garden for lunch or dinner while in town.

_____

_____

_____

_____

_____

2. Due to the fact that the board meeting is in the near future, a decision needs to be made on what to order in for lunch. We must make these arrangements early in spite of the fact that the restaurant is very accommodating.

_____

_____

_____

_____

3. As a result of last week's study session, Mark's and Lucy's test grades are up.

_____

_____

_____

Exercise 14-7 • Messages (*continued*)

4. In my opinion, this is the most successful fund-raiser we have ever had; and I think a decision should be made to have it again next year.

_____

_____

5. There are some issues that I want to be sure to discuss with each and every student at the next student council meeting.

_____

_____

Exercise 14-8 • Spelling and Word Usage Check

*Compare the words in Column **A** with the corresponding words in Column **B**. Use the appropriate proofreaders' marks to correct the misspelled or misused words. If both columns are correct, write **C** to the left of the number.*

Column A	Column B
1. adequate	adquate
2. admissable	admissible
3. capacity	capacity
4. continueing	continuing
5. dependant	dependent
6. familiar	familar
7. miscellaneous	miscellanous
8. practise	practice
9. referrence	reference
10. resturant	restaurant
11. accessable	accessible
12. immediately	immedaitely
13. The audit went quite well.	We had quiet a scare.
14. Bring a resent photo.	I re-sent the bill.
15. Dr. Orozco sees only babies.	Our motto is "Seas the Day!"

Exercise 14-9 • Word Division

*If a word is divided correctly, write **C** to the left of the number. If a word is divided incorrectly or in a manner that is not preferred, use the appropriate proofreaders' marks to correct the division.*

Ex. power	pres~~t~~ent	sym- phony	*present*
1. ac- knowl- edge	com- pan- y	li- a- bil- i- ty	_____
2. grad- u-ate	ad- a- mant	legit- imate	_____
3. spokes- person	president- elect	presump- tuous	_____
4. horserad- ish	self- rule	affilia- tion	_____
5. in- tro- duc- tion	pit- y	re- li- gious	_____
6. jumped	equiv- a- lent	ob- ject- tive	_____
7. exten- uating	memory	inter- ception	_____
8. fal- ling	re- called	father- in- law	_____
9. hyper- tension	dis- tres- sing	con- tami- na- tion	_____
10. cir- cum- stan- tial	reconstruc- tion	domi- nant	_____
11. in- cen- di- ary	re- mov- ing	over- slept	_____
12. crit- i- cal	remark- able	han- di- cap	_____
13. sub- stan- tial	jour- nal- ist	co- in- ci- dence	_____
14. ex- ces- sive	co- op- er- ate	cat- a- clys- mic	_____
15. ad- van- tage	profes- sor	sis- ter- hood	_____

Exercise 14-10 • Business Letter

Work with a partner to edit the following letter for correctness, conciseness, and clarity in content. Supply additional information, if necessary, to make the message more complete and clearer. Facts: Letter was addressed to Ms. Nereyda Garza-Lozano, 1101 East University, Fresno, CA 93741-0765, in block style with open punctuation. The correct information is printed in the table on page 265.

STATE CENTER COMMUNITY COLLEGE DISTRICT
1525 East Weldon Avenue, Fresno, CA 93741-2312
509-555-0110 Fax: 509-555-0170
E-mail: scccd@brakenet.com

September 8, 20--

Ms. Nereyda Garza-Lozano
1101 East University
Fresno, CA 93741-0765

Dear Ms. Garza-Lozano

Congratulations are in order! Your proposal for a study abroad program to Salamanca, Spain, was approved by the board of trustees during the time that they met last night. You are authorized to move forward with plans at the present time.

In spite of the fact that the budget is tight, the board believes that a trip such as this is one that each and every one of our students should have the opportunity to experience. Our office staff will prepare a flyer for you pursuant to your request. We will print copies in the amount of 500 for distribution to students. If you require more, feel free to request them. Due to the fact that there are so many details, please check the following information for accuracy.

Academic Courses

Spanish 1	Beginning	4 units
Spanish 2	High Beginning	4 units
Spanish 3	Intermediate or Spanish 3NS (for native speakers)	3 units
Spanish 4	Intermediate or Spanish 4NS (for native speakers)	4 units
Spanish 5	The Short Story (Spain)	3 units
Spanish 6	The Short Story (Latin America)	3 units
Spanish 7	Advanced Grammar and Composition	3 units
Spanish 8	Advanced Conversation	3 units

Exercise 14-10 • Business Letter (*continued*)

Ms. Nereyda Garza-Lozano
Page 2
September 28, 20--

Flights
Departure from Fresno to Madrid: June 2, 20--. Our flight is scheduled to leave at 7:15 a.m. Be at the airport by 5:15 a.m.

Return from Madrid to Fresno; July 20, 20--. We are scheduled to arrive in Fresno at 8:45 p.m.

Passports
Because this is an international flight, you will be required to carry a passport. If you do not have a current passport, please apply for one immediately. The process can take up to two months. You can obtain an application form at any post office (or online at http://www.usps.com) or at many public libraries.

Payment Information
Program fee is $4,500, which includes round-trip air and ground transportation from Fresno to Salamanca and housing with a Spanish family (including breakfast and lunch and dinner). Application deadline is March 1, 20--, with a deposit of $550; balance of $3,900 is due by March 24, 20--. Deposit is nonrefundable. Students are enrolled on a first-come, first-served basis.

Please notify me immediately of any necessary corrections. Keep up the good work—this is a wonderful opportunity for our students. Thank you for your service.

Sincerely

Mr. Kim Quesada
Administrator

rrh

Exercise 14-10 • Business Letter (*continued*)

Ms. Nereyda Garza-Lozano
Page 3
September 28, 20--

Academic Courses		
Spanish 1	Beginning	4 units
Spanish 2	High Beginning	4 units
Spanish 3	Intermediate or Spanish 3NS (for native speakers)	4 units
Spanish 4	High Intermediate or Spanish 4NS (for native speakers)	4 units
Spanish 5	The Short Story (Spain)	3 units
Spanish 6	The Short Story (Latin America)	3 units
Spanish 7	Advanced Grammar and Composition	3 units
Spanish 8	Advanced Conversation	3 units
Flights		
June 2, 20--: Fresno to Madrid; 7:15 a.m. departure		
July 2, 20--: Madrid to Fresno; 8:45 p.m. arrival		
Payment Information		

Program fee is $4,500, which includes round-trip air and ground transportation from Fresno to Salamanca and housing with a Spanish family (including breakfast and lunch or dinner). Application deadline is March 1, 20--, with a deposit of $550; balance of $3,950 is due by March 24, 20--. Deposit is nonrefundable. Students are enrolled on a first-come, first-served basis.

Exercise 14-11 • Brochure

Edit the following brochure text for correctness, clarity, and conciseness. Then proofread for mechanical errors.

SENSIBLE EATING ON THE ROAD

Don't be a stick-in-the-mud about your eating habits while you are traveling. It is easy to follow a sensible diet while you're at home where everything is familiar. When you travel, however, you must practice a different discipline. Try these healthy, easy-to-follow rules for eating on a plane or in a restaurant.

Eat a good, healthy breakfast. A healthy breakfast includes whole wheat toast, cereal (hot or cold with skimmed milk), and fresh fruit—not canned. Special dietetic menus are sometimes available pursuant to your request on flights, so check on this before the departure date.

If you are eating later than usual, counting lunch as dinner and keeping the entree on the lean side is a good idea. The amount of food served in restaurants at lunch is usually smaller than what is served at dinner—and it costs less too. Use salad dressing sparingly. If you are dining buffet style, take only one small serving. Don't go back for seconds in spite of the fact that you may want to.

Develop a habit of eating healthful snacks, such as fresh fruits and vegetables, and keep them handy. You can use them to keep your head above water between meals. Another good habit is to drink a lot of water; it fills you up. The fact of the matter is that you should drink eight cups of water each day. Water is a great substitute for sweet, syrupy soft drinks. If possible, avoid caffeine; it stimulates your appetite and may cause nervousness and insomnia.

Use these tips whenever you travel, never throw in the towel. Eat right and stay healthy!

PROOFREADING AT THE COMPUTER

Exercise 14-12 • Manuscript

1. Open 14-12 from the Chapter 14 folder on the student CD. (This is a computer copy of Exercise 14-11.)
2. Edit the text for correctness, conciseness, and clarity, using the marked copy for Exercise 14-11. Use the spelling checker.
3. Produce the manuscript following the standard procedures described in the previous chapters.

Exercise 14-13 • Letter

1. Open 14-13 from the Chapter 14 folder on the student CD.
2. Edit the text for correctness, conciseness, consistency, and clarity. Use the spelling checker.
3. Produce the document following the standard procedures.

Exercise 14-14 • E-mail Message

1. Open 14-14 from the Chapter 14 folder on the student CD.
2. Edit the text for content, correctness, conciseness, consistency, and clarity. Use the spelling checker.
3. Produce the document following the standard procedures.

CUMULATIVE APPLICATION

Exercise 14-15 • Business Letter

Proofread and correct all errors using the appropriate proofreaders' marks. Facts: Letter was addressed to Mr. Alfonso Farentino, 4098 Bellflower Road, Aiken, SC 29808-8616, in block style with mixed punctuation.

TWENTIETH CENTURY BUSINESS COLLEGE
400 Broadway • Aiken, SC 29802-1532
803-555-0122 Fax: 803-555-0123
E-mail: century@sccom.com

Mr. Alfonso Farentino
4098 Bellflower Road
Aiken, SC 29808-8616

Dear Mr. Farentino

Dean Stephanie Quiring informed me that you have completed all of the requirements for the advanced course in Business Administration. I understand that you are now submitting your application for employment to a number of inter-national companies recommended by our Placement Department.

Congratulations! I am confident that you will be successful in obtaining employment within a very short time.

While obtaining employment is your primary concern now, I strongly encourage you to take the long view and to consider your career in relation to other factors that will come into play as you advance in your profession—your work, your family, you continuing education, and your social life.

Your work. Because work will be a major part of your life, you must be prepared to make adjustments, if not sacrifices, to accommodate yourself to the urgencies and requirements of your chosen field. You may be asked to work a few hours of uncompensated overtime, you may have to come in early and leave late when the workload is heavy, or you may be forced to postpone a vacation during the busy season. This is the name of the game, and it may well be the pattern for many years—at least until you establish yourself in your career. Don't be stubborn; accept it graciously.

Your family. Your family must come first. But there's no denying the fact that there will be times when you must make a difficult decision concerning the little League game you promise to attend but can't, the school play starring your daughter that gets lost in your're busy schedule, and the class reunion your wife is looking forward to attending but can't because of an unexpected visit by your company president.

Your continuing education. Education is an invaluable tool in your career path. It prepares you for greater responsibility and keeps you up to date on the changes and developments in your chosen field. Take advantage of this opportunity because education has an impact on your future.

Exercise 14-15 • Business Letter (*continued*)

Mr. Alfonso Farentino
Page 2
(current date)

<u>Your social life.</u> Socializing is important in many businesses. Train yourself to be not only an interesting dinner partner but also a desirable one. Learn how to initiate or hold a conversation, take time to learn, if not master, the basic dance steps; and develop an interest in art and music and painting. Besides being enjoyable in and of themselves, these skills can also be a factor in your career development as well as position advancement.

Before excepting any job offer, ask yourself if the company is a good fit for you. You should also stay organized; the interviews can come quickly, and the follow-up process is important in your job search. Don't underestimate the importance of thank-you letters.

Remember that a career is more than an occupation; it is a way of life that has a bearing on the lives of everyone with who you come in contact. You will have choices to make; and if you make them wisely, they will sustain you throughout your lifetime.

Again, congratulations! I wish you the very best in what, I am confident, will be a very successful career.

Sincerely,

Eldon R. Goodsen, Ph.d.
President

tcp

Bookmark It!

Want more practice? Go to www.cengage.com/keyboarding/pagel for more proofreading activities.

Investment Company

PageNors Investments

Instructions: You work as a student intern for Lynn Fallgastarr. Lynn is the general manager of PageNors Investments, located in Madison, Wisconsin. Your responsibilities include proofreading all of Lynn's internal company documents and ensuring that all information is current and correct. The following pages show a variety of business documents prepared by Lynn as she carries out her duties as general manager of PageNors Investments.

Objectives

- Demonstrate an understanding of the importance of accurate proofreading through the careful review of typical business documents.

- Identify a variety of proofreading errors.

- Use appropriate proofreaders' marks to show what corrections should be made.

>> PageNors Investments

Document 1 lists the correct names, addresses, and telephone numbers of the people Lynn corresponds with in this project. As you read through these documents, you will need to compare the names and addresses in Document 1 with the names and addresses used in the other six documents.

Document 1 • Names and Addresses for PageNors Investments

Miss Jayne J. Branch
3904 West Avenue
Boscobel, WI 53805-1234

Ms. Lynn Fallgastarr, General Manager
PageNors Investments
89037 State Street
Madison, WI 53701-0087
608-555-0173   608-555-0175 (Fax)

Mr. Kyle J. LaCrosse
63024 Mineral Point Road, #501
Madison, WI 53705-4399

Mr. Jackson Norstern, President
PageNors Investments
89037 State Street
Madison, WI 53701-0087
608-555-0170   608-555-0175 (Fax)

Ms. Sally Page, CEO
PageNors Investments
89037 State Street
Madison, WI 53701-0087
608-555-0171   608-555-0175 (Fax)

Document 2 • PageNors Investments Web Page

Proofread the following Web page letter and apply proofreaders' marks. Open P2-D2 from the student CD and make corrections.

PageNors Investments was originated by Sally Page and Jackson Norstern in 2006 as a premier investment firm serving the needs of individuals living in the Madison, WI, area. Madison is located in Dane County in south-central Wisconsin, 77 miles West of Milwaukee and 122 miles Northwest of Chicago. Madison is also home to the University of Wisconsin-Madison. The Madison Metropolitan Statistical Area has an estimated population of 570,000 people and is one of the fastest growing regions in the state.

The University of Wisconsin-Madison and Wisconsin state government is Madison's two largest employers. The Madison economy continues to change with the times and is now based primarily on consumer services and technology, particularly in the advertising, health, and biotech sectors. Many Madison businesses are attracted to the area because of the high educational level and the strong work ethic of it's employees.

The main office for PageNors Investments is located at 89073 State Street in downtown Madison, just blocks from the state capitol. Office hours are Monday through Friday from 8:30 a.m. – 5:30 p.m. and Saturday from 8:30 – 11:30 a.m. If these times are not convenient for you, call 608-555-0173 to discuss a time that fits into your schedule.

PageNors Invesments provide the following services: meeting individually with clients, providing investment advice, purchasing stocks and bonds, selling stocks and bonds, providing educational seminars, and we also provide information about mortgages.

We are eager to meet with new clients, regardless of their income level or ability to invest. It is our philosophy that everyone needs to learn how and when to invest, and we are eager to educate people on planning for retirement. Whether you plan to retire next year or forty years from now, we can help you meet your short-term and long term goals.

Our fee schedule is based on the services we provide—not on the investments we sell you. We encourage you to meet with us as often as you feel necessary, but we recommend you schedule at least an annual meeting with us. No one can know too much about their investments and how well those investments are doing in today's economy.

The main office staff for PageNors Investments are as follows:

Ms. Susan Page, CEO
Mr. Jackson Norstern, President
Ms. Lynn Fallgastarr, General Manager

We look forward to serving you investment needs. Please call us today to set up an appointment!

Proofread the following letter and apply proofreaders' marks. Open P2-D3 from the student CD and make corrections.

April 5, 20--

PAGENORS INVESTMENTS
89037 State Street
Madison, WI 53701-0087
608-555-0173
608-555-0175 (Fax)

Miss Jayne O. Branch
3904 West Ave.
Boscobel, WI 53805-2134

Dear Miss Branch,

Thank you for meeting with us last week to discuss your investments and a strategy to move forward in these difficult times. We understand your concern about the loss of capitol in your retirement accounts and we hope you have reached a decision your about future investments.

We continue to encourage our clients to develop a strategy for dividing there investments between a variety of stock, bond, IRA, and other accounts. This is good advice, regardless of economic times. No one should invest more than 10 percent of their account value in only one stock. Diversity in your investments will help your account(s) to grow in value through out the year.

As we discussed on February 30, you would be wise to select stocks from the following categories; energy, consumer staples, health care, industrials, or utilities. Many of these stocks provides quarterly dividends and are expected to increase in value within.

The enclosed brochure provides information you will find of value in selecting potential investments? Please call us if you have any questions.

Sincerely,

Ms. Lynn Fallgastar, general manager

Enclosure

Document 4 • Memorandum to PageNors Investment Employees

Proofread the following memo and apply proofreaders' marks. Open P2-D4 from the student CD and make corrections.

TO: Staff/Employees

FROM: Lynne Fallgastarr, General manager

DATE: April 9, 20--

SUBJECT: Mutual Funds

When you meet with prospective clients, please discuss with him the importance of investing in mutual funds for long-term growth. Our clients recieve a number of advantages. When they purchase mutual funds through PageNors investments:

- Ease of purchase and selling of mutual fund shares
- Automatic diversification
- Automatic reinvestment dividends of
- And finally, they have expert portfolio management

Our clients should also be informed about the differences between "load" and "no-load" funds so they can make wise financial decisions. More than half of all mutual funds charges a front-end load when mutual fund shares are first purchased. This load is usually somewhere between 3.00 - 5.75%, and is often based on a sliding fee which decreases with the size of the purchase.

Some funds may charge a back-end load Back-end loads are also called redemption fees as it is charged when you sell the mutual fund. The net affect of this fee is to reduce your profit or to add to your loss. Another type of fee is a deferred load. This fee is sometimes called a contingent deferred sales fee as it is levied when you sell shares of mutual funds within a certain time after you first purchase these shares. The purpose of the deferred load is to discourage your from jumping into and out of mutual funds too quickly.

Most funds also charge a marketing fee, often called a 12b-1 fee. 12b-1 fee are charges for marketing and advertising the fund and typically are around 0.25 - 1.25%. Their is only 1 reason to pay a load of any kind and that reason is to pay your investment broker or advisor for financial planning or analysis they do on your behalf.

Finally, you should discuss with your clients management fees. All funds, weather they are load or no-load funds, charge a management fee to compensate portfolio managers for their services, pay for rent, etc. The more your clients know, the better will be the relationship you have with him/her.

Document 5 • E-mail to Ms. Sally Page, CEO, and Mr. Jackson Norstern, President

Proofread the following e-mail and apply proofreaders' marks. Open P2-D5 from the student CD and make corrections.

TO:	Sally Page, CEO
	Jackson Norstern, president
FROM:	Lynn Fallgastarr, General Manager
DATE:	April 15, 20--
SUBJECT:	Meeting to Discuss New Satellite Office

Please check your schedule for the week of Sep. 5 to discuss the possible edition of a new satellite office in either Lansing, Michigan or St. Paul, Minnesota, in 20--. In preparation for this meeting, please do the following:

1. Analyze our balance sheet for the previous fiscal period.

2. Read the financial reports prepared by our CPA.

3. Review comments from our current employees.

4. We would also like you to think about a strategy for strategically moving forward in these difficult economic times.

The edition of a new office for PageNors Investments. Would mean significant risks, but it could also mean increased income for our shareholders. However I believe that now is the apropriate time to consider growth of our company. I am confident that our growth depend on expanding to other neighboring states.

If you have any questions for I in preparation for this meeting please call me to discuss your concerns or questions. I am eager to discuss this issue while.

Document 6 • PageNors Investments Newsletter Article

Proofread the following article and apply proofreaders' marks. Open P2-D6 from the student CD and make corrections.

RETIREMENT STRATEGIES

Most of you is investing your money today for one basic reason: to be able to retire one day and not have to work past a certain age. But to be able to retire, especially given todays economy, you need to make wide investment choices along the way.

There are three fundamental truths for investing for retirement. 1st, you need to have one or more goals for retirement. Second, successful investment means taking risk. Thirdly, you must diversify.

Retirement Goals

Every investor should have a goal—such as building a new house, sending their children to college, taking a long vacation, retiring early, or to start a new business. Goals for retirement generally need to be long-term goals. Fortunately, time is usually on your side. Time helps you reach your goals, because of compound interest. This means that you earn interest on the interest already earned. For example, if you invest $10,000 at 8%, the original investment of $10,000 grows to $14,700 after five years, $31,700 after 15 years, and $68,000 after 25 years. This is true even if you never add another Dollar to your original investment!

Taking Risk

Investing for the long term may be risky. Markets sometimes go up, but sometimes they go down as well. One fact on your side is this; the more time you have until retirement, the more risk you can afford to make. The benefits of compound interest outweigh the risks within the marketplace. While no investor want to lose money, they still have time to make up for any potential losses that might occur in the short-term.

A willingness to take risk provides you with the oppporsunity to earn increased returns. Some investments, like a savings account or a CD, provides little risk and a reduced potential to earn higher levels of interest. Other investments, like stocks and commodities, have the potential to have much higher levels of risk. But that investment also provides the potential for a higher rate of return. Which would you rather have? Would you rather have an investment that earns only two or three percent interest or an investment that has the potential for a high rate of return.

Diversification

No investment performs best all of the time. During any period of time, some investments will increase in value while other investments will go down in value. When one investment provides a dividend, another investment may provide no dividend. When you diversify your portfolio, you place you investments in various types of investments: stocks, bonds, mutual funds, CDs, etc.

Long-Term Investments

Over a period of time, the best long-term investments. Have been stocks. As a buyer, you may purchase stocks either directly from a company or through a broker. Stocks may or may not pay dividends to individual owners. When paid, a dividend is usually paid quarterly. Buying stocks through a broker provides you with professional management and expert advice. Buying stock through a discount broker may save you money in the short-term, but they won't generally offer any advice on what stocks to buy. In the long term, stocks have outperformed all other investments by a big margin.

Generally, you will find 6 general categories of stocks: growth stocks, blue-chip stocks, income stocks, cyclical stocks, small company stocks, and international stocks. Growth stocks have the potential for growing faster then the economy in general, and investors like growth stocks because of the likelihood that share prices will go up significantly in the long run. Blue-chip stocks are stocks from industry leaders. These stocks have a consistent earnings growth and share prices generally go up in the long term.

Income stocks pay out a large portion of profits their in the form of quarterly dividends. These companies are usually mature companies that carry little risk. Even if the economy does fail, income stocks provide a cushion beneath the share price, because investors still receive the dividend.

Small company stocks are usually newer, fast-growing companies. Their share price is risky because prices tend to be volatile over a period of time. Finally, international stocks, help diversify your portfolio because foreign markets may perform differently than U.S. companies.

Conclusion

When you meet with your broker, come prepared with a list of questions you want answer. Don't be afraid to ask for advice; come prepared with a list of questions about why common stocks might be a better investment then preferred stocks or why one stock is riskier than another stock. Your broker is available to help you make the decisions that will prepare you to retire and live comfortably at the level to which you are accustomed.

Document 7 • Letter to Kyle LaCrosse

Proofread the following letter and apply proofreaders' marks. Open P2-D7 from the student CD and make corrections.

April 9, 20--

PAGENORS INVESTMENTS
89037 State Street
Madison, WI 53701-0087
608-555-0173
608-555-0175 (Fax)

Ms. Kyle J. LaCrosse
63024 Mineral Point Rd., #505
Madison, WI 53705-4399

Dear Mr. LaCrosse,

As we discussed during your portfolio review last week, we believe that the economic recovery is well underway and that now is the time to return to investing in stocks which are most likely to appreciate in value, and provide a dividend of 4 percent or more.

My recommendation is that you read the enclosed analysis provided for each of the following stocks: AT&T, Chevron, Coca-Cola, ConocoPhillips, Duke Energy, Home Depot, Illinois Tool works, Johnson & Johnson, Kimberly-Clark, Kraft Foods, and Eli Lilly. These are all top notch stocks which promise to provide dividends that will continue to increase the value of your investment portfolio in years to come.

The sectors that have the greatest momentum now. Appears to be in consumer staples, energy, health care, industrails, and utilities. You might also wish to look into stocks from technology and real estate as these sectors may also have great potential in the years ahead.

Once you have had an opportunity to read the stock analysis, please narrow your list down to 4 or 5 stocks to discuss them in detail. I look forward to answering your questions and to provide you with additional information so you can select the stock you want to purchase.

We certainly believe that the recent financial crisis has reshaped many peoples attitudes about money and investing. While investing always involves risks, you can decrease that risk by investing with a long term perspective, diversifying your portfolio, and focus on quality investments.

Sincerely,

Ms. Lynne Fallgastarr, General Manager

Enclosures

GUIDELINES FOR WORD DIVISION

RULE 1   Divide a word only between syllables. A one-syllable word cannot be divided.

SYLLABICATION	MARKED WORD	HYPHENATED WORD
per fec tion	per/fec/tion	per- fec- tion
pho to graph	pho/to/graph	pho- to- graph

RULE 2   Do not divide a word with five or fewer letters. Avoid dividing a word with six letters.

SYLLABICATION	MARKED WORD	HYPHENATED WORD
pow er	—	power
cit y	—	city
lo cate	—	locate

RULE 3   At least two letters must appear at the *end* of a line (*in-*crease), and at least three letters must appear at the *beginning* of the next line (larg- *est*, but not larg-*er*).

Note: Although it is acceptable to divide after a two-letter syllable at the beginning of a word (*re-* pairing), it is better to avoid doing so (*repair-* ing).

SYLLABICATION	MARKED WORD	HYPHENATED WORD
in ter cept	inter/cept	inter- cept
sym pho ny	sym/phony	sym- phony

RULE 4   Generally, divide between double consonants. However, when the root word ends in double consonants and a suffix is added to the word, divide between the root word and the suffix.

SYLLABICATION	MARKED WORD	HYPHENATED WORD
ha rass ment	harass/ment	harass- ment
suc cess ful	success/ful	success- ful

RULE 5   Divide between double consonants when the final consonant of the root word is doubled before adding a suffix.

SYLLABICATION	MARKED WORD	HYPHENATED WORD
ad mit tance	admit/tance	admit- tance
pro gram ming	program/ming	program- ming

RULE 6   Divide after a single-vowel syllable except when the single-vowel syllable is followed by the ending *ble*, *bly*, *cle*, or *cal*.

SYLLABICATION	MARKED WORD	HYPHENATED WORD
pos i tive	posi/tive	posi- tive
res o nance	reso/nance	reso- nance
log i cal	log/ical	log- ical

RULE 7   Divide between two single-vowel syllables when each of the two vowels is pronounced separately.

SYLLABICATION	MARKED WORD	HYPHENATED WORD
sit u a tion	situ/ation	situ- ation
e val u a tion	evalu/ation	evalu- ation

RULE 8   Divide compound words between the words. If the compound word is hyphenated, the only acceptable point of division is after the hyphen. In such cases, use the diagonal mark without the hyphen symbol.

	MARKED WORD	HYPHENATED WORD
Insert diagonal mark. /	self/control	self- control
Insert diagonal mark and hyphen. /	tax/free	tax- free
	senator/elect	senator- elect

RULE 9 Do not divide abbreviations, numbers, contractions, acronymns (initials that represent words), times, or units of measure (a number with a descriptive word). Units of measure must always be written together.

mdse.	UNICEF	15-ft. board
9.25 percent	7 1/2 lb.	6 min.
couldn't	8 kg	C.A.R.E.
Flight 12	10:15 a.m.	No. 10

RULE 10 Avoid dividing proper names, titles, addresses, or dates. If it is necessary to divide these elements, choose a logical point that will give the best readability.

RULE	EXAMPLE
Divide before a surname (or after the middle initial if it is used).	Carl T. Santos
Divide between the city and state, not between the state and the ZIP Code.	Green Bay, Wisconsin
	San Diego, CA 92110-2134
Divide dates between the day and the year.	April 15, 20--.
Divide between parts of a city name.	Santa Barbara

CONFUSED WORDS

accept *v.* to agree to; to receive
except *prep.* but; other than

addition *n.* process of summing; an added part
edition *n.* copies of a published book

advice *n.* recommendation
advise *v.* to give advice; to inform

affect *v.* to influence
effect *v.* to bring about; *n.* result

all ready *adj.* (two words) completely ready
already *adv.* before now or a specified time

all right *adj.* (two words) all correct or appropriate
alright unacceptable spelling of *all right*

all together *adv.* (two words) gathered into a single unit or group; collected in one place
altogether *adv.* entirely, completely, utterly

allot *v.* to allocate or distribute
a lot *n.* (two words) a large amount; many
alot unacceptable spelling of *a lot*

allude *v.* to make an indirect reference to something
elude *v.* to avoid or escape notice

among *prep.* comparison of three or more persons or things
between *prep.* comparison of only two persons or things

any one *adj./pro.* (two words) certain person; use when the pronoun is followed by an *of* phrase
anyone *pron.* anybody; any person at all

assistance *n.* help
assistants *n.* helpers

assure *v.* to give confidence to; to feel sure; to convince
ensure *v.* to make sure, certain
insure *v.* to cover with insurance; to guarantee; to secure from harm

can *v.* to be able to do something
may *v.* to be possible; to give permission

capital *n.* official seat of government; money to invest
capitol *n.* a building in which a legislature meets

cent *n.* 1/100; penny
scent *n.* a distinctive odor; perfume; a sense of smell
sent *v.* past tense and past participle of *send*

cite *v.* to quote; to acknowledge
sight *v.* a vision; *v.* to see or observe
site *n.* a location

complement *n.* something that adds to or completes a whole; *v.* to complete or make perfect
compliment *n.* an expression of praise; *v.* to praise

cooperation *n.* working together
corporation *n.* a legal entity

correspondence *n.* a communication by exchange of letters
correspondents *n.* those who write letters

council *n.* an assembly of people
counsel *v.* to give advice or guidance; *n.* a lawyer or group of lawyers; *n.* advice received

currant *n.* small, seedless raisin
current *adj.* up-to-date; *n.* electricity

dairy *n.* a commercial firm that processes and/or sells milk and milk products
diary *n.* a daily personal record of events, experiences, and observations

device *n.* a machine or gadget
devise *v.* to invent or to plan

envelop *v.* to cover with a wrapping
envelope *n.* a paper container for correspondence

farther *adv.* more distant
further *adj.* to a greater degree; additional

foreword *n.* an introduction; a preface
forward *adj.* at or near the front; *v.* to send mail

its *adj.* possessive form of *it*
it's contraction of *it is* or *it has*

later *adv.* after
latter *adj.* the second of two

lay *v.* to place or set down an object
lie *v.* to rest; to recline

lean *adj.* thin; not fat; meager; *v.* to slant away from a vertical position
lien *n.* the right to sell property of a debtor

loose *adj.* not fastened; free
lose *v.* unable to find; to fail to win
loss *n.* a person or thing lost; a defeat

may be *v.* to be allowed or permitted to
maybe *adv.* perhaps; possibly

moral *adj.* concerned with goodness or badness of human action and character; *n.* lesson contained in a story or an event
morale *n.* attitude of an individual

personal *adj.* private; pertaining to a particular person
personnel *n.* people employed; staff of a company

precede *v.* to come before in time or rank
proceed *v.* to go forward

principal *adj.* main; *n.* money that earns interest; *n.* head official of a school; chief
principle *n.* a basic truth; a rule or standard

quiet *adj.* calm; opposite of noisy
quit *v.* to stop; to resign
quite *adv.* completely; considerably

raise *v.* to lift; to move upward; to bring up or rear; to grow things; *n.* an increase in pay
rise *v.* to get up; to move upward by itself; to increase in intensity, volume, or speed

recent *adj.* occurring at a time immediately prior to the present; modern or new
resent *v.* to feel anger from a sense of being injured or offended
re-sent *v.* (past tense of *resend*) sent again

right *adj.* correct, truth, proper; opposite of left
rite *n.* religious or solemn ceremony
write *v.* to form letters of the alphabet on a surface with a tool such as a pen or pencil

seas *n. pl.* continuous bodies of salt water
sees *v.* (third-person form of *see*) to perceive with the eye; to observe; to view
seize *v.* to grasp suddenly and forcibly; to take or grab

stationary *adj.* immovable; fixed
stationery *n.* writing materials

than *conj.* used in comparison
then *adv.* at that time

their *adj.* possessive form of they
there *adv.* in or at that place
they're contraction of they are

to *prep.* toward; for the purpose of
too *adv.* also; more than enough
two *n.* one more than one

vain *adj.* without success; not resulting in the desired outcome; conceited
vane *n.* a rotating device that indicates the direction of the wind
vein *n.* a blood vessel

weather *n.* conditions in the atmosphere; *v.* to endure
whether *conj.* if

who's contraction of *who* is
whose possessive form of *who* and *which*

your possessive form of *you*
you're contraction of *you are*

FREQUENTLY MISSPELLED WORDS

absence
accessible
accommodate
achieve
acknowledge
acknowledgment
adequate
admissible
advantageous
advisable
already
analyze
anxiety
anxious
appearance
appropriate
approximately
arrangements
assessment
attendance

beginning
believe
beneficial
benefit
brochure
business

calendar
canceled
cannot
capabilities
capacity
categories
cautious
censor
changeable
clientele
commission
commitment
committee
communication
compel
compelled

compliance
conceited
conceive
conference
congratulations
conscientious
conscious
consensus
consistent
consultant
continuing
controlling
convenience
cooperate
corporate
correspondence
counseling
courteous
criteria
criticize
curriculum
customer

decision
defendant
definition
dependent
description
design
desirable
desperate
development
disastrous
dissatisfied
dominant

efficient
eligible
eliminate
embarrassed
emergency
emphasis
enclosing
encouragement

environment
equipment
especially
evaluate
exceed
excellent
existence
experience
extension
extraordinary

facilities
facsimile
faculty
familiar
February
finally
financial
foreign

gauge
government
grammar
grievance
guarantee
guidance

harassed
hierarchy
hindrance
hors d'oeuvres
hygiene

ignorance
illegible
immediately
impatient
implement
indispensable
influential
installation
institution
intelligence
interfere

interference
interrupt
irate

jealousy
judgment

knowledgeable

legitimate
leisure
liability
library
license
lieutenant
likelihood

maintenance
manageable
mathematics
maximum
mediocre
millennium
miscellaneous
misspell
mortgage
mysterious

necessary
negotiable
noticeable

obstacle
obvious
occasionally
occurred
occurrence
offered
offering
omitted
opportunity
optimism
ordinarily

palette
parallel
parliament
partial
participation
particular
pastime
pedestrian
percent
permissible
perseverance
pertinent
phenomenon
plagiarism
plagiarize
possibility
potential
practice
precede
precedent
preferable
preference
preferential
preferred
prejudice
preparation
prior
privilege
proceed
processing
proficiency
proficient
pronunciation
psychology
pursue

questionnaire

realize
receipt
receive
recognize
recommendations
reference

referred
regard
representative
resemblance
responsibility
restaurant

salary
schedule
self-confident

separate
session
similar
simultaneous
situation
sophomore
submitted
substantially
succeed
sufficient

susceptible
symmetrical
synonymous

technical
tendency
thorough
tournament
transferred
truly

unanimous
unique
unnecessary
usable
usage
usually
utilization

vacuum
vague

valuable
vegetarian
vehicle
vendor
vengeance

warrant
worthwhile

yacht

COMMONLY MISSPELLED U.S. CITIES

Abilene, TX

Albuquerque, NM

Berkeley, CA

Bismarck, ND

Boise, ID

Butte, MT

Charlotte, NC

Chattanooga, TN

Cincinnati, OH

Cleveland, OH

Decatur, GA or AL

Des Moines, IA

Dubuque, IA

Durham, NC

Everett, WA

Fayetteville, NC or AR

Fremont, CA, NE, or OH

Gainesville, FL or GA

Hialeah, FL

Honolulu, HI

Indianapolis, IN

Milwaukee, WI

Pasadena, CA or TX

Philadelphia, PA

Phoenix, AZ

Pittsburg, CA or KS

Pittsburgh, PA

Raleigh, NC

Roanoke, VA

San Bernardino, CA

San Francisco, CA

Savannah, GA

Schenectady, NY

Shreveport, LA

Sioux City, IA

Sioux Falls, SD

Tallahassee, FL

Tucson, AZ

Worcester, MA

SPELLINGS AND ABBREVIATIONS OF STATES AND U.S. TERRITORIES

Alabama	AL	Illinois	IL	Nebraska	NE	South Carolina	SC
Alaska	AK	Indiana	IN	Nevada	NV	South Dakota	SD
Arizona	AZ	Iowa	IA	New Hampshire	NH	Tennessee	TN
Arkansas	AR	Kansas	KS	New Jersey	NJ	Texas	TX
California	CA	Kentucky	KY	New Mexico	NM	Utah	UT
Colorado	CO	Louisiana	LA	New York	NY	Vermont	VT
Connecticut	CT	Maine	ME	North Carolina	NC	Virgin Islands	VI
Delaware	DE	Maryland	MD	North Dakota	ND	Virginia	VA
District of Columbia	DC	Massachusetts	MA	Ohio	OH	Washington	WA
		Michigan	MI	Oklahoma	OK	West Virginia	WV
Florida	FL	Minnesota	MN	Oregon	OR	Wisconsin	WI
Georgia	GA	Mississippi	MS	Pennsylvania	PA	Wyoming	WY
Hawaii	HI	Missouri	MO	Puerto Rico	PR		
Idaho	ID	Montana	MT	Rhode Island	RI		

Index

A

abbreviations, 63–64, 72
  general style, 64–67
  informal or technical style, 67–69
academic courses, capitalization rules for, 47
academic degrees, capitalization rules for, 50
academic titles
  abbreviations for, 64–65
  capitalization rules for, 50
accuracy, 3
acronyms, 191
action verbs, 113
active voice, 257
added copy errors, 12–13
addresses
  abbreviations for, 66–67
  commas in, 174, 175
  letters, 207, 208–9
adjectives
  capitalization of, 47–48
  consecutive, 172–73
age bias, 155
agencies, abbreviations for, 66
align copy (proofreaders' mark), 204
a.m., 48, 67, 86
American Psychological Association (APA) citation styles, 338
amounts, expressed as words, 85
antecedents, 130–33
apostrophes, 189–91
application letter, 232, 233, 234
appositives, 170
appropriate words, 252–53
articles, capitalization rules for, 51
artistic works, capitalization rules for, 51
as, pronoun usage following, 138
associations, abbreviations for, 66
attention line, 209

B

balanced appearance, in letters, 205–6
begin new paragraph (proofreaders' mark), 204
bias-free language, 152–56
block letter format, 213, 214
body
  letters, 207, 210
  reports, 226

brand names, capitalization rules for, 47
buildings, capitalization rules for, 47
business correspondence, abbreviations and, 67
business forms, abbreviations in, 67–68
business reports. *See* reports
business terms, bias and, 153

C

capitalization, 45–52
capitalize (proofreaders' mark), 46
case, of pronouns, 133–38
categories, numbers in, 84
center (proofreaders' mark), 204
change copy as indicated (proofreaders' mark), 112
change letter (proofreaders' mark), 13
chronological resume, 229
citations, 228
city names, abbreviations for, 67
clarity, editing for, 251–55
clauses, 148
  colons and, 188
  independent, 186
  introductory, 168
  restrictive, 171
  semicolons and, 186, 187
clichés, 252–53
close up space (proofreaders' mark), 12, 64
clubs, capitalization rules for, 47
collective nouns, 118–19, 131–32
colons, 188–89
combination resume, 230
comma errors, 165, 176
  consecutive adjectives, 172–73
  dates and addresses, 174
  direct addresses and titles, 175
  direct quotations, 173–74
  Inc. and *Ltd.,* 175
  independent clauses, 166–68
  nonessential elements, 170–72
  punctuation marks, importance of, 166
  series, 169
  word usage errors, 176
company names
  abbreviations for, 65–66
  capitalization rules for, 47
company officials, capitalization rules for, 50

comparative proofreading method, 6
compass points, capitalization rules for, 51
complements, 113
completeness, editing for, 248–49
complete sentence, 112, 114
complimentary close, 207, 210–11
compound antecedents, 132
compound sentences, 166
compound subjects, 116–17
computer proofreading and editing, 27–28
  e-mail, 31–32
  information processing tools, 30–31
  on-screen method, 6, 28–30
conciseness, editing for, 256–58
confused words. *See* word usage errors
conjunctions, 166–67
  capitalization rules for, 51
  correlative, 149
consecutive adjectives, 172–73
consistency, editing for, 250
content, editing for, 248–51
content errors, 4–5
contractions, 137. *See also* apostrophes
copy editors, rough drafts and, 69, 70
copy errors
  added copy, 12–13
  omissions, 14–16, 249
correctness, editing for, 248, 249
correlative conjunctions, 149
correspondence, abbreviations and, 67
country abbreviations, 67
courteous request, 185
courtesy titles, abbreviations for, 64–65
cover letter, 232, 233, 234
cover page, in reports, 226, 227
cursor movement check, 29

D

dangling modifiers, 150–52
database, 31
dates
  commas in, 174
  in letters, 207, 208